POLICE DOG HEROES

POLICE DOG

HEROES

MICHAEL LAYTON AND BILL ROGERSON

AMBERLEY

Front Cover: Police dogs for patrolling goods yards being introduced by the railway at Sighthill (Glasgow) 6 September 1949.

First published 2016

Amberley Publishing
The Hill, Stroud
Gloucestershire, GL5 4EP

www.amberley-books.com

Copyright © Michael Layton and
Bill Rogerson, 2016

The right of Michael Layton and Bill Rogerson to
be identified as the Authors of this work has been
asserted in accordance with the Copyrights, Designs
and Patents Act 1988.

ISBN 978 1 4456 5547 5 (print)
ISBN 978 1 4456 5548 2 (ebook)

British Library Cataloguing in Publication Data.
A catalogue record for this book is available
from the British Library.

Typesetting and Origination by Amberley Publishing
Printed in the UK.

CONTENTS

FOREWORD

The British Transport Police (BTP) has a long and proud history of innovation in policing, which is part of the inheritance it gratefully received from its constituent parts in the form of the old railway, docks and canal police forces. Back in 1908 a forward-thinking police inspector of the North Eastern Railway police force learned about developments in Belgium and decided to establish the first Police Dog Section in Britain. The massive goods yards and depots that were policed by these forces and later BTP were, before the motorways and the growth in ever-larger goods vehicles, the hunting grounds of both opportunist and organised gangs. Police dogs were ideal for this kind of terrain and the radio call 'suspects on' inevitably meant that dogs would be called up and deployed.

The decline in goods transported by rail and the cessation of dock policing saw the numbers of dogs in service fall. However, as the type of tasks for which dogs could be used widened, the challenges of twenty-first-century policing saw a renaissance in the number of dogs used by the force. During my service I saw and experienced the decline in numbers, and so I was delighted to be able strongly to support the increase in the Dog Section as a Chief Officer, and to see the professionalism and pride of our dog handlers as they became integral to successful operations combatting robbery, knife crime, football violence and countering the threat of terrorism. Our forward-thinking predecessors of 1908 would be extremely proud of how their idea took hold and evolved into one of the biggest and most effective Police Dog Sections in Britain. This is their story.

The book has been co-written by two former British Transport Police Officers with more than eighty years of collective police service between them. While neither of them were ever dog handlers themselves, they have been privileged to witness the skills and courage routinely displayed by handlers and dogs alike.

In addition to detailing the history of the Dog Section, the book also contains numerous recollections from retired officers of incidents that have taken place over the years. Occasionally humorous, frequently chaotic, and sometimes 'nail-biting', these stories bring to life the relationships between handlers and 'man's best friend'.

Paul Robb QPM
(President of BTP History Group)

INTRODUCTION

THE ORIGINS OF THE BRITISH TRANSPORT POLICE

The railway police have a very proud history and were actually on duty three years before the formation of the Metropolitan Police, on 29 September 1829.

British Transport Police's policing of Britain's railways is considered to be one of the most sophisticated and successful railway policing models in the world. Working closely with the rail industry and community partners, they provide a specialist dedicated service protecting passengers, staff and the rail network from disruption and crime.

The history of policing goes back to the Roman times. Methods of combatting crime have varied in success throughout the ages. In Tudor times the ineffectiveness of the hard-pressed magistrates and constables at that time meant that methods of combatting crime were not always successful. In Tudor times magistrates sat four times a year in courts of law called 'Quarter Sessions' to deal with criminal business. At other times, they were constantly dealing with less serious offences. In addition to seeing that proclamations and laws were carried out, they were responsible for a wide range of things, from repair of bridges to licensing of alehouses. They were not paid;

they were chosen from the gentry and, as Justices of the Peace, they had great social status.

The origins of modern police forces came with the establishment of the Bow Street Runners – the original 'thief takers' – and the Thames Marine Police in 1797 to combat piracy, which was rife on the Thames. The Bow Street Runners were successful at dealing with crime as they covered only a small part of London. Even with the Metropolitan Police, success was slow in coming, as the public was against an organised form of policing. However, the Metropolitan Police proved themselves.

In 1825 the Stockton and Darlington Railway made its inaugural run and, just a few months later, on 30 June 1826 came the first recorded mention of a police establishment of one superintendent, four officers and a number of constables or 'gate-keepers'. One of the constables was PC Metcalfe, and a crude oil painting of him in his red tunic can be seen at the National Railway Museum in York. The railway police were therefore on duty three years before the formation of the Metropolitan Police on 29 September 1829.

Over the next fifty years the railway network expanded at an extraordinary rate, using a huge workforce of men previously used to dig canals, or 'navigations' – hence the word 'navvy'. People used to think of these navvies as being Irish, but the majority came from the English agricultural classes, while others came from Germany and France to gain work.

In the days before county constabularies, large gangs of navvies brought fear to genteel Victorian Britain, provoking Parliament to pass an act on 10 August 1838 requiring all railway companies to provide constables to patrol and protect the railway. Some railway police forces were quite large and had several hundred staff, although the Ffestiniog Railway in Wales employed just one officer.

The navvies kept the early railway policeman very busy. In 1839 a fight broke out during the construction of the Chester and Birkenhead Railway. It took four days and the threat of military intervention to restore order. Across the country, gangs of navvies fought each other and there are many tales of murder and mayhem.

Early railway police also had a role in running the railways, with a policeman based along every mile of the line to regulate the trains and operate each set of points. It has been suggested that the term 'point duty', for an officer on duty at a road junction, comes from the railway police – as does the then railway term 'Bobby' for the signaller. The word 'Bobby' is believed to come from Sir Robert Peel, who founded the Metropolitan Police. His first name was shortened to 'Bob', and the policemen were known as 'Bobbies'.

When the trains first started running, people were very nervous of this new 'Iron Horse', and some nervous travellers going from London to York even made out their wills on King's Cross station.

Another first for the railways came in 1845 when John Tawell became the first person to be arrested with the help of IT. Mr Tawell had murdered a former servant at Slough and escaped aboard a London-bound train. A message was sent to Paddington on the newly installed telegraph, and Sergeant William Williams of the Great Western Railway Police met him off the train and arrested him.

In the early 1900s many railway forces reorganised. The North Eastern Railway Police were the first police force in the United Kingdom to use police dogs in 1909. Their Chief Constable, Capt. Horwood, went on to be the Commissioner of the Metropolitan Police.

With the outbreak of the First World War, many railway policemen responded to the call to arms. The Midland

Railway Police lost 56 per cent of its staff to the military. To replace them, paid Special Constables and women were taken on, making railway police one of the first forces to recruit women.

After the war, returning officers found their wages cut, and conditions worsened, leading to the creation of the Police Federation and Britain's only police strike in 1919. Railway police also went on strike in support of their colleagues from other forces.

In 1921 the Railways Act amalgamated hundreds of railway, dock and harbour companies into four large organisations: Great Western Railway; London North Eastern Railway; London, Midland & Scottish Railway, and Southern Railway. Each had a police force led by a Chief of Police.

The Second World War brought more challenges for the railway police, who temporarily amalgamated into one police force, making it the second-largest force in the United Kingdom with around 4,000 officers. Over 500 railway stations were permanently staffed by railway policemen and women, supplemented by hundreds of paid special constables.

Hitler's Luftwaffe targeted the railways and, in 1940, sixty-eight people were drowned when a bomb fractured an underground river near Balham station in which people were sheltering. It took the railway police three months to remove and identify the dead.

In 1943 panic at Bethnal Green Underground station left 173 people crushed to death. It was during the war that the decision was made to open a railway police training school on a site at Tadworth in Surrey, which eventually closed in 2010.

The wartime amalgamation of the railway police worked well and on 1 January 1949 the British Transport Commission Police was established, formed from the four old railway forces, the canal police and several dock forces. The London Transport Police, with just one hundred officers, was not to amalgamate for another ten years.

In 1957 an arbitrator granted parity in pay and conditions with the home department forces, but the railways established an inquiry to decide if there needed to be a separate police force at all. The Maxwell Johnson enquiry not only found that there should be parity, but recommended that the force should have a Chief Constable and headquarters, and these were duly established at Park Royal in north London. The first Chief Constable, Arthur West, is noted as the last-ever police officer to arrest a witch under the Witchcraft Act of 1735.

This was certainly not the last review that railway policing was to undergo. In 1961, Lord Beeching made savage cuts in the mileage of the rail network and, as a result, the strength of the British Transport Commission Police was nearly halved. The following year the word 'Commission' was dropped from the name.

The force also covered the ports of Dun Laoghaire and Dublin North Wall in Southern Ireland until 1965, and Belfast Donegal Quay until the early 1980s, with a full-time establishment of officers.

Having pioneered the use of the telegraph in crime detection, in 1979 British Transport Police became one of the first forces in Europe to computerise crime recording.

Despite losing the buses, docks and harbours in the 1980s, British Transport Police pioneered contingency planning and the use of live and tabletop exercises and, as it was earlier in the twentieth century, was in the front line of combating terrorism in its last decades with Provisional IRA bombs exploding on stations, trains and tracks across Britain.

Bringing the story up-to-date, in 2001 an Act of Parliament resolved the historic jurisdiction problems, and in 2004 an

Independent Police Authority replaced the former Police Committee. The establishment of a Special Constabulary and the recruitment of Community Support officers has enhanced the way the force can provide a uniformed presence of around 2,914 warranted officers, 322 Community Support officers, 190 special constables and 1,316 support staff, to protect and reassure those 6 million people travelling and working on Britain's railways every day on 10,000 miles of track, over 2,500 stations and numerous trains. The London Underground has nearly 5 million people using its system and 270 stations every day. Today the force is responsible for the railways of Great Britain including London Underground, Glasgow Subway, the Docklands Light Railway in London, Eurostar, and the trams in Croydon and the West Midlands. They also provide a police service for the Emirates Air Line cable car link across the River Thames.

The use of dogs on the railway was confined to the Hull area from 1909 until 1949, when some were sent to Glasgow after a number of railway policemen had been attacked while patrolling the sidings. They were introduced for special operations in and around London in 1951.

I

THE CONCEPT OF USING DOGS TO SUPPORT POLICING

Pound for pound, a dog is twice as strong as a human being. Throughout history, mankind had used this fact to his advantage, and there is evidence that the Greeks used dogs during battles over 2,500 years ago, using 'war dogs' that were even provided with armour.

In May 1985 Inspector John Harrison, from the BTP, submitted a thesis as part of his Inspectors Development Course entitled 'Police Dogs – Use or Ornament!' The document provides a valuable insight into the use of dogs in policing but, moreover, it travels back in time to elaborate on man's relationship with dogs. With his kind permission, parts of his thesis are reproduced in John's own words:

Dogs are mentioned in the Bible and, if one considers the tombs of Ancient Egypt, the wall paintings display the dogs favoured by those people who lived in 1,000 or 2,000 BC. The dog was venerated by the Ancient Egyptians, although not in the same way as the hawk or the cat.

Alexander the Great introduced the mastiff to Greece. It is believed that he obtained these dogs during his march into obably Tibetan mastiffs. Watch-dogs were fortresses.

Roman occupation of Britain, many of the s were brought over here, one of them being the d, of which the St Bernard is a descendant.

Bloodhound was noted as being a dog of a distinct spe es in the early eighth century and, as the fame of this dog's hunting prowess spread throughout parts of Western Europe, they were introduced to Britain at the time of the Norman Conquest. The Bloodhound's ability to follow a scent was even used in those early days, and these dogs were deployed in the border skirmishes between England and Scotland, including against Robert the Bruce in the thirteenth century. It is recorded on one occasion how he escaped from them by wading down a brook until he arrived at a tree with overhanging branches and climbed up into the dense foliage.

Dogs have been used to track down criminals such as cattle rustlers and sheep stealers since before the days of the police. Robbers and marauders crossed the borders of England and Scotland to murder, pillage and rape, and were often then pursued by Bloodhounds. In the border country a tax was introduced on the inhabitants of the area to maintain these hounds. There was a law in Scotland that whosoever denied entrance to any of these hounds should be treated as an accessory to the crime.

As police forces began to be established, some forces, including North Riding of Yorkshire, Wiltshire, and West Sussex, trained and used Bloodhounds for tracking down criminals and finding missing persons.

In Germany in 1896 a process of selective breeding and intensive training of the German Shepherd dog began until every division in Germany had its own Police Dog Section.

In later years this breed of dog was to become the preferred choice of many police forces in the UK.

There are accounts of dogs accompanying parish constables in England in the fifteenth century. However, it is likely that these dogs were pets used for company rather than any other police duties. This position continued into the nineteenth century, when pet dogs often accompanied officers on night duty.

In 1888 Charles Warren, the Commissioner of the Metropolitan Police, tested the effectiveness of two Bloodhounds with a view to using them in the search for the infamous Victorian murderer, Jack the Ripper. The experiment was a painful and embarrassing failure; one of the dogs bit the Commissioner, and they both ran off, requiring a police search to find them again.

In 1897, following a series of attacks on police officers at night, Police Inspector Franz Laufer, who had no experience of dogs, introduced them to the Prussian Police to accompany his officers in order to ward off any attackers. His preference was to use Great Danes. As he was 'breaking new ground', there were no books or experts to assist him in his task but, eventually, he found a police sergeant who had worked with dogs in his previous employment as a gamekeeper. Sergeant Lange thought that the Alsatian was best suited to the task, but Inspector Laufer disagreed and thought that the Great Dane would be more intimidating to criminals. Sir Arthur Conan Doyle had recently promoted this breed in his *Sherlock Holmes* story, 'The Hound of the Baskervilles', which had been widely read throughout Europe.

Laufer believed that the dogs could be used not only for protecting the Police, but also for the tracking of criminals. In 1901 his first dog, a Great Dane called 'Caesar', entered the service. He was kept muzzled and always remained on a lead.

Others were soon recruited. Local people were dubious but, when one of the dogs traced a criminal after a track of over 2 miles, the dogs and Inspector Laufer got some well-earned publicity.

Meanwhile the Police Chief, Mr Van-Wesemael, was also using dogs to accompany his officers on patrol at night in Ghent, Belgium. He used Belgium Sheepdogs (Flemish Shepherd Dogs), which could be well trained and were found to be highly effective.

Mike Morris retired as an Inspector with the British Transport Police and produced a document outlining one hundred years of the history of the Dog Section, which covered the period from 1908 to 2008. He has very kindly allowed the authors to reproduce extracts from this document, which contains valuable insight into the world of police dogs, as well as some great 'human interest' stories.

During the course of Mike Morris's research, he identified that police dogs are one of the few 'custodians of the law' that are capable of engendering a complete range of emotional responses from the public.

Place a number of dogs at a main railway terminus awaiting the arrival of a train full of football supporters, and the majority of the public will generally give them a very wide berth indeed.

But, allow one dog handler to patrol in public with his, or her, dog, and they will generally be stopped every few yards by someone who asks if they can 'pat the dog', or have a photograph of their child with the dog. Sadly for the handler, their inclusion in such pictures is often merely background for the undoubted star, which is invariably the dog.

Again the public have often evidenced a great affection for police dogs. I have a personal recollection of a display of British Transport police dogs at a school charitable fête that raised some £2,400 for the school, whereas a similar event held the previous year, without the dog display, raised only £400.

Famously, prior to the construction of the first Tadworth Dog School, Chief Inspector Lloyd attended a Tadworth Residents' Association meeting. Armed as he was with a wealth of information as to how the Dog School would be operated, and soundproofed, he submitted the proposals to the assembled residents. Sitting down he waited for the anticipated, and to a degree, expected objections. CI Lloyd was somewhat taken aback when he was asked as to whether this proposed school would mean that police dogs and their handlers would be routinely passing through the woods at the rear of their homes. When he answered that that was in fact the case, the residents provided no objections to the proposals.

Mike Morris continued,

To list every incidence of successful dog work would take a volume far larger than this article; however, the following instances have been selected to illustrate examples of the variety of their duties throughout their history.

The visible presence and deterrent:

The opinions of one ship's captain in Hull: 'Fifty policemen could not do the work of one dog; when I see a dog patrol go past my ship, I feel a great sense of security. Many a drunk has been brought back to this ship escorted by a policeman on one side, and a dog on the other. Once I saw a drunken man stumble and fall against his handler but the dog knew his master was not being attacked. He helped his handler to get the fellow on board. The dog was wagging its tail, as amiable about it all as a dog could be.

A few nights later I saw this same dog chase and catch a criminal, and hold him while his handler went to get help. No wagging the tail this time! The huge body sat astride the struggling man, and fangs were bared ready for action while a warning growl was rumbling in the dog's throat. I thanked my lucky stars I was not that man.'

Crowd management and control:

At midnight one St Patrick's night, Police Dog 'Bruce' and his handler were on duty in the Old Oak Common area, when they received an urgent request from the superintendent of a local hostel. The inhabitants had used St Patrick's Day as an excuse to indulge in the excessive consumption of alcohol, and a disagreement had broken into a violent brawl, involving some thirty participants. The handler was unable to restore order until 'Bruce' began to bark, and plunged into the general mêlée. The effect was electrical – in a matter of seconds the fight was over, and the men were persuaded to retire to their beds, thus avoiding a great deal of damage, and probably many injuries.

Searching for criminals:

Police Dog 'Major' was patrolling with his handler in the Cricklewood district, when he suddenly stopped and refused to walk past a warehouse. His interest in one of the doors clearly displayed to his handler that the dog believed someone was on the premises.

'Major' and his handler gained entry, and discovered three offenders in the process of burgling the warehouse. However, not only had 'Major' found the offenders, he had also herded the three into one corner of the premises. After arrest one of the offenders admitted to committing twenty-three previous local burglaries.

Searching for children:

One Sunday afternoon, Police Dog 'Roger' and his handler were on patrol near a timber yard. 'Roger' began to indicate towards a large stack of timber, and on investigating the officer found a man behind the timber stack in the process of indecently assaulting a very young child. Two other very young frightened girls were present, and would no doubt have been subject to a similar assault had not 'Roger' sensed something was amiss and indicated to his handler, thus capturing an offender, and fortunately rescuing one child and saving two other children from the most monstrous violation.

Tracking criminals:

Tracking criminals, and finding evidence, is a task that, if correctly trained, dogs can excel at. In many cases the detection and successful prosecution of offenders would simply never happen without the involvement of dogs. The following three instances clearly indicate the truth of this statement.

Following a burglary at an address in Stockport, Police Dog 'Jasper' was deployed to assist the Greater Manchester Police. 'Jasper' soon picked up a scent from the rear of the premises, and began to track across fields and open country. The weather was appalling, with high winds and heavy rain. Despite the conditions 'Jasper' continued to track over a variety of surfaces for approximately one and a half miles.

Eventually 'Jasper' led the officers to the front door of a house, where, after entry had been gained, property was recovered from the burglary, and a suspect was arrested. 'Jasper' and his handler were later commended for their diligent work, and the difficult nature of the track was recognised when the pair earned the 'Dog Action of the Year Award'.

Cable theft and criminal damage to railway signals and equipment is a crime with potentially fatal consequences for everyone using the railway and, as such, has a high priority among a range of duties. While on an operation specifically undertaken to protect the safety of persons travelling on the railway, Police Dog 'Zeke' and his handler spotted three persons cutting and removing signal cable. Outnumbered, 'Zeke's' handler requested support, but it soon became clear that the thieves had spotted the handler and they began to run. 'Zeke' was deployed to chase and detain one suspect, who was subsequently handed over to arriving officers. 'Zeke' was then deployed to search the area where the suspects were last seen; he soon picked up a scent, and began to track over a variety of surfaces, including roadways and rubbish-strewn waste ground. The scent led 'Zeke', and his handler, to a large steel works, and a subsequent search of the huge premises found the remaining two suspects. Not content with this success, 'Zeke' and his handler returned to the site of the crime, and began an 'area search'. 'Zeke' found hacksaws and the blades used in the commission of the crime, evidence that could be linked directly to the suspects, which eventually led to a successful prosecution. Quite rightly, 'Zeke' and his handler were later awarded the 'Outstanding Police Dog of the Year' Award 2007.

Following a burglary at a Cash and Carry warehouse, Police dog 'Jac' was deployed to search the premises. 'Jac' soon indicated the presence of a person, and his handler was surprised to see 'Jac' running back and forth over a twenty-yard stretch. The handler could then see that there was indeed a person on the top rack of the warehouse shelving, some 40 to 50 feet above the ground. The handler then became aware of another figure, and gradually he detected no less than five suspects, which had been the reason for 'Jac's' initial, and slightly puzzling, behaviour. 'Jac' and his handler challenged and detained the suspects until assistance arrived, when it became clear that it had been the burglar's intention to drop a suitably heavy object upon any searching police officer to facilitate their escape. The fact that 'Jac' had spotted the five, some 50 feet in the air, in the dark, saved the officers from a potentially fatal attack, and successfully apprehended criminals.

Searching for drugs:

Suspecting that drugs were being routinely brought into the country through the Southampton Docks, Police Dog 'Cap' was among the first of many to be specially trained, and soon proved his worth when on an early patrol he indicated the presence of drugs in the back of a lorry. A search unearthed several concealed sacks of cannabis, with a street value of many thousands of pounds.

Searching for bodies:

Following the terrorist bomb on board a Pan-Am 747 flight in December 1989, which crashed on the town of Lockerbie, two Scottish BTP dog handlers attended, and commenced a search that lasted for some thirty-three hours. The officers and their dogs discovered a grim total of twenty-three bodies.

It took time for some members of the community to come to terms with the concept of using police dogs on the railway, as evidenced by a comment in the book *A Force on the Move* by Pauline Appleby:

> The idea of dogs aiding in police work took some time to be accepted by the general public. One old lady, who spotted tracker dogs at work, is known to have remarked: 'Fancy hunting the poor man with those dogs, it's dreadful and inhuman.' She was duly informed that the 'poor man' was being pursued for beating and severely injuring a similar old lady to herself.

2

ARRIVAL OF 'VIC' AND THE ESTABLISHMENT OF THE BTP DOG SECTION

The British Transport Police were the first force in the Country to use dogs and the Section is now over one hundred years old.

Mr Geddes, who was Chief Goods Manager for Hull Docks, visited Ghent in Belgium to observe the work of police officers working with dogs. He was very impressed with what he saw and on his return to work arranged a meeting with Superintendent J. Dobie of the North Eastern Railway Police, who were responsible for policing the docks at Hull.

Geddes was able to convince the Police Superintendent that the dogs would assist his officers in maintaining security at the docks and, on 26 November 1907, the two men and some other officers attended Ghent on a 'fact-finding' mission. They were met by the Ghent Police Dog Section, which by then numbered forty officers and dogs.

Superintendent Dobie was suitably impressed and decided to set up a similar scheme at the docks at Hull. Back home, Dobie gave the task of setting up the new scheme to an Inspector Dobson. Unlike the Ghent Police, however, Inspector Dobson opted to use Airedale Terriers, as he considered them to be stronger, hardier and to have a keener sense of smell. Another consideration was that their wiry coat was less likely to pick up mud from the docks and therefore they would need less grooming.

So it was that in 1908 Airedales 'Jim', 'Vic', 'Mick' and 'Ben' began a tradition that endures to this day, some 107 years later.

'Jim' was handled by Sergeant Allinson, who was pictured in the local press, and the nationally circulated *Pall-Mall* and *Penny Pictorial* magazines. 'Jim' later became well known in the local press for capturing two criminals by jumping through a window.

Below is an extract from an article that tracked this early progress and appeared in *The Railway and Travel Monthly* [1910; NERA library B9], titled, 'The North Eastern Railway's Police Dogs'.

Most docks are fenced, but those at Hull are not. Therefore the NER Police are accompanied on night duty between 10 p.m. and 5 a.m. by dogs. The dogs' employment is due to the number of thefts, attacks by thieves on policemen at night, and frequent fires set by vagrants. The NER sent representatives to Belgium to see the police dogs – Flemish sheepdogs – working there. Airedale terriers are used in this country, on account of their extraordinary gameness, and staying powers. The dogs are muscular, rough, hardy and strong.

The experimental use of dogs has been a success, and large kennels are now provided at the entrance to Albert Dock. The docks and the Riverside Quay are patrolled by policemen with dogs. The dogs are trained to view anybody not in Police uniform as an enemy.

They are taught to obey the Police whistle. First they are taught to chase and hold thieves; next to guard a prisoner; and later to jump a wall or through a window in pursuit of a thief, and to knock a man off a bicycle. On duty, the dogs are muzzled. On wet nights, the dogs wear a waterproof cover on their backs. Policemen carry dog biscuits in their pockets.

Inspector Dobson was the first British policeman to be entrusted with the establishment of police dog kennels.

On 26 November 1908 the scheme was extended to the Hartlepool, Middlesbrough, and Tyne Docks, all of which were policed by the North Eastern Railway Police. It was therefore down to one dog called 'Charlie', who went from the Hull Dog Section to the Hull & Barnsley Railway Police to spread the message.

The dogs were trained at Hull, where kennels had been erected. Each dog had his own kennel space with a run. The dogs were also issued with a coat to wear during bad weather. The kennel man was a PC, who had previously been a gamekeeper before joining the force. They were only used at night, and probably not allocated to a specific handler. They were trained, by the use of 'treats', to 'protect police uniform' – indeed, to attack anyone not wearing a uniform. It is reported that the dogs would growl at their handlers when they were out of uniform.

The *Penny Pictorial* for 25 June 1910 produced an article called 'The Dog Detectives', an extract of which reads,

> The novel experiment by the North Eastern Railway Police of employing dogs as detectives on the docks at Hull has been fraught with such success that several other ports are now about to follow the example. Each dog has to undergo special and most elaborate training and the first thing he is taught is that every person not dressed in a police uniform is an enemy. The dogs are trained to obey a police whistle, and then to chase and stop a man who is running away, and hold him

till the officer arrives. If a thief is escaping on a bicycle these canine detectives are taught to race after him and to knock him off by turning the front wheel aside. It is necessary for the dogs to be muzzled when not on duty as otherwise any tramp they came across would be badly mauled.

In 1910 the *North Eastern Magazine* printed an account of an early arrest by the dogs:

Early one morning a policeman accompanied by a dog was patrolling St Andrew's Dock, Hull and, on seeing a man loitering in a suspicious manner, called upon him to stop. The man took no notice, so the officer slipped the dog (one of the best, it is reported), [which] soon had the man down and begging for mercy. Having secured this man the officer made a search and found the window of a refreshment room broken. He entered and called upon those inside to surrender. Receiving no response he called out that he had taken the dog's muzzle off, when the reply came back, 'Put the muzzle back on sir, and we will come out,' and two burly fellows came from behind the counter. They, along with their companion, were marched by the officer and his dog to the police station, a distance of about half a mile without the slightest resistance. The offenders turned out to be notorious burglars and received their just desserts.

Another story appeared in the same magazine:

An officer was passing a wagon when his dog scented something inside. The wagon was opened and two men were found sleeping next to an amount of stolen property. When told the game was up they said that they would not come out for a 'slop' (the local slang name for a bobby) but when the officer said he would take the muzzle off the dog they changed their tune and walked to the police station with the officer 'like lambs'.

They were also used for crowd control, the magazine reports:

On an occasion where there was a fire on board a ship a number of hooligans congregated and, taking advantage of the small number of police present, became defiant. Two dogs were brought to the scene, and it was amusing to see the desperados falling over each other in their haste to leave the dock.

The following newspaper article, 'Railway Police Dogs are Terrors to Evil-Doers', appeared in the *Dundee Evening Telegraph* on 29 July 1910 and is reproduced courtesy of the British Newspaper Archives:

Most docks, particularly those belonging to private corporations, are protected by unscalable walls, but Hull Docks differ with others in this respect, as they are not fenced in any way, and are consequently open to the depredations of thieves and the unenviable attention of tramps and others. As an additional protection to those docks, a scheme has been formulated by which the police constables of the North Eastern Railway on night duty will be assisted by dogs.

The dogs, which are Airedale terriers, are so brave that they will attack a man even though he is armed with a revolver or a club. On duty the dogs are muzzled, as otherwise they would tear any tramp to pieces.

At three o'clock one morning an officer was passing along the quayside, says a writer in *The Railway and Travel Monthly*, when suddenly his dog – a favourite named 'Whisk' – flew to a very large hamper, which was standing alongside several more. The dog jumped on top of the hamper, and a voice said, 'Oh, my head'. The owner of the voice proved to be a rough-looking navvy, who said he had walked all the way from Leeds the other day. Rough-looking fellow as he was, he was grateful when he was given his liberty. On another occasion an officer with his dog was passing a railway carriage when his canine companion commenced to growl and jump around him. On investigation two men were found inside the carriage. One of the best and keenest dogs in the Hull kennels is 'Jim', and it was this splendid animal that was responsible for the arrest of two notorious thieves who were plundering a coffee house.

In 1912 'Charlie', and his handler, PC Easton of the Hull & Barnsley Railway Police, came across a man armed with a knife. The officer attempted to arrest the man but was stabbed in the chest. Luckily his thick greatcoat saved him from serious injury. 'Charlie' leapt onto the man to defend his master and held him down until he could be arrested. As a result of his good work, 'Charlie', with PC Easton, was invited to Crufts Dog Show in London the following year where he was awarded a shield and a medal by the Canine Defence League. 'Charlie' was the first police dog in the country to receive such an award.

The under mentioned press cutting is courtesy of the British Newspaper Archives:

'Charles', Airedale-Collie – saved the life of his master on March 24 1912. Mr Easton, who is a police-constable, while on duty at the Alexandra Dock, Hull, was attacked by a Norwegian sailor, who attempted to stab him. The affray took place on a bridge only 4 feet wide, with simply a chain hand rail to prevent falling into the dry dock, 45 feet deep, and had not the dog flown at his master's assailant and knocked him down there is little doubt that Mr Easton would have met his death.

The following newspaper article appeared in the *Sheffield Evening Telegraph* on 26 March 1912 and is reproduced courtesy of the British Newspaper Archives:

Policeman's Dog – Officer Rescued by Canine Friend

A striking illustration of the value of the North Eastern Railway Police dogs was given before Hull magistrates when a Norwegian seaman named Ole T. Olsen was charged with being drunk and disorderly, and also with assaulting Police-Constable Easton.

It was explained that Olsen was drunk and refused to go on board his ship. When the constable remonstrated with him he became very violent, and was taken into custody, but knocked the constable down and kicked him in the head. In a violent struggle which ensued, the man stabbed the constable with a pocket knife.

One of the police dogs, however, came to the assistance of the officer, flying at Olsen and knocking him down. The constable attributed his escape from serious potential injury, and perhaps death, to the pluck and sagacity of the dog.

Olsen was fined 5s and costs for being drunk, and 40s and costs for the assault, or in default thirty days with hard labour.

With the coming of the First World War in 1914, ten dogs were conscripted from Hull Docks to the war effort. The dogs from Hull Docks were conscripted into the Army to accompany the 17th Northumberland Fusiliers (North Eastern Railway Pioneer Battalion). The *North Eastern Railway Magazine* pictured the dogs in France, with a photograph entitled 'The Sentry Dogs'. The handlers, although in khaki, were thought to be railway policemen who had joined-up with their dogs.

During the war the work of the Police Dog Section at Hull continued, still led by Inspector Dobson. By the end of the war no fewer than 185 suspects had been detained at the docks, many with the assistance of dogs.

They were not the only dogs to make their presence felt in the First World War on the Allies' side. America's first war dog, a stray Pit Bull/Terrier mix named 'Stubby', who later became 'Sergeant Stubby', was the most decorated war dog of the First World War and the only dog to be promoted to Sergeant through combat.

One day he simply appeared at Yale Field in New Haven, Connecticut while a group of soldiers were training, stopping to make friends with soldiers as they drilled. One soldier, Cpl Robert Conroy, developed a fondness for the dog. He named him 'Stubby' because of his short legs. When the time came for the unit to leave, Conroy hid 'Stubby' on board the troop ship, and they went on to see active service.

The German Army had some 6,000 'war dogs', while the British Army had just one in the initial stages.

After the First World War the BTP Dog Section was reviewed and by 1923 the Hull trainers decided to use Alsatians, which at the time were the favoured dog of the German Army, after they had tried Airedales, Labradors, and Doberman Pinschers.

As can be seen from this brief initial history, the use of dogs has been the subject of much division of opinion, not only at the outset, but throughout the career of the Dog Section. Initial opposition to their establishment was voiced in an early Metropolitan evaluation report, which stated, 'The dogs are useful, but their expertise has been exaggerated. We feel that London is no place for police dogs.'

3

'PRINCE' GETS HIS MAN

An early use of these new dogs is recorded in the *LNER Magazine* of 1924, which reported on an incident at Middlesbrough Docks the previous year:

> PC Leitch was on patrol with police dog 'Prince', when they caught three men breaking into an office. The men ran off but 'Prince' was slipped from his lead and pursued and caught one of the men. In court the burglar ruefully related his capture: 'I knew nothing until the dog butted me, got between my legs and forced me down. The Constable kept shouting to the dog, 'Go on "Prince"', and it frightened the wits out of me. And I was so terrified I could not speak.'

Viv Head, who has done a lot of research into the policing of docks in Wales, and is a retired Detective Inspector with BTP, recalls that,

> some old kennels were attached to the police house at Subway Road at Barry Docks, suggesting that dogs were in use at Barry at some point, though it is not clear when.

Certainly a small number of Airedale dogs were kept at Cardiff Docks in the 1930s but these were used for general patrol by any officer on duty. Neither the dogs nor the officers were given any formal training. Perhaps surprisingly, there is no record of police dogs being used at the South Wales Ports during the Second World War. Trained German Shepherd dogs were in regular use at Hull Docks by 1940.

During the Second World War, police dogs were subject to the 'blitz' of German bombing, along with the rest of the population. After one raid that had damaged the kennels on Hull's Albert Dock, several dogs escaped, some dogs were recovered, and some returned of their own accord; however, one dog that at the time was described as an 'enterprising and sagacious animal' was found on Paragon Railway station, apparently attempting to board a train bound for Brough in the Yorkshire Wolds. The rumour soon began that he had had enough of city life and decided to join the ever-growing army of evacuees.

In 1939, at the outbreak of the Second World War, railway police, including dog handlers, were armed. A photo of the period showed six dog handlers, each carrying a gas mask, and armed with a revolver while on patrol, with their dogs at Alexandra Dock at Hull. There are no recorded instances of the handlers discharging their firearms at the 'enemy', but one instance is noted of an officer losing the toe-cap of his boot while cleaning his firearm.

On September 3 1939 at 11.00 a.m. the sirens were heard all over Britain as we went to war with Nazi Germany. The transition from peace to war was dramatic. Yet through all the violence of the destruction experienced in the war, Britain's railways ran. Women replaced the male workers who had been called up to fight the enemy.

It goes without saying that the Second World War was a difficult time for the four main railway companies and the railway police. Continual vigilance was required on all movements, particularly the goods traffic, to protect them and their premises from thieves and Hitler's Luftwaffe. Goods depots all over the railway system, particularly in the London area, were bombed relentlessly by the Luftwaffe.

During this war, due to a lot of their staff being called up for war service, it was virtually impossible to keep their goods secure. They did try to lock the vans and wagons, and to remove identification labels. The railway companies had to rely on inexperienced staff, who were working in blackout conditions, to ensure that the goods remained relatively secure.

However, these bombing raids did not deter the thieves from raiding the vans in the depots up and down the country. In London, for instance, the sounding of the air raid sirens became a signal for the thieves – not to go to a place of safety, but to risk their lives to raid the vans in the sidings during the blackout and the absence of staff.

Their ill-gotten gains would then be sold on the black market. It was something of a war within a war. The railway police, along with their dogs, despite their low numbers, were particularly successful in arresting culprits, even when the bombs were actually falling and anti-aircraft defences were hard at work shooting away at the enemy bombers in the sky. For instance, in 1944, 36,000 prosecutions were undertaken.

On 27 July 1940 at West Hartlepool station, sadly PC William Race was struck by a train and killed while on patrol. His faithful dog stood guard over his body, and attacked the railway staff that went to his assistance.

During the course of further research, Viv Head established the following:

During the Second World War the city of Hull, like many other British towns and cities, was subjected to sustained bombing raids; 1,241 of its citizens were killed during enemy air raids between 1939 and 1945. It became the most bombed city in Britain outside of London.

Returning RAF pilots crossing the coast of Denmark reported seeing the glow of fires at Hull during the worst night of bombing on 7 May 1941. It was a night when 120 enemy aircraft focused their attention on the city for more than six hours, and 279 people were killed with many more injured and nearly 7,000 made homeless. As always, one of the main targets that night was the city's docks area and the Dockmaster's house on King George Dock took a direct hit by a parachute mine.

Albert Eastwood and his wife Ethel survived, but their two eldest children – Kenneth, aged eighteen, and his sister Muriel, aged twenty-three – were killed instantly. Two other children, Roy and Winifred, suffered serious injuries but later recovered at Driffield Hospital.

The King George Dock was a prime target for the German Luftwaffe as they attempted to destroy the port, but their efforts were in vain, as the Dockers did not miss a single day's work, at least up until 1941.

Kenneth and his brother Roy, aged seventeen, had just returned from Home Guard training and were standing outside their home when they spotted incendiary devices falling from the sky near the house, next to the main dock gate entrance and opposite the police station. Two dock constables – PC John Woods, fifty-two, and PC George Barker, sixty-five – were helping the young men to extinguish incendiary bombs when a parachute mine floated down from the sky and became snagged on a poplar tree next to the family's house.

Although eighteen-year-old Kenneth Eastwood realised a bomb was falling and was able to shout a warning to the others, he and his sister Muriel and the two policemen were killed instantly when the bomb exploded seconds later.

Constable John Woods was a Police dog handler, teamed with an Alsatian dog. Had it not been for the war, PC George Barker may have already been retired or would certainly have been on the point of doing so.

All the officers at Hull Docks were armed with pistols kept in holsters slung over one shoulder, alongside their gas masks, on the outside of their tunics.

Following the Second World War, the Government amalgamated the various railway and docks police forces into the British Transport Commission Police. This new force had a total of twenty-four police dogs.

Even the deployment of the dogs was subject to varying opinion. Initially, Transport Police dogs wore leather-strap muzzles during their working hours. In the late 1940s and early 1950s this muzzle gave rise to the erroneous belief that Transport Police dogs were more vicious than those used by the City Police.

The muzzle was deemed necessary to prevent 'accidental' bites; however, while the muzzle did not hinder the dog to a great extent, it was soon found that it could prove a hindrance if the dog was dealing with a particularly violent criminal.

So, the muzzle was dispensed with, which had two advantages: the dogs looked less aggressive to the public, and potential criminals were plainly aware that the dog was always 'ready for action'.

Even the transporting of railway police dogs was the subject of contention for a long time. For many years, the instruction was that police dogs should be temporarily kennelled in the guard's brake van of the train. This instruction lingered long after the removal of such guard's vans, when it was suggested that the handler and dog should travel in the passenger compartments with the general public.

In the early 1950s a new Police Dog Training Centre was established at Inman's farm, Hedon Hall, near Hull, which had previously been a convalescent home for horses. The Officer in Charge was Inspector John William Morrell and during his tenure the Dog Section increased to seventy-five dogs.

Henry Wreathall – a Yorkshire man, now a youthful ninety-four years, and a member of the BTP History Group – joined the British Transport Commission Police at Hull Docks in November 1952. Shortly after completing his probation he became a dog handler, completing his training at Hedon, near Hull. He was later made Acting Sergeant and, upon the death of John William Morrell, he took charge of the Dog Training School at Hedon until a successor was appointed. He was then promoted in the substantive rank of Sergeant and went to the Metropolitan Police Dog Training School for a short secondment. When Hedon closed, he transferred to Grimsby and Hull Paragon railway stations as a patrol Sergeant. He completed his service at Hull Docks in November 1982, when he retired.

He remembers the school at Hedon as being an old farm, and it was set in beautiful countryside not far from the sea – a far cry from the hustle and bustle of Hull Docks where Henry had previously worked. The air was always fresh and invigorating. But it could be really bleak and uninviting in the winter with the icy blast blowing in from the North Sea.

Henry remembers his days at Hedon and, in particular, he recalls Harold Philbin from Manchester who attended Hedon as a trainee dog handler. Henry introduced Harold to his first dog 'Tollo', who was to last for about eight years. He remembers that 'Tollo' was a very good and enthusiastic tracking dog; in fact he was unique among his fellow breed. He believes that Harold attended his retirement evening in 1982.

At the early stages of dog training, there was no official course structure, and new police officers were given just two days to learn the rudiments of handling their new dogs. Inspector Morrell had not only obtained 'gift' dogs, but began to breed pedigree dogs for use by the force.

Tragically on 18 February 1960 Inspector Morrell died suddenly at the early age of forty-six years. The John William Morrell Trophy was later donated by Mrs Winifred Morrell, widow of the late Inspector John William Morrell. In the April 1960 edition of the *British Transport Commission Police Journal* the following obituary appeared:

The death occurred suddenly on 18 February of Acting Inspector John William Morrell, the officer in charge of the BTC Police Dog Establishment at Hedon, Hull. Acting Inspector Morell had attended a conference at Force Headquarters and was returning to Hull when taken ill at King's Cross station. Acting Inspector Morrell joined the former London North Eastern Railway Police Force in 1946 after previously serving with the Hull City Police and was transferred to detective duties in 1949. He was promoted Sergeant in 1951 and Acting Inspector in 1955. He had been responsible for the care and training of police dogs for many years and his skill and efficiency in this work was widely recognised. Acting Inspector Morrell had, with his team of police dogs and handlers, taken part in many demonstrations at public functions, with great credit to the British Transport Commission Police Force. His loss will be keenly felt by the Force as a whole, and the deepest sympathy of all members of the Force is extended to his widow and family.

The funeral took place at Hedon Parish Church and Hull Crematorium on 24 February, when a police escort of some sixty uniformed officers was on parade. Sergeants Stubley, Harness, Hartley, and Griffin acted as pallbearers, and the cortège was accompanied by Constables Edson, Baker, Dewson, and Murrey with their dogs.

Superintendent J. Lewins, representing Mr A. C. West, Chief Constable, and Mr E. C. Brashier, Area Chief of Police, York, with many other senior officers was present. The Hull City Police Force was represented by Chief Inspector Ingham with a detachment of some twenty officers, together with Inspector Baker of the Transport Section with four dog handlers. The East Riding Constabulary was represented by Inspector Lofthouse. The British Legion, with their standards, were at the church at Hedon, and the Worshipful Master of the Thesaurus Lodge of Freemasons, was accompanied by a number of the brethren.

4

'ZIP' DOES THE BUSINESS – POLICING THE DOCKS

At 7 a.m. on Tuesday 5 December 1950, the SS *Solbritt*, a Canadian freighter, was docked at Quay 12 in King George Dock, Hull. At this time a well-known thief by the name of 'Ginger' Sharpe, with previous military service as a Regimental Sergeant-Major, boarded the ship with theft on his mind. Unfortunately for him, also on Quay 12 that day was PC Cook, together with police dog 'Zip'. The officer at first thought that Sharpe was a returning crew member but, on finding his bicycle, realised that the man was up to no good and maintained observations to await his return.

In due course 'Ginger' reappeared from the shadows of the ship, carrying a bag, and returned to his bicycle, where the officer stepped out and confronted him. Initially in shock Sharpe revealed that he was in possession of 'uncustomed cigarettes'.

The officer had to walk over a mile and a half to the Revenue Office with his prisoner, carrying the bag, and holding his dog and the cycle. Sharpe began to recover his composure and decided at one point to make a break for it. What he didn't know was that PC Cook was an ex 'Red Beret' who had served with distinction in a famous airborne division, and that the dog was not prone to giving up.

As they were walking Sharpe suddenly pushed the officer off balance, grabbed his cycle, and tried to ride off. PC Cook released 'Zip', who soon caught up with Sharpe and returned the compliment by jumping at him, knocking him off the bike, and standing over him, snarling, until the officer arrived.

Now ninety-one years of age, Bob Cook recounts this story in his own words. It is a fascinating story, which still stands the passage of time:

I joined the British Transport Police in 1948, aged twenty-four, at Hull and became a dog handler. We were the only police force in the country that used dogs, although I believe the Ministry of Defence Police had a Dog Section at that time.

We trained the dogs at a village called Hedon, near Hull, in an area of fields and a farmhouse, which had been used as a hospital for sick horses. The dogs were trained for obedience and tracking and tackling criminals.

When I joined the Dog Section, which was used on the Eastern Docks, i.e. King George Dock, Alexandra Dock and Victoria Dock, all the docks were busy with shipping, bringing a lot of cargo of various types. This was usually stored in dockside warehouses or some yards, outside in the open, when the warehouses were full.

At that time we were not allowed to train the dogs without muzzles, but each dog learned to tackle runaway criminals. Some dogs leapt up and hit the man in the back, knocking him down. They would stand over him until receiving orders from their handler. One dog learned to use his forelegs and make a rugby tackle on the man, and another dog ran in between the man's leg to bring him down. Once the man was down the dog stayed with him until we called him off with the orders 'leave' then 'heel', and the dog returned to his handler.

One dog called 'Zip' was able to bite through his muzzle and nip the man on his ankles. I often went home after a training session with bruised ankles after 'Zip' tackled me when I was the criminal. We did training once a week at Hedon. Those of us on duty were paid overtime. The trainer in charge was Sergeant Morrell, later promoted to Inspector. I believe he was promoted to Chief Inspector, but he died of a heart attack on his way home from receiving his promotion from the Chief of Police.

In obedience training, it consisted of sending the dog away in a certain direction until ordered to stop and face the handler. He was then told to sit and lie down on all fours and then stand. The handler called 'come' to the dog and he would come to the handler and sit in front of him. The dog was then ordered to 'heel' and the dog went round the right side of the handler and sat on his left side.

We gave demonstrations locally and for three years running gave demonstrations at the Great Yorkshire Show; we also gave demonstrations to the police at Bootle in Lancashire and the police at Durham. The Metropolitan Police had given a demonstration at Durham a few weeks earlier but the final attacks were made some distance from the people watching and they could not see clearly what happened. They could not hear the commands given to the dogs. When we gave the demonstration, the tracking by the dogs was closer and the handlers giving their commands were clear to those watching. The Durham Police considered our performance to be much better than that of the Metropolitan Police.

Another demonstration was in London, about 1951. The Royal Artillery were putting on demonstrations regarding their army duties and were at Walthamstow Stadium for a week. It was called 'Gunners Week'. We gave the demonstration; the dogs did the job perfectly and they were pleased with the applause from the watching crowd. Some members of the public came to see the dogs after the show, as they were delighted with the dogs and said, 'You stole the show'.

An amusing arrest I made was with the dog 'Zip' at King George Dock. I was on early turn and I took 'Zip' on patrol with me, as his handler was on leave and he needed some exercise. I took 'Zip' out on patrol at 6 a.m. and it had been snowing, with a couple of inches laid on the ground. I saw some cycle tracks in the snow. I followed them to a ship's gangway and the bicycle was leaning against a crane on the quayside.

I waited and a man left the ship onto the quay. He was a known thief called 'Ginger' Sharpe. I stopped him and found the bag he was carrying was full of cartons of duty-free cigarettes, which he had bought from members of the crew. I took hold of the bag but I couldn't hold him, his bike and the dog.

'Ginger' snatched the bike and rode off. I let him go a few yards and then told 'Zip' to attack. 'Zip' ran after the man, and jumped up and knocked him off his bicycle. 'Ginger' stood up and 'Zip' immediately went for his ankles, nipping him through his muzzle. 'Ginger' was hopping from one foot to the other and, after a while, I called the dog off. I told 'Ginger' I was arresting him and he replied, 'If I had a gun I would shoot that dog and you an' all.' He was later fined heavily at the Magistrates' Court.

One of our dogs was called 'Major'; he was a very good tracker and the Hull City Police sometimes used him and his handler to track down thieves. A kiosk near Alexandra

Dock on the main road was broken into and a lot of cartons of cigarettes had been stolen. 'Major' had a sniff around the interior of the kiosk and then led the police officers along the main road over a street, which went over the railway. He then went through two more streets and sat outside the front door of a house. A man came out of the house carrying a bag containing stolen cigarettes. The police officers went into the house and found another man with a lot of stolen cigarettes. The two men were arrested and appeared at the Magistrates' Court.

The Hull City police officer who accompanied Bob was Ken Ogram, who later became the Chief Constable of the British Transport Police. He was on extended night turns to evaluate the use of Police Dogs as the Chief Constable of the Hull City Police was thinking of establishing a Dog Section.

In the *BTP Journal* of January 1951, Sergeant R. Galway wrote a letter espousing the value of police dogs and encouraging the force to take on more. He described the success of the dogs used in the North East Area, and the editor confirmed that there had been one dog in London for some time, and that its establishment would soon be increased to twelve. The officer commented that we should not lose sight of the fact that 'a police dog can and would detect a would-be felon much quicker than any officer, owing to the fact that the dog's ear and nose is more sensitive'.

In the July 1951 edition of the *BTP Journal*, a photograph appeared of six of the London Area police dogs, all of which were Alsatians, with their handlers.

In the October 1951 edition of the BTP Journal an article appeared which described dog-training at that time. Inman's Farm, at Hedon, near Hull, was an old-fashioned farmhouse set in forty acres of green pasture. This was home to the British Transport Police Training Centre for the training of police dogs, normally pedigree Alsatians, aged between one and two years. Discipline was strict for both handler and dog, with the maxim being 'work or quit'.

The selected dogs were either bred 'in house' or came from private homes. After initial fitness tests, the dogs went through a three-week probationary period and were kept in isolation from other animals, while receiving individual attention from their handler.

The dogs then went through a phase known as 'conditioning' and, if they showed any signs of undue nervousness or inherent weakness, they were rejected. Rigorous training for those successful then continued for a three-month period, where dogs were taught to scale an eight-foot-high wall, jump over a five-bar gate, and creep on their bellies for one hundred yards. The final stage of their training dealt with how to tackle human beings.

In 1951 BTP police dogs and handlers patrolled King's Cross Goods Yard, which was an eighty-four-acre site, capable of handling 17,000 tons of goods per week. With property valued at £2 million per year stolen in transit, dogs were seen as a vital component of policing the transport networks.

In November 1951 a female student nurse was travelling from Willesden to Bletchley when she was joined at some point in her compartment by a man who indecently exposed himself, and tried to assault her. She fought back and he left the train at Cheddington when he realised that she had alerted the train staff.

After making off across fields, rail staff and a member of the public surrounded him in a wooded area, and the police later arrived with a dog. The offender was discovered hiding in some undergrowth by the dog and gave up without a fight. He was later sentenced to four years' corrective training, to be followed by twelve months' supervision.

On Saturday 12 July 1952, during the early hours of the morning, plain-clothes officers, accompanied by police dog 'Bruce' and his handler, were keeping watch at St Rollox Yard in Glasgow. The officers were concealed near to an embankment at a point between the sidings and a main thoroughfare, when they became aware of four men leaving the sidings, fifty yards in front of them, carrying cartons. They made off on seeing the officers but 'Bruce' was released and caught one of them, who came off 'second best' in a struggle with the dog. The offender was sent to prison for thirty days.

In 1952 four police dogs based in Scotland were instrumental in the apprehension of seventeen people for theft. The four dogs – 'Bruce', 'Rex', 'Major 2', and 'Chappie' – were kennelled at Sighthill Goods Yard in Glasgow, where dogs had been present for nearly four years.

Prior to their introduction officers were regularly attacked by gangs of 'Neds', but they were not so keen on taking the dogs on, one of which became even more alert when the word 'Ned' was used in his presence.

Normal feeding arrangements in those days consisted of more than two pounds in weight of cooked horseflesh, and half a pound of hound meal biscuits, per dog, per twenty-four hours. The average weight of a dog was six stone and two pounds.

In the middle of July 1954 a BTC Police investigation commenced following a number of incidents where signalling equipment was interfered with in the Hull district. Operation 'Quanta' was set up by the force, in conjunction with the East Riding Constabulary, and this included a number of observation points, as well as the provision of police dog patrols.

On 22 July 1954 Constable Donald Hancock was keeping observation when he saw a man acting suspiciously near to the railway lines. As he approached him cautiously, he lost his footing and fell down a cliff edge, 35 feet into a quarry. He lost consciousness for twenty-four hours, and suffered arm and leg injuries, although he later made a full recovery. The suspect made good his escape.

On Saturday 24 July 1954 a man riding a bicycle along a lane near the railway was seen to enter a plantation. The cycle was later found abandoned in the plantation and police dog 'Quanta' tracked the suspect to an area situated on top of a tunnel, where he was spotted cutting down trees. As the officers closed in, the suspect spotted them and made off into a barley field. The dog was released and found Victor Albert Thompson lying on the ground in the middle of the field. 'Quanta' stayed by Thompson until the arrival of officers who arrested him. While it soon became clear that the officers had got their man, his reasons for interfering with equipment, and generally being disruptive, were less than coherent and it was soon established that he was of unstable mind.

In the mid-fifties two police dogs, 'Rajah' and 'Sweep', worked at Carlisle with their handlers PC Millray and PC Donoghue, and on occasions patrolled Denton Holme Marshalling Yard.

When two youths escaped from Hull Borstal Institute in the summer of 1957 they were caught after being at liberty for just three hours. East Riding and BTC Police Dogs were called out and tracked the escapees towards Hedon where they were finally cornered and detained. One of the officers involved was PC 201 Edson BTC based at Hull, with police dog 'Rinty'.

On Saturday 17 August 1957 a riot broke out at the Borstal Institute. Officers from the Hull City Police, under the command of Superintendent Lessels, went to the scene and tried to drive the principal offenders from the top floor of the building, where they had barricaded themselves in. They were met with a hail of missiles, and the senior officer requested the attendance of BTC dogs. PC Higgins with dog 'Van', PC Moss with dog 'Kim', PC Bielby with dog 'Rex', and PC Hooper with dog 'Pedro' attended and quickly managed to bring about a change in the situation, leading to the inmates surrendering.

The Blackhill area of Glasgow in the mid-fifties was known as 'Blackfeet' territory. Its residents had previously been known as 'Neds' and some were well known to the British Transport Commission Police for the wrong reasons. For a while coal trains were routinely raided until police-dog patrols started to deter them. They then, however, turned their attention to the coal stockpiles in a gas works, adjacent to the railway line.

On 19 December 1957, under cover of darkness, three men entered the gas works and stole 9 cwt of coal but, instead of taking the long way home via the streets, they made the mistake of taking a shortcut across the railway line.

They were spotted by police dog 'Caro' and, after ignoring shouts from the dog's handler to stop, dropped their bags of coal and ran off. From a distance of about fifty yards the dog was released and easily caught up with one of the offenders, who had the wisdom to stand completely still. The other two made good their escape.

A telephone call at the Gate House brought assistance from the Civil Police and the prisoner, plus the stolen coal, were taken to the local police station. The following morning the prisoner was sentenced to fourteen days' imprisonment. He remarked to a Civil Police Officer, 'These railways cops don't give you a dog's chance. As for the dogs, they look at you as though you were a tin of "Lassie".'

Meanwhile, similar problems were occurring in the railway yards in Motherwell in Lanarkshire and, after local BTC police officers lost patience in endless foot chases, they sought help from their Glasgow colleagues. Police dog 'Chappie' and his handler were the first to deploy to the area and, in one go, rounded up eleven offenders who were put before the court on charges of coal-stealing. Peace broke out for just two weeks until the local thieves regained their confidence and once again started stealing. On this occasion police dog 'Ranger', with handler PC 370 J. W. Miller, was deployed from Glasgow and seven offenders, including two railway servants, were caught. While this was going on, 'Caro' and 'Major' continued to focus on Blackhill and made further arrests.

At 11.30 p.m. on Saturday 7 June 1958 PC Wreathall received a call to go to 270 Anlaby Road, Hull, where a man had been assaulted and robbed after being invited inside by a woman. On arrival with police dog 'Sandy' the officer was shown by Inspector Pick of the Hull City Police the scene of the crime. 'Sandy' was taken into a room where a serious fight had obviously taken place and picked up a scent.

He set off down five flights of stairs and through various passages, before leaving by the back of the house. The dog then continued to track through gardens, across roads, and a grass paddock adjoining the edge of the Hull–Doncaster railway line. Eventually the scent was lost in some allotments but, during the 'track', a 'grip' and a suitcase containing clothing was recovered. As a result of evidence recovered during the search, a man and a woman were arrested shortly afterwards.

In the April edition of the 1958 *BTC Police Journal* an article appeared by Dorothy Campion, who was described as a well-known author on dogs and horses. She carried out extensive research into the establishment of Police Dog Sections in various police forces in the UK, during the course of which she paid close attention to the BTC Dog Section at Hedon, in Hull.

She met Inspector Morrell and described him as 'one of the most brilliant trainers in this field. Inspector J. Morrell brought 'Condor' onto the training ground, and I saw man and dog work as one. PC Edson and his dog 'Raff' marched side by side like old soldiers.' She was even more impressed that the dogs worked free from their muzzles.

Miss Campion was also able to go out on patrol with officers and was able to witness at first hand an arrest by 'Condor' and PC Craddock on St George's Dock on No. 2 Shed, which was stacked with bales of wool from Australia. The large black-and-sand-coloured dog caught the scent of a man and leapt over the bales to corner him. He wisely gave up without a fight.

During the course of her contact with officers she was also privy to stories relating to other arrests such as when police dog 'Bruce' joined an 'all-in' brawl and broke up a fight involving forty drunken men. On another occasion police dog 'Zip' visited the catacombs of a church and found five men in hiding, while police dog 'Buller' once gave chase and retrieved stolen property valued at £80, and on yet another occasion police dog 'Sweep' chased and caught an escaping convict.

Her visit was arranged by Superintendent Lewins, who went out on patrol with her on the docks. She went on to conclude that the BTC police dogs were among the best trained, and that she had seen no better dogs during her quest to write a book about the subject, during which she had travelled 1,500 miles. The book she was commissioned to write was to be called *The Perfect Team*.

In August 1958 four officer cadets from the Thailand Police Force, and an Assistant Superintendent from the Kenya Police, visited the BTC Police Dog Training Establishment at Hedon, hosted by Superintendent J. Lewins, the Chief of Police for the North Eastern Area. During the visit they observed the dogs in training.

At 1.10 a.m. on Monday 8 December 1958 two police officers from Hull City Police, working in plain clothes, disturbed two men who were trying to break into Sutton Golf Club in Salthouse Road, Hull. The suspects made good their escape. A crime alert was circulated throughout the city and PC 99 of the BTC Police attended the scene, together with police dog 'Kondor'. The dog followed a track across the fields in the direction taken by the men towards Bilton. As a result of joint working between both forces, three men were subsequently arrested and charged.

In the January 1958 issue of the *BTC Police Journal*, mention is made of the fact that, following a request from the Chief Constable of Monmouthshire, PC David Edwards and his dog 'Bronks' was loaned to the local police following a serious fire at Barry Docks.

In the January 1959 *BTC Police Journal*, mention is made of a dog display taking place at Beverley, near Hull, which involved PCs Dewson, Edson, Maycock, and Craddock, and Inspector Morrell, together with their five Alsatian dogs.

In July 1959 the *BTC Police Journal* highlighted a slightly unusual case involving PC Rochford, who normally worked with police dog 'Dane':

> A message was received at Leeds that a 'parcel' travelling from St Pancras to Leeds was causing considerable trouble on the train. The train was met by PC D. Rochford who, on opening the brake van door, was confronted with the 'parcel', which proved to be an Alsatian dog in transit from the War Dog Training School. The dog's muzzle was hanging loose on its neck and, although chained to the side of the van, the dog bared its teeth and attacked the officer. PC Rochford managed to subdue the animal but, in doing so, received a nasty bite to the knuckles of his right hand necessitating hospital treatment.

In 1962 the Southampton Docks Dog Section was formed.

Following Inspector Morrell's death in 1960 Inspector Herbert Shelton was recruited from another force in 1962 to take over his role. He had originally joined the Metropolitan Police Dog Section in 1946 as one of the six handlers, who were part of a Home Office experiment to measure the effectiveness of dogs as an aid to policing. He subsequently helped to establish a Dog Training School within the Metropolitan Police.

Terry Shelton was a very private man and what was not known among the many thousands of handlers he trained was that Terry was not his real name, nor that he was one of the heroic Marine Commandos who invaded Norway during the Second World War. It seems that a PC called him Terry by mistake just after the war and he liked it so much that he answered to it for the rest of his very long active service, just short of forty years to be accurate.

By the time Inspector Shelton had arrived at Hedon Hall, there were some thirty dogs employed at different locations around the country. They were generally kennelled in whatever premises were available, which included sidings, goods yards and, in some cases, stables in the London area, Glasgow, Leeds, West Hartlepool, Carlisle, Crewe and Derby.

Inspector Shelton established the practice of building kennels and runs at handlers' homes, so that dogs and handlers could establish that closeness necessary to form professional and effective working partnerships. He further established the concept of 'refresher training' for two weeks of every year. The plan was to raise the total number of BTP dogs to seventy-five, which required a replacement rate of twelve dogs a year.

5

'SHEP' DIES IN THE LINE OF DUTY AND THE ARRIVAL OF THE 'GUVNOR'

Terry Shelton was affectionately known as the 'Guvnor' by his many students and was widely respected for his skills and total commitment to his work. One of his first tasks was to reduce the amount of paperwork, which dog handlers had to complete after an arrest. He introduced a much simpler system that enabled the handler and his dog to be back on the patch with the minimum of delay. He also introduced a trophy for presentation to the highest scoring dog in the BTP Dog Trials, called the Big Ben Trophy, which was named after a Labrador he handled.

This book touches on a number of sad stories involving police dogs. One such case relates to police dog 'Shep' from Liverpool, who was five years old and worked in Liverpool from 16 August 1962. The dog had many successes in dealing with the criminal fraternity, or controlling unruly crowds, but was tragically killed while chasing a suspect on the railway line, who was wanted for theft.

In October 1962 Sergeant L. Austin, from the Dog Section at King's Cross, wrote an article in the *BTP Journal* entitled 'The Police Dog – From Pre-Palaeolithic to Present Times'.

At the conclusion of the article, he wrote an amusing anecdote about one particular handler:

> There was one handler who, when entering the canteen, for the benefit of a visitor would 'sit' his dog outside the door. After solemnly consulting his watch he would address the dog thus: 'It is now five minutes off ten; you will give me a call at twenty past the hour.' The handler would then enter the canteen, obtain the refreshments desired, and retire to a quiet table in the corner. The visitor is of course watching all this. At fifteen minutes past he sees that the handler is 'buried' behind a newspaper, deep in the sports page, all thoughts of the dog and time forgotten. Then, at the time stated, the door was pushed open. The dog walked up to the handler, gave a short bark, and sat down. The handler just patted the dog's head and said, 'Good lad, time for off, eh?', while the visitor tried to get his chin off the table. The secret of this little effort was a silent dog's whistle blown from behind the newspaper, the dog being trained to come when he heard the whistle.

Roger Wilks ('Wilksy') served in the Dog Section from 1963 to 1969 and recalls,

> Prior to immigrating to Australia I served with the Force between 1963 and 1969 at London St Pancras and London Euston, part of my service was as a dog handler. My collar number was 'M78' I completed my initial training at Elstree.
>
> At Elstree we not only trained our dogs but also those from South Africa. My dog, an Alsatian, was called 'Rhap', with the Kennel-Club-registered name 'Rhapsody of Bellevue'. If he didn't like anybody he would show it straight away by growling at them. On one of my courses around 1965 there was a police officer from South Africa and he was to be my 'criminal'. 'Rhap' didn't like him one bit, and he

growled and growled at the man. We gave him a head start and I could see that 'Rhap' was itching to go. I let him off the lead, telling him to fetch. The officer was running as fast as he could, shouting, 'My body is in danger.' He managed to scramble up a tree before 'Rhap' got to him.

Those days I lived in New Cross, South London and travelled to and from work with 'Rhap' by train, as we had no kennels at St Pancras. Needless to say, I never had any trouble from anyone, it was quite an experience, and the railway staff were always pleased to see me.

Stanley Peck, a former Staffordshire Police Chief Constable, was a big supporter of police dogs. He was later appointed as Her Majesty's Inspector of Constabulary in 1964 and, when he became a member of the British Transport Police Committee following his retirement, he did much to encourage the resurrection of the BTP Dog Section.

Police Dog 'Tex' from Birmingham, who was handled by PC 'M' 133 Ivor Kerslake, became well known for his prowess in tracking. On one occasion he followed the scent of a number of youths who had been interfering with railway vans, as a result of which thirteen arrests were made.

Michael Layton remembers the dog well:

Tex was unusual because he was nearer to being golden rather than the more traditional brown and black. He also had shorter hair and therefore did not carry that feeling of size that other Alsatians did. That said, in a public order situation Tex's colour and size made no difference and I personally witnessed many errant football fans making a quick exit as he advanced on them.

Ivor Kerslake joined the British Transport Commission Police in 1958, aged 22 years, and was initially posted to Lawley

Street Parcels Depot in Birmingham. He became a dog handler in 1964.

Ivor recollects his initial training:

I did my training at Hedon Hall. Actually, my first dog was called 'Vince' but after two weeks the staff realised that he could not be trained as he was too 'possessive and protective'. I could go into his pen to feed him but if anyone else went in he wouldn't let them out again, and he simply wouldn't let anyone get near to me. He went as a guard dog to a tyre company in Carlisle, but he was that good that he wouldn't let anyone into the place, including his handler.

After this Terry Shelton came back from London with four German Shepherds and just said to me, 'You can have that one', and that was it. 'Tex' was a gold-coloured German Shepherd, about eleven months old with big ears, who had been donated by a family who were having a child and were nervous about having the dog in the house.

When the Dog Section was set up in Birmingham in 1964, for a while there was just me and PC John Sutcliffe, whose nickname was 'Snowy'. His dog was 'Prince' and was the only dog to bite me and draw blood while I was at Hedon. John and I knew that we would sometimes have to feed both dogs, so we used to swap around for feeding from time to time. One day I was doing this and, just as I started to have a conversation with the trainer Sergeant Henry Wreathall, the dog just bit me.

When we first started at Birmingham there was a bit of 'anti-dog' feeling, as some officers thought that we got special treatment. Sergeant Edgar Smith was put in charge of the Dog Section at Birmingham. It was an admin role but he had two of his own German Shepherds, 'Ricky' and 'Jan', who were show dogs, and sometimes used for guarding. He was a member of the British Alsatian Association, and he also used to do some judging, so they thought that he was well qualified. Sometimes, if the press wanted a photograph, he would bring one of his out – neither of them was a trained police dog, but it just made for a better photograph. One such media opportunity was billed as 'Dogs join Parcel Patrol', and showed a picture of me with 'Tex', who by now was two years old, and Sergeant Smith with five-year-old 'Ricky' at British Railways Central Parcels Depot at Suffolk Street, which was crammed full of Christmas parcels during the holiday period.

On one occasion, Sergeant Smith was acting as the 'criminal' during a dog display, but 'Tex' took him by the unpadded right hand, instead of the 'padded' right arm. The incident made the media and Sergeant Smith, displaying a heavily bandaged hand, commented, 'I think his teeth slipped really. The trouble was that like a good dog he would not let go.'

John Sutcliffe eventually left the job after a few years, and PC Vic Batchelder took his place as the other handler.

Early on in his service as a dog handler, Ivor recalls one incident where 'Tex' became somewhat famous in the force for his tracking skills:

Basically, what happened was that we were keeping observations at Wednesbury sidings due to the railway wagons being raided. We were there from 6.30 p.m. one night until midnight and nothing happened, so we went home. I then got a phone call at 2 a.m. in the morning to say that the vans had been broken into and that they were sending a car for me. I got to the location and set 'Tex' to track. He circled around and then started to track with a couple of officers behind me. Every now and then he stopped to indicate items that he had found, mainly foodstuffs, which were collected by the officers. He tracked for a couple of miles at least and eventually identified where the offenders were getting into the sidings, and where they were leaving.

The following night observations were kept at these two locations and a couple of arrests were made, with eventually thirteen people being arrested.

On Wednesday 26 August 1964 Detective Constable Maycock, together with PC Rodmell and police dog 'Kurt', commenced observations inside Number 8 Quay canteen, in King George Dock, Hull, following a number of break-ins. At the same Detective Sergeant Deighton, together with PC Baker and police dog 'Tosca' were in Number 1 Quay.

At about 2.15 a.m. on the morning of the 27 August, DC Maycock and PC Rodmell heard voices coming from the canteen, and then heard the sound of the padlock on the kitchen door being forced with a metal instrument. From their observation point they saw two youths enter the building, at which point they challenged them. Despite the presence of the dog, the two offenders ignored warnings to stop, and ran off, one of them dropping a crowbar as he tried to escape, with a third youth who had been keeping watch outside. During the ensuing chase, one of the suspects appeared to fall over and knock himself out, while 'Kurt' was released to chase the other two.

After running about 150 yards they jumped into a small motor boat, but when PC Rodmell arrived he saw them having difficulty in unfastening the mooring rope because of 'Kurt's' presence. They were duly arrested and handcuffed together. All three suspects were subsequently dealt with for a number of canteen break-ins, with two of them being sent to a detention centre, and the third fined.

On Monday 12 October 1964 Captain Carlos Roggiero, the Chief of Police for the Province of Pichincha, in Ecuador, paid an official visit to Hull Docks. He made a specific request to see a police dog at work and PC Rodmell duly obliged by putting 'Kurt' through his paces. The captain was so impressed that he said at the conclusion of the visit that he would be lobbying for a police-dog-training facility in his home country.

On Tuesday 24 November 1964 PC G. Atchinson and Police Dog 'Flash' were on duty at the Station Master's House in Waterhouses near Durham, in connection with the theft of copper wire from lineside telephones. At about 5.40 p.m. he observed an indicator at the location that showed that wire had been cut to the east of the station. Initially he was unable to contact other CID colleagues who were involved in the observations, so he made his way along the track and, after walking for just 300 yards, saw a man on the track near to a quantity of newly cut copper wire. He called out to the man and warned him to stand still otherwise he would release the dog. The suspect did as was told and the officer arrested a man by the name of Albert Morson, handcuffing him to a nearby fence while he continued with his search.

As he was walking along a nearby bridle path, he noticed two men talking to each other. 'Flash' then tracked to a pile of empty sacks, and finally made his way to a vehicle, which turned out to be owned by the son of the first man arrested. Enquiries later connected Albert Morson, and his son Alexander Morson, who was in fact one of the two men seen on the bridle path, to the thefts and they were subsequently both fined at court.

In 1964 four new police dogs were deployed at Southampton Docks, after their initial training at the BTP Dog Training Centre at Hedon, in Hull. The dogs, including eighteen-month-old 'Blackie', were specifically trained for dock patrol work, guarding ships and warehouses. The handlers were PCs Thomas Murphy, Raymond Nias, Donald Hill, and Leonard Boughton. In charge of the new Docks Police Dog Section was Inspector P. Longland.

Over 200 arrests of criminals and 'hooligans' were attributed to police dogs in 1965, the highest figure ever, and as a result of their success the number of dogs was to be increased from forty-seven to seventy-five. Forty arrests were attributed to just one dog alone, namely 'Storm' based in Manchester, who was then just three years old.

'Rebel' from Glasgow and 'Rinty' from Southampton attended two week refresher courses at the new facility in 1966, alongside four newly trained dogs who spent ten weeks with their new handlers during initial training. The oldest dog used by the BTP at the time was 'Romulus', aged ten years, who worked at Euston, while the youngest at the time was 'Boss', just one year old and based in Crewe. Another dog that became very well-known was 'Chance' from Southampton Docks, who, along with three other dogs, had helped to cut crime by 25 per cent since their introduction.

Malcolm Clegg, who retired as a Detective Sergeant at Cardiff, recalls:

1 January 1964 saw the formation of two divisions in South Wales, Docks and Rail and it was soon decided that a 'Dog Section' would be formed in South Wales. The dog handlers would serve in the Docks division, with the exception of one handler who would perform duties as a divisional dog handler for the rail division. The docks division handlers would be stationed at Cardiff Docks, Newport Docks, and Swansea Docks, and serving officers interested in becoming dog handlers were invited to apply for these positions.

The successful applicants were: John Perry, later transferred to Cardiff Docks; John Mellor, also at Cardiff Docks; Brinley (Bryn) Morgan, at Newport Docks, and Mervyn Davies, at Swansea Docks. The handler appointed as divisional handler of Cardiff Rail Division was Constable Lovat Stuart McGregor, who was of Scottish descent. He had joined the BTC Police in Scotland but transferred to Cardiff in 1959.

I was working as a Police Cadet at the Divisional H.Q. in 1964 when Superintendent Voyle visited the premises and, after a meeting, Police Constable John Perry was summoned to the office to see him. I was present when Superintendent Voyle said to PC Perry, 'Congratulations, son. You are in trap one. You are officially our first dog handler.'

PC Perry was the first South Wales officer to attend a dog training course, after which he was transferred to Cardiff Docks to become the first dog handler in South Wales. However, he resigned after about twelve months and, as far as I recall, Derek Harris was the officer who replaced him as dog handler at Cardiff Docks.

Ian Murray retired as a District Inspector at Aberdeen and recalls,

During my police service I served in five locations in England and Scotland. The only post to have police dogs was Carlisle. When I arrived there from Preston in around 1961 two police dogs were based there under the care of their handlers, Harry Thursby and Stan Millray. Shortly after my arrival at Carlisle PC Millray left the force, and no replacement was allocated.

I frequently assisted Harry Thursby in the training of his dog. My contribution mainly consisted of running for the dog. That is, I played the part of the villain. When I was 50 to 75 yards away, Harry would release the dog, which halted my progress. During these episodes I was fitted with padding on my right arm and instructed to hold this out to the dog when it came up to me. I was further instructed to stand perfectly still and the dog would not harm me.

Also, on at least three occasions, I concealed myself in the goods warehouse. Harry would then release the dog, which ran along the warehouse platforms, but never detected my presence there!

Pete Hempton joined the British Transport Commission Police at Crewe in 1960 and in 1965 he joined the Dog Section, completing his training at Elstree. He was allocated an Alsatian called 'Boss'. Upon the retirement of 'Boss' in 1973, Pete worked at Elstree as an Instructor and kept in touch with 'Boss' as he spent his retirement there. Pete was later promoted to Uniform Sergeant and later Detective Sergeant at Crewe. He recalls:

One of my first arrests came in the days leading up to Christmas 1965. In those days the railway carried a high volume of Post Office mail and parcels traffic, and a lot of it arrived at Crewe for sorting and was the subject of thefts.

At 1.10 a.m. on 23 December 1965, I was on duty with dog 'Boss' and two other colleagues in the sidings just off Hungerford Road, Crewe, when we saw a car parked without lights. A number of mailbags and parcels were found scattered on its seats. I removed the ignition keys, released 'Boss' and told him to 'find'. He made straight for a hut and found a man hiding in there. Realising that there was a police dog looking for him, the man shouted, 'I will come out.' He emerged and was arrested, and two others were subsequently arrested and all three charged with the theft of the mail bags and parcels in rail transit.

The offenders subsequently appeared at Crewe Magistrates' Court and one man received six months' imprisonment after admitting to previous thefts of mail. The other two received fines. The Chairman of the bench, Mr Consterdine, said that the magistrates appreciated the work of the police in dealing with the matter and added that the public should know what 'wonderful dogs the police had.'

Peter and his colleagues subsequently received a Commendation for good police work from George East, Area Chief of Police, Manchester.

6

'TEX' BECOMES A BLUES SUPPORTER AND 'BOSS' CLEANS UP CREWE

Roger Wilkes recalls another incident involving 'Rhap':

On another occasion – I believe in 1966 – 'Rhap', a Detective Constable and I were on duty in the goods yard at St Pancras, keeping observation for thieves. A thief was spotted. He started to run away. As I shouted a warning to him and was about to unleash 'Rhap', the Detective set off running after the thief. By the time I realised he was in hot pursuit, I'd let 'Rhap' off the lead. The inevitable happened – 'Rhap' brought down the Detective, while the thief got clean away. There were some red faces and swear words that night.

Frank Street served in the Military Police before joining the British Transport Commission Police in Birmingham in 1959. He became a dog handler in 1968, much to the annoyance of his wife Molly, who had just given birth to their daughter, and was facing the prospect of him being away from home for a lengthy period. He did his initial training at Elstree under the supervision of Chief Inspector Shelton, whom Frank described with a degree of affection as being 'a brilliant guy – if not a bit bolshie'.

Frank's dog 'Rebel' was a traditional brown-and-black-haired Alsatian and was just under twelve months old when he started training. Frank describes his experiences of working with 'Rebel' as follows:

He was a good dog and very strong. He wasn't very good at tracking, as he was far too excitable, but he was great with football crowds and was more of an 'attack' dog. He could jump over a wall 8 feet high, and do a long jump of some 13 feet. Mr Shelton once acted as 'the runner' at a show we gave to the public and commented that, when 'Rebel' went in to take his arm, you could tell that he 'meant business'.

When we were trying to control football supporters you could see that he did indeed mean business. He had a thing for anything that sort of flowed so I had to keep him away from football scarves. On one occasion the robes of a passing nun even caught his attention and I had to hold him back, while on another occasion a man with a walking stick passed by a little bit too close for comfort.

I remember being involved in serious football-related disorders with him at Smethwick Rolfe Street, and Leicester where we had trouble with Tottenham fans, and at Sheffield for a semi-final, where I saw a dog from the local force rip the back out of PC Dave Wickham's uniform coat. I always felt safe with him though. I used to travel on the football special trains with him and would let him go through the carriages on a long lead or tie him up in the brake van at the rear until we arrived.

Sometimes he would do the unexpected – we were patrolling the shopping centre above New Street station one night and we found the front doors to a furniture store open. I put 'Rebel' inside and he promptly 'cocked his leg up' on every sofa as he passed through searching for intruders! On another occasion, I was on night duty patrolling the goods yards in Lawley Street, Birmingham when we disturbed some men on the 'V' shed. I called for them to stop but they ran, so I released the dog. He shot off after them but unfortunately in the dark he ran into some protruding metal bars at the back of a Scammell trailer and finished up taking out one of his large front teeth.

Molly Street recalls the softer side of having a police dog in the household:

He was great with the kids and they loved him. We also had a Staffordshire Bull Terrier at one stage and he used to play 'Rebel' up until, one day, 'Rebel' just put his paw on him to hold him down and snapped at him – enough was enough and he didn't do it again. 'Rebel' was ten years old when he died. He had a growth and had to be put to sleep. We were all so upset that we put off going on holiday.

Frank concludes,

The dog handlers tended to be characters in those days, but very committed to their dogs and the jobs they were doing. There was a handler on each shift in the Midlands area: myself, Ivor Kerslake, and Ron Woollaston at Birmingham, and Don Hughes at Wolverhampton. Ron was ex-military – always immaculately turned out, and with a real skill in woodwork, so much so that he was forever collecting pieces of wood to work on. Ron had his dog's kennel in the middle of a big shed in his back garden but he had so much wood in it at times the dog could hardly get in!

Ivor Kerslake continues his recollections:

They eventually decided to increase the Dog Section at Birmingham to three and we were joined by PC Ron Woollaston and 'Brutus', who had originally been handled by an officer at Crewe but got into trouble for barking at cattle on board some railway trucks. To say the least, 'Brutus' was initially very aggressive but, within a few weeks, Ron had changed his personality completely and he became a great dog.

Ron was very laidback and placid unless someone went too far. He was a typical guardsman and 'always obeyed the last order'. On one occasion I remember being told by an Inspector to patrol the railway line between Vauxhall and Aston because of problems with kids on the lines. I refused to do it because it was not safe. The following week Ron was on duty and the same Inspector gave him an instruction to go to Vauxhall, due to the problems with trespass, and then to go to Aston. Ron duly completed his task and, when I questioned why he had done it when it was dangerous, he said that the last part of his instruction was to go to Aston so he went there and simply sat on the station.

In those days we didn't have a dedicated vehicle for the dogs so the shift Inspectors used to send someone out to pick us up from home. One of the Inspectors resented having to do this, so when Ron rang up one day to ask to be picked up, the Inspector refused and told him to make his own way in. Ron duly travelled on the bus to work with 'Brutus' and the job quickly realised that having a big German Shepherd on a bus was not the best way of doing things so they got us a vehicle.

We used to train regularly at Springfield Farm in Sutton Coldfield and at the British Railways Sports and Social Ground in Eastern Road. The BTP Cadets at Birmingham regularly acted as 'criminals' and, between 1968 to 1971, Cadets Michael Layton (co-author), Paul Majster and Paul Turner frequently donned the 'padded sleeve', which was covered by a raincoat, and tried to outrun the dogs – always unsuccessfully unless they were quick enough to get up a tree. The idea was to wear the padding on the right arm and to offer that arm to the dog when they attacked. Sometimes it didn't always go to plan! On other occasions the Cadets were tasked with hiding in hedges and up trees to see if the dog could find them.

We used to have one PC at Birmingham who was always goading the dogs saying, 'Come get me', and trying to wind them up. I got one of the Sergeants, Ted Graham, to tell him one day that he had been selected to help with the training. He refused point blank to do it but never teased them again.

Ivor recalls some of his experiences policing football supporters in about 1970:

On one occasion Birmingham City were travelling away and we had a full football special train to take out. It was going to be a full train and, as usual, they were a bit noisy. I think that there were five of us on the escort. In the office, as I was getting ready, I took a 'Blues' scarf from my locker and put it around 'Tex's' neck. As we went down onto the platform all the fans started cheering and shouting, 'He's one of us!' A bit later on, as we were on the train, a fan came up to me and asked me if the dog was in fact a 'Blues' supporter. I politely informed him that he was wearing the scarf so that he knew which supporters to bite!

On another occasion, Ivor and 'Tex' escorted Aston Villa fans on a special train to Huddersfield and the media were on hand to witness them wisely giving 'Tex' a wide berth on the platform, as Ivor commented: '"Tex" is a veteran of seven years now. He is the best crowd controller we have.' 400 Villa fans made the trip north and on this occasion an officer was placed in each of six carriages, in addition to 'Tex'. On the same date another dog handler boarded a special train at Birmingham New Street to escort Wolverhampton fans travelling to Sheffield.

Ivor also has memories of some other crime-related incidents:

We were keeping observations one day in some sidings where people had been stealing phosphor bronze bearings from wagons. We were at the top of an embankment, when we heard a noise and the dog indicated. The CID officers that I was with told me to let the dog go and a few minutes later the dog started barking. We got down the embankment and found 'Tex' guarding a man who was standing 'to attention' against a wagon. He was arrested, but it turned out that he wasn't a thief at all and that he had been using the railway to spy on courting couples – a bit of voyeurism. His wife was none too happy after his house was searched but he wasn't charged.

On another occasion we were keeping observations on booking offices that were being broken into in the early 1970s. I was out late one night with DS Stan Jones, and DC Harry Reeves, and we saw two figures walking away from the direction of one office and crossing the railway lines. I shouted to them to stop but they started to run so I released the dog. One of the men thought better of it when the dog caught up with him and stopped while the second escaped. Harry Reeves got to him first and said proudly, 'We got you!' At which point, the prisoner said, 'No you didn't – he did!'

and indicated to the dog. I was supposed to go out with the CID next day to get the second person but, by the time I came back on duty, they had already got him in so I never got a mention!

Ivor recalls another incident on a football special train where nerves were tested:

I was moving through the train at regular intervals with 'Tex' and every time I went through one particular coach someone imitated a dog barking. I eventually managed to identify the culprit, who obviously thought it was hugely funny and was playing up to his mates. During the course of the journey, one of them came up to me quietly and told me to watch it as the 'dog barker' was intending to smash a bottle over the dog's head in the usual confusion on arrival at our destination. I decided to confront the issue and took 'Tex' back to the coach where the troublemaker was sitting. We had 'words' and I pointed to a bottle and said to him, 'There is the dog and there is the bottle – your move, then, young man.' At this point 'Tex' sat there looking at him with a sense of anticipation. As I expected he backed down completely and lost total face in front of those around him, who all laughed at him.

'Tex' was great with children and my niece Kim used to come round to see us when she was about four years of age, and liked to hold the dog on his lead. Sometimes she would go to sleep with 'Tex' on the floor and rest her head on his stomach. Her mother had to ask me to pick her up when it was time to go because he used to growl at her, being protective.

'Tex' was retired in about 1975 at the age of eleven years and I kept him at home. He lived until he was about fourteen years of age but, over a period of time, his health suffered and eventually he went blind. I had another dog that used to guide him around the garden. Finally it was time to do the right thing because of his failing health and a friend of mine drove me to the vets so that he could be put to sleep. I knew I wouldn't be in any fit state to drive afterwards and it was a very sad day for us as a family.

Without doubt the dog always came first in the house. When I got home he always had to be groomed, fed and exercised first. That was the difference between being a working dog and a pet.

At one stage Ivor recalls that PC 'Nobby' Clarke, based at King's Cross, was given a Rottweiler to handle and the dog was so strong that, on one occasion while playing with it, his arm got broken.

In March 1966 PC Dan Donovan and his dog 'Fritz' were featured on an ITV programme highlighting the dangers associated with committing crime on the railways. The officer and 'Fritz', based at King's Cross, had been working together for fourteen months and had already made five arrests.

From time to time occasions arose that questioned the value of tracker dog evidence in bringing accused persons to justice. Although not involving British Transport Police dogs, the following are two cases of interest in relation to arresting suspects:

R. V. Montgomery 1966 N.I. 120

A police constable in Northern Ireland saw three men apparently stealing wire from a telegraph pole but, before he could approach closely enough to be able to identify them, they made off across some fields and he lost sight of them.

About an hour and a half later, a police dog handler brought his tracker dog to the base of the telegraph pole, where the dog picked up a scent and went off in the same direction as the escaping men had gone. The dog followed the scent for some time and eventually stopped at a place from which the three accused men had previously been driven away in a car. In upholding convictions and ruling that the evidence of a dog handler as to the behaviour of the tracker dog was admissible, the Court of Criminal Appeal of Northern Ireland said that there was nothing to require the trial judge to warn the jury that it would be dangerous to convict the accused on that evidence without corroboration.

The members of the Court thought that it would be unrealistic to close one's eyes to the fact that it had been known for a long time that dogs can follow human scent. It was also common knowledge that dogs can be trained to obey commands, and there's no reason to doubt that a dog can be trained to obey a command that tells him he is to look for a scent and follow it.

Paterson v. Nixon 1960. S. L. T 220

In 1960 there is a Scottish case concerning tracker dog evidence of Paterson *v.* Nixon 1960. S.L.T 220. It appears that the facts, in this instance, were that a lady returned to her house after an absence of about three hours and found that it had been broken into. She herself did not enter at that time but called a neighbour who immediately called the police. They were very quickly on the scene with the dog.

The history of the dog was that it was an Alsatian and had been trained at the London Metropolitan Police School. Its training included tracking, searching, man work, and discriminating between and detecting the scents of persons and the tracking of them by their scent. It had completed its last four months of training with its present handler, been tested, and passed fit and up to a high standard for its work. It had been kept in rigorous training and worked regularly to maintain that standard.

The case further set out that, on being taken into the house, the dog appeared to get a scent from an article that had been moved after the occupier had left. It also got scents on two rugs, one standing before a wardrobe and the other before a dressing chest, both of which had been opened. From their knowledge of the mode of commission, the police suspected Paterson, and took the dog to the common stair in which he lived. At the entrance to that stair the dog was again allowed to smell the rugs. It then sniffed along the passage and up the stairs. There were six houses on the top flat where it stopped. In response to the police knocking, Paterson opened the door. Two further tests, or a similar test in duplicate, were then carried out. When they arrived at the police station, the police took Paterson's shoes from him. They then obtained shoes from five police officers who had come on duty shortly before.

First, they placed all the right shoes together and again, after smelling the rug, the dog went along the line of shoes and back, and then brought Paterson's right shoe to the handler. A similar test was then made with the left shoes with the same result. In considering the value to be placed on the evidence of these actions, the Lord Chief Justice Clerk (Lord Thomson) gave it as his opinion that no general rule could be laid down, and sustained the conviction, citing that the dog was reliable.

Pete Hempton further recalls,

In the spring of 1966 I, together with police dog 'Boss' and four other colleagues were called to the main West Coast

Railway Line, half a mile south of Winsford railway station, which is north of Crewe. A British Railways overhead line inspector had found a gap in the copper return conductor wire, the cable on either side of the section hanging slack. I would estimate that around 500 feet of copper cable had been stolen; I put 'Boss' to work on tracking in the area. He found a crumpled sheet of paper on the lineside, which turned out to be a time-sheet belonging to man from Nantwich, near Crewe. This find led us to the arrest of the man from Nantwich and two others. They subsequently appeared at the Cheshire Quarter Sessions at Knutsford on a joint charge of stealing cable to the value of £60. They were convicted of the offence.

Peter and his colleagues subsequently received a Commendation for good Police work from George East, Area Chief of Police, Manchester.

Pete continues,

In 1966 myself, 'Boss' and some colleagues had to board a football special train at Crewe, which was travelling from Birmingham to Manchester conveying Manchester United fans, due to the fact that a carriage had been wrecked by the fans returning from a match with Aston Villa, which United lost 2-1. Seats had been ripped, windows broken and every light bulb was smashed. More than £700-worth of damage was done to the six-coach train. There was no more trouble for the rest of the journey, but the damaged coach was a virtual write-off.

Again in 1966, in company with 'Boss', I was called to the British Railways-owned car park in Gresty Road, regarding the suspicious activities of a twenty-year-old local youth and his accomplice, who was sixteen years of age. One of the youths was seen by me stealing a wing mirror from a car. On seeing me they ran off. I shouted for them to stop but they continued running, so I let 'Boss' off the lead. 'Boss' soon caught both of them. They were arrested and found not only to have stolen the mirror but also a car aerial and a petrol filler cap. They had also caused damage to a wing mirror and a car aerial. The thieves appeared at Crewe Magistrates' Court and the sixteen-year-old was fined £20 and ordered to pay restitution of £1 6s 3d, which was a lot of money in those days, while the twenty-year-old was jailed for a total of six months.

On 12 August 1966 Harry Roberts murdered three plainclothes Metropolitan Police officers, in Shepherd's Bush, London. He went on the run. Shortly afterwards we received a call from the Metropolitan Police in Shepherd's Bush to the effect that they had a tip to say he was on the 11.35 p.m. train from Glasgow to London. At 5 a.m., when the train arrived at Crewe, myself, along with 'Boss' and uniformed officers from the British Transport Police and Cheshire Constabulary, met the train with truncheons drawn to search for Roberts, but found nothing.

In 1966 'Boss' and I were called to assist the Cheshire Constabulary to search for six boys who had escaped from an approved school in the Crewe area. Due to the diligent tracking of 'Boss', the boys were found in Basford Hall railway sidings. They were subsequently detained and returned to the school.

While on routine patrol on nights with 'Boss' in the railway sidings in Cliff Vale, Stoke on Trent, I came across five men who were sleeping in the railway carriages. As they were of no fixed abode, they were arrested and appeared at Fenton Magistrates' Court, Stoke on Trent, where they pleaded guilty to trespass on the railway and received different forms of punishment.

During an evening Crewe Alexandra *v.* Chester football match in 1966, I was on duty with 'Boss' at the rear of Crewe's ground, which actually borders railway property, when I saw a fourteen-year-old Chester boy with a steel spanner fastened to a wooden shaft. The boy claimed it had been thrown at him and he had picked it up to defend himself if he was attacked. He was fined the maximum of £20 when he appeared in the juvenile court.

One night while I was on patrol with 'Boss' and a colleague in Gresty Road, Crewe, I saw a local man, who had just come out of prison, climb over the fence into a cable compound at the signal and telegraph stores in Gresty Road, and start to throw what appeared to be coils of wire over the fence. When we approached him he then ran away and I released 'Boss' to go after him, calling the man to stop. The man shouted, 'All right, I give in – call the dog off'. He was arrested. The cable, which was scrap, weighed around 1.5 cwt and was valued at £35. He was given a six-month prison sentence, suspended for two years. The Chairman of the bench commented, 'The circumstances of this case point to the advantages of a well-trained police dog, "Boss". I think it should be entered on "Boss's" record.'

A member of the railway staff informed me that he had seen two men with shotguns in the North Staffordshire railway sidings, Crewe. I went to the scene with 'Boss', who quickly picked up the scent of the two men and found them hiding in an adjacent field, with a girl. One of the men stated that he was protecting the girl, who was on the run from the police, and did not want her to get caught. The other stated that he was just doing some shooting. They were arrested and it was subsequently discovered that the two men had been released from prison the previous year and had been automatically prohibited from carrying a firearm for five years. They appeared at Crewe Borough Magistrates' Court and were each sent to prison for two months for trespassing on railway land with firearms and four months concurrently for being in possession of firearms as convicted men

At 7.45 p.m. on 26 February 1967, after a local coal merchant had complained to us about the theft of coal from his yard, I, along with 'Boss' and another officer, went to the Cumberland Coal Wharf, Crewe. 'Boss' was quickly on the case and picked up a very recent scent of someone. I let him sniff around the area further and he found a local youth hiding behind a coal stack with a sack of coal at his feet. He was arrested and was convicted at Crewe Borough Magistrates' Court.

Most major railway stations issued platform tickets for members of the public to use the facilities of the station, without purchasing a travel ticket. These tickets usually cost around 2d. At certain times, particularly during the night, it became necessary to stop issuing these tickets. Crewe Railway station was no exception to this rule. On one particular night, while I was on night duty, four local men came to Crewe Railway station and were refused admission as they were not travelling by train and that the sale of platform tickets had been suspended for the night. They became abusive towards the ticket collector and other members of the railway staff. They made their way to the refreshment room via another route. I was called with 'Boss' and a colleague to them. On seeing us, they became abusive. I commanded 'Boss' to bark, which quietened them down considerably. The offenders were ejected from the refreshment room. However, in view of their conduct, they were arrested and later appeared at Crewe Borough Magistrates' Court to be fined, with a threat that if they appeared before the Bench again they would be sent to Borstal.

One evening in 1967 a Liverpool soccer fan from Lancashire, who was travelling to Liverpool on a football special was seen by a railway worker to leave the train while it stopped at Crewe, pick up a mailbag, throw it over his shoulder and carry it just like Father Christmas and get back onto the train. I attended with 'Boss' and arrested the culprit. He appeared at court and was fined.

Over the years the Electric Traction Depot, Wistaston Road, Crewe, has been subject to the theft of copper wire. Therefore it was necessary for us to carry out observations from time to time. At 8.30 p.m. on 12 November 1967 I was on observations with 'Boss' and a colleague, in the sidings at the depot, when I saw three local men, who were well-known thieves, carrying two rolls of copper cable between them. This cable weighed approximately 1.25 cwt with a value of £40. I released 'Boss' and told the men to stand still. At this, one of the men shouted, 'All right. Keep that dog off me.' One of the others replied, 'It's a fair cop'. All three were arrested and interviewed. During the interview they admitted other similar offences. On appearing at Crewe Borough Magistrates' Court, they were each given suspended prison sentences. The Chairman of the Bench praised the work of 'Boss', stating that if it were not for him they might not have been caught.

One of my most unusual cases was one evening when I was patrolling with 'Boss' in the old disused section of Crewe locomotive works off Forge Street, Crewe. Sniffing about, 'Boss' suddenly began to dig frantically and exposed to view part of a horse box. Eventually the whole horsebox, which had been dismantled section by section and buried under earth and timber, came to light. Enquiries by our officers established that it came from Alme, near Alcester, Warwickshire. It is not known what motive could inspire anyone to dismantle it and bury it in Crewe.

Just before Christmas 1966 or 1967 I, 'Boss' and some colleagues were keeping observations on the Christmas mail, which was in transit on the platforms of Crewe railway station, when we saw two men leave a car in Station Street and enter the station over the railway lines. A short time later they returned, carrying parcels. When spoken to by one of my colleagues they dropped the parcels and ran off. A police dog was sent after them but was injured, and I released 'Boss', who caught them both. Both men received prison sentences.

One evening, while I was patrolling the Crewe to Chester railway line with 'Boss' in the vicinity of the old locomotive works, I saw two railway shunters picking up pieces of scrap brass and copper from the ground in the yard of the works. They were arrested and during interview they admitted theft of other property from British Rail. They were subsequently fined at court.

On Saturday 19 February 1966 PC F. White and police dog 'Mark' were on duty in the North sidings at Hartlepool when the officer saw a John Patrick Ryan walking towards him carrying coils of cable around his shoulder. Ryan was well known to the officer as a local thief, a well-built man who was 6 feet 3 inches tall and always difficult when in drink. He was also prone to running away when he saw the police. PC White saw Ryan drop the cable and turn round as if to make off, at which point he released the dog and commanded Ryan to stop and stand still, which he wisely did. The officer then called off the dog and arrested Ryan, who was eventually sentenced to three months' imprisonment.

The Southern Alsatian Training Society held their Championship Working Trials under Kennel Club Rules between 29 September and 1 October 1966 at Ashsown Forest, Hartfield, East Sussex. The force entered police dog

'Chance' registered name, 'Laddie of Clan Dhai' – in the Utility Stake. Thirty-one dogs were entered, seven of which were police dogs from five civil forces. PC Murphy with his dog 'Chance' were second, obtaining 198 marks out of a possible 220 marks, the dog qualifying U.D. excellent and gaining a Certificate of Merit.

'Chance' was born on 23 July 1962, and was donated to the force by a Mr Davidson of Hull. PC Murphy, the handler, commenced a basic course of dog-handling with the dog in August 1963. At the completion of the course, the dog and handler gained 372 marks out of a possible 405. As mentioned previously, in 1964, the John William Morrell Trophy Competition was initiated in the force, with a team of dogs and handlers from each area competing for the trophy on a knock-out basis. PC Murphy was selected to represent the Southern area and that area won the trophy. On this occasion PC Murphy was the second-highest scorer in the final, the top marker being PC Philbin of Manchester with his dog 'Storm'. PC Murphy went on to achieve great success in other competitions. Before taking up police-dog work, PC Murphy had no previous experience in this field. The dog 'Chance' was just four years old at the time.

John Warner served with the British Transport Police from 1967 until 1994 at London Euston, King's Cross, Liverpool Street, Mansion House, Baker Street and Liverpool Street London Underground and he recollects the following incidents while he was a dog handler at London Euston:

> I was with Police Dog 'Hobo' from 1967 to 1974, as PC 'M' 54. We had a good bond and he lived at my home. During training he was good at obedience and agility, excelled at man work but gained about 60 per cent in tracking. We were attached to the Euston Division.

During mid-December 1969, due to burglaries relating to theft of furs taking place at Watford Rail Depot, I was directed to carry out observation with 'Hobo' and Police Constable Matt Crowley who is now deceased. For four nights, we took up observation at 10.00 p.m., and maintained the observation to about 03.00 a.m. The depot was in complete darkness and, it being winter, very cold.

We took up our observation under a wagon about 50 yards from the parcels bank. Because of the freezing weather, I managed to obtain three blankets from the sleeping cars, one for 'Hobo', and one each for ourselves. I actually saw the puddles freeze by my side. We also had a flask of soup to keep us warm.

On the fourth night, about 02.00 a.m., 'Hobo' sat up and pointed in the direction of the warehouse. I said to Matt that it could be a cat or somebody could be in. I said that I would give it three minutes and then release the dog. 'Hobo' remained silent. It was the longest three minutes I have ever spent. Then I released him. A short while later I heard him bark. Matt went one side of the parcels bank and I went the other side. I found 'Hobo' still barking and indicating under the bank. During the excitement I forgot my torch, so I struck a match and saw a male under the bank. He then ran from the bank and, in doing so, knocked Matt over. Under the street lighting, I could see him running up the road chased by 'Hobo', who apprehended him. First aid was rendered and he was advised to attend his doctor for a tetanus injection.

A search was carried out and three parcels containing furs were found cut open, their value about £500. He was charged with burglary at Watford Police Station and received a six-month suspended sentence. After court and having a sociable pint he told me that he was the one with the least convictions as there were four more waiting to enter the warehouse. So, really I should have waited a little longer. 'Hobo' may have at least detained one more. 'Hobo' received a Chief Constable's Commendation.

During August time the following year on night duty at about 03.00 a.m., I was off my patch at Broad Street station car park. I released 'Hobo' for his exercise when I heard him bark. I located him; he was on his hind legs with his paws on the driver's side of a Daimler car. I thought to myself, 'I am in trouble if he has scratched the car.' Through questioning the male occupant and enquiries made by radio, I found that the car had been stolen. He admitted that he was a chef at a hotel in the Euston area and that he had taken the keys to the vehicle from the bedroom of a customer. I called for assistance and he was conveyed to City Road Police Station. It later transpired he was wanted by Special Branch and was suspected of IRA activity in Belfast.

I was in plain clothes with 'Hobo' walking from King's Cross station to Euston late one evening when I saw four youths, who were football supporters, cross the road and commence beating another supporter. I released the dog and arrested all four. They were charged with public order offences and received suspended sentences at Clerkenwell Magistrates' Court. The supporter received minor injuries.

On another operation, when whisky thefts were reported at Cricklewood sidings, observations were carried out for a couple of weeks with some CID officers. I lay under a wagon with the wind blowing from the bonded wagons towards us. One night, during the early hours, I heard the locks break, and released 'Hobo'. The dog detained one male by the wagon and the second male remained in the wagon with the whisky. Both were arrested and dealt with by the CID.

'Hobo' was also used for crowd control in respect to football supporters. On one occasion, while on a long lead he dispersed some one hundred rowdy fans from Euston station. The Inspector was so impressed that he patted my shoulder; at the same time 'Hobo' bit him on the arm, causing bruising, but nothing was further said.

British Rail was, as it is today, experiencing cable thefts. During my dog-handling days, cable thefts were taking place from trunking alongside tracks in North London. This line was operated by signal boxes. Once the cable was cut the signalman lost his circuit detail. I spent a couple of weeks or so hidden in the bushes with 'Hobo' between two signal boxes. I had made arrangements with the signalman at one box to flash his hand lamp. Early hours of one morning, I saw the lamp flash. I waited for a while when I heard footsteps on the ballast. In the moonlight I saw a tall and well-built male carrying a quantity of cable. When he was level with me, I broke cover with the dog. He made no effort to run. I told him he was under arrest. In reply to the caution he said he wanted the cable to string up his runner beans. He was a likeable Irishman. He received a suspended custodial sentence.

During his service 'Hobo' did a few displays at fêtes and schools. To keep up to standard, 'Hobo' and I had one day's training each month and two weeks every two years. The initial course had totalled six weeks. On my rest days, with permission from the local farmer, I practiced tracking with 'Hobo.' As a team we successfully managed to track for about half an hour after the track was laid, but my young daughter, Julie, who was about six years old then, would lay a track covering most of a large field. She would leave small items, such a buttons, on her way round. Believe it or not, 'Hobo' would follow the track some three hours later.

The reason for this was that the dog loved Julie as she gave him the odd sweet or two – the loving memory of a faithful animal.

As an aside, while he was operational, 'Hobo' was chosen to play the 'werewolf' in a Dracula film starring Jack Palance and Simon Ward. The reason being that he was a grey long-coated dog, with a good record of detaining a running person. The film company had difficulty in finding a dog that would perform the required scene. The filming was completed at Slough. The brief I had was to train 'Hobo' to jump through French doors. The doors were made of balsawood and toffee glass. I commenced training 'Hobo' by jumping through an open window. Then we covered the window with loose cooking foil so it had no resistance. Eventually he would jump through the window with the foil stuck to the frame with sellotape.

The storyline was that Dracula attended the zoo and put a spell on the wolf, which then attacked and killed the zookeeper. On the set 'Hobo' stood and growled beside Dracula. The wolf ('Hobo') went to the next scene where he then ran up a platform and, at a command from me, jumped through the French doors and landed on the carpet in the lounge. The wolf ('Hobo') then attacked the butler, who was the actor Simon Ward. In fact it was a stuntman. The wolf was then shot during the struggle.

A lookalike dummy of 'Hobo' was used, as I refused to allow 'Hobo' to be sedated, much to the annoyance of the director. Incidentally two stuntmen attended initially and both requested that they run for the dog to gain experience. I told them not to run but jog. One decided to run and the dog hit him at speed and knocked him over, thus injuring his arm. He was out of action and I was not paid!

During 1977 the second film he was involved in after he retired was *The Seven-Per-Cent Solution*, starring Laurence Olivier. As Sherlock Holmes was a drug addict, a scene showed him in bed having hallucinations, with snakes floating in the air and a wolf jumping out of the wardrobe. After about two months I managed to get 'Hobo' to run in darkness and jump on command through the backless wardrobe, strike and spring the doors open. On this occasion I received a cheque for £300.

Below are extracts from British Transport Police General Order Number 245, dated November 1967 and headed, 'Police Dog Handlers and Police Dogs':

OWNERSHIP – Police dogs are the property of the British Railways Board and must not, without authority, be used for training purposes outside official duties, or be entered in any Dog Show, exhibition, or demonstration, or registered with any Society or organisation; handlers will not have the use of any police dog for stud purposes.

LICENCES – Licences for all police dogs, in compliance with the Dog Licences Act 1867, as amended, will be obtained by the Divisional Superintendent of the division concerned and held by him. They will be taken out in the name of the Chief Constable, British Transport Police, and the name of the place, i.e. Manchester, Glasgow, etc.

USE OF POLICE DOGS – Police dogs are trained to:

– Track from a scene of crime, i.e., breaking into a warehouse, van or building, removing bearings from wagons, larceny of telephone wire, or where objects have been placed on the track.

– Search buildings, yards and open spaces for hidden persons, usually after thieves have been disturbed.
– Search stabled stock for vagrants, missing persons etc.
– Search for and recover property at the scene of a crime; stolen property relating to the crime; housebreaking implements; or property belonging to the thief and dropped by him.
– Chase, hold, and detain fleeing criminals found committing a crime.

The practical application of dog and handler is to employ them on a patrol on foot; mobile and foot patrol:

– To prevent or detect the theft of property.
– To prevent or detect acts of vandalism.
– To detect or prevent trespass.
– To assist in combating rowdyism at stations, especially when trouble is expected, e.g. football specials.
– To assist in escorting large sums of cash, bullion, etc.
– To assist the CID on observations where gangs are likely to be encountered where terrain is difficult, e.g. unlit sidings, during the hours of darkness.
– Aggressive attacks against suspects and prisoners are to be avoided.

DOG HANDLERS – Exercising, grooming, feeding, etc.

– On a working day, allow forty-five minutes. On a rest day or annual leave day, allow one hour and thirty minutes. Any time spent on this outside of duty hours is to be regarded as being within the commuted allowance arrangements.

FEEDING OF DOGS – The food requirements of the dog are 1.5 lbs of meat a day and 0.75 lb of biscuits. In some cases certain dogs may require a little more meat or biscuit, but where this is thought to be necessary the Chief Instructor should be consulted.

ALLOWANCE FOR KEEPING DOG AT HOME – An allowance of £1 7s 6d is allowed for keeping a dog at the handler's home. If cases arise where it is alleged that the allowance does not cover the cost of feeding the dog, the Chief Instructor should be consulted. (Allowance based on meat at 2s 0d per lb = 10.5 lbs per week = 21s 0d; biscuits at 1s 2d per lb = 5.25 lbs per week = 6s 1.5d. Total 27s 1.5d).

DOGS SICK, INJURED ETC. – A dog handler is responsible for the fitness of his dog in so far as it lies within his power to ensure it.

Dog Unfit – If a dog shows any symptoms of unfitness for duty through sickness or injury, it should be reported to the handler's Inspector at once. The Chief Instructor should be consulted before taking the dog to a veterinary surgeon (approved), except in cases of emergency, when the circumstances should be reported afterwards for the information of the Chief Instructor. If treatment by the approved veterinary surgeon is authorised, the dog handler must comply strictly with his instructions. Handlers will ensure that the medical history sheet provided for each dog is produced to, and completed by, the veterinary surgeon at each consultation. At the conclusion of the treatment, the dog handler will submit a report for the information of his Chief of Police, Divisional Superintendent, and Chief Instructor at the Dog School.

Visit to Sick Dogs – Sick dogs will be visited by the Chief Instructor at his discretion, or if asked by the local Divisional Superintendent. A register of sick dogs is maintained at the Dog Training School. If, in the opinion of the Chief Instructor or approved veterinary surgeon, a dog is so ill or injured as to be unfit for duty, the handler will perform ordinary duty during the time the dog is so incapacitated.

Nursing – In cases of serious illness or injuries the handler will, with the authority of his Superintendent in consultation with the Chief Instructor at the Dog School, or the approved Veterinary Surgeon, devote up to a maximum of four hours daily to the care of his dog.

Removal to Dog Training School – In cases where the treatment is likely to be prolonged, or where the handler is unable, for any reason, to give proper attention, the sick dog must be removed to the Dog Training School.

INITIAL TRAINING – Initial training of police dogs and handlers is carried out at the Dog Training School, Elstree. The dogs are trained in obedience, agility, to search for persons and property, to track, and to chase and hold a running person. If the person stands still before the arrival of the dog, the dog does not bite, but stands guard on the person until the handler arrives.

Duration of the Course – the basic course lasts ten weeks. The course commences on a Monday and the handler travels on the first day of the course. He returns to his home station on the last Friday of the course with his dog.

Travelling – handlers attending basic courses will be met at Bushey and Oxhey or Elstree stations if time of arrival is notified in advance. Time of arrival should be arranged as near 1 p.m. as possible to avoid unnecessary use of transport.

Lodgings – Handlers other than those who live close to the School in London will be accommodated in the British Rail Hostel, Old Oak Common. Sleeping accommodation is provided at 35s od – a single room per week, 31s 6d.

Two men sharing a room, 5s od per night, for odd nights. Meals can be purchased from a varied menu at the Hostel as required.

Transport – handlers are issued with passes to travel to and from the Hostel between Bushey and Willesden. Handlers are met at Bushey in the morning and returned to Bushey in the evening by police transport.

Allowance – Handlers are allowed £4 5s od per week while in the Hostel to cover lodgings and meals, plus £1 5s od social allowance.

RE-ALLOCATION COURSES – Re-allocation courses are arranged from time to time where a trained dog becomes available, i.e., through the resignation or promotion of the dog's handler. The dog is then allocated to a new handler, with or without previous experience. Preferably one who has had a basic course.

Multi-handlers – this method of handling dogs can only be done on a very restricted basis. To be successful, the necessary ingredients are as follows: the selected dog must be several years of age, and have received a great deal of training. The dog must have an ideal temperament to accept more than one handler and work satisfactorily for them. The number of handlers for one dog should be restricted to few as possible, i.e. two.

Local Refresher Training – This is arranged locally where facilities and duties permit. A minimum of one day a month is necessary to keep the dog up to a high pitch of efficiency. One day a fortnight is preferable. When there is only one handler at a station, arrangements can usually be made for the handler to train with the Local Constabulary handlers. If this cannot be arranged and training cannot be fixed up within the Force owing to distance etc., the Chief Instructor should be consulted for advice. Night training in yards or docks is preferable to day training on a sports field.

EQUIPMENT – The equipment listed hereunder is supplied to each dog handler (except multi-handlers) for use in connection with police dogs: Kennel, Compound (where applicable), Leather Collar, Chain Choke Collar, Leather Lead, Tracking Harness, Tracking Line, Dog Brush, Dog Comb.

GENERAL – *Reports* – Crime and Other Good Work – a police dog 'Incident Report Form' B.R. 6565 should be submitted in all cases where a police dog is concerned, even when there is no arrest made. These should be submitted in triplicate, one copy to the Chief Constable, one copy to the Chief of Police, and one copy to the Divisional Superintendent.

Offers of Dogs to Police by the Public – Persons offering dogs to the police should be told that the Force accepts only Alsatian dogs, not bitches, between the ages of ten months and two years. Particulars of all offers coming within the above description, either by way of gift or sale, should be forwarded to the Dog Training School, Elstree, where arrangements will be made through the Division concerned to inspect the dog, complete the acceptance forms if suitable, and arrange for the dog to be brought to the School.

7

'STORM' IN ACTION – CLEANING UP THE NORTH-WEST

The BTP Dog Training School at Elstree was designed by Dr F. F. C. Curtis, Chief Architect to the British Railways Board. It had fifteen kennels, and a veterinary inspection room, as well as a two-storey block with offices for the Instructors, a classroom, and a two-bedroom flat for the Sergeant Instructor. The remainder of the two-acre site was used as a training field. The officer in charge of the facility, Inspector Herbert Shelton, was assisted by Sergeant Instructor Len Austin, and Constable Tom Jakeman, who acted as the kennel man.

Other well-known dogs at the time were 'Flash' from Bradford, who, before being transferred from Newcastle, had secured three arrests for the theft of telephone wire, while 'Sean' and 'Rebel' from Glasgow caught six boys throwing stones at trains.

Dogs were stationed at West Hartlepool, Derby, Middlesbrough, Nottingham and Grimsby, while 'Fritz' and 'Shaun' were based at King's Cross, 'Czar' at Newcastle, 'Jock' at Leeds, 'Brutus' and 'Prince' at Hull, 'Rex' at Carlisle, and the aptly named 'Duke' at York. Two incidents involving

South Wales-based dog handlers are recalled by Malcolm Clegg, retired Detective Sergeant, based at Cardiff:

In the summer of 1967 I was on duty as a uniform constable one Sunday afternoon at Newport Docks. The dock was quiet, and it was a warm sunny day. My duties that day consisted of foot patrol. As I prepared to leave the docks' police station at the main entrance, I was in conversation with Police Constable Brinley (Bryn) Morgan, a close friend of mine and the station dog handler. Bryn asked if he could accompany me on patrol, together with his dog, so that he could exercise the dog by letting it off the leash at the top end of the dock on the waste ground adjacent to the dry dock. The weather was ideal and, due to it being a Sunday, the Dockers, and most other workers, were not in work and the dock was quiet and almost isolated.

After walking for a couple of hours, we reached the waste ground in question and PC Morgan let his dog roam freely, throwing him the odd stick now and again, which the dog would retrieve. After some time, I observed a wild rabbit several yards away from the dog. The dog appeared to spot the rabbit, which turned and ran away towards the dry dock. The dog chased after the rabbit at great speed and they both disappeared from view. PC Morgan, who had shouted at the dog to no avail, gave chase. I quickly followed and, when I arrived at the dry dock, I saw PC Morgan peering over the edge of the dry dock. He turned to me and said, 'He's gone over the top.' I then saw the dog lying in the bottom of the dry dock, which was empty of water, and it did not appear to be moving.

We then climbed down into the dock; PC Morgan picked up his dog and we climbed back out. The dog was conscious, but barely moved and did not make a sound. I cannot recall whether I returned to the police station to pick up a vehicle or whether we walked back to the main gate. When we arrived back at the police station, PC Morgan telephoned Sergeant Len Preece, who was the officer in charge at Newport Docks, at his home to explain what had happened.

PC Morgan took the dog home. The dog did initially survive the fall and received extensive veterinary treatment, but sadly it died a few days later. PC Morgan returned to normal dock duties and gave up his position of dog handler at Newport Docks. I believe that he was succeeded as dog handler there by Constable Mike Lambert.

Malcolm Clegg recalls the second incident:

Once again at Newport Docks – I believe it was in the winter of 1967–68 – Detective Sergeant Charlie Nunn of the Newport Borough Police Crime Squad received information that a serious burglary was going to take place at the premises of the National Dock Labour Board at Newport Docks. The NDLB was located on Newport Docks, and was a detached brick-built office block. A part of the building was used by Dock cashiers to store money and pay out the wages of the Dockers, who were paid in cash on a weekly basis every Friday morning. A Docks BTP officer would perform duty there by sitting inside the cashier's office while the wages were being paid out. The wages in question were withdrawn from a local bank every Thursday and taken by security escort to the NDLB where the money was sorted into pay packets by Docks Board cashiers, and then placed into a large secure safe, where it remained overnight for payments to be made the following morning. The amount of cash on hand at the time was in the region of £40,000, which in today's money would be about £500,000.

The information received by Detective Sergeant Nunn was that a gang of men would break into the offices on a

Thursday night, and would break open the safe by using a thermic lance and oxy acetylene equipment. Meetings were held between BTP CID at Cardiff and officers from the Newport Borough Constabulary, and a police operation was put in place to catch the culprits after they had stolen the money.

My duties at that time consisted of being one of three motorcycle patrol officers working on Newport Docks. It was decided that I would play a minor part in the operation. A briefing of officers to be involved in the operation took place at Pill Police Station (Newport Borough Constabulary), which was in close proximity to Newport Docks. A brief outline of the police operation was that a number of officers would surround the building, keeping some distance away. I was to carry out routine motorcycle patrols of the dock, visiting and making a thorough examination of the NDLB offices on two separate occasions during the night, the first being at 10 p.m. and the second between 4 a.m. and 5 a.m.

Apparently, the gang would enter the building, prior to my first patrol, via a skylight on the roof of the building, which would go undetected during my examination of the premises, unless I climbed onto the roof. After I rode away, the gang would have six or seven hours to carry out the raid before I returned. I had been told not to return in between to check the premises a second time. We were told at the briefing that the operation would take place on two consecutive Thursday nights, the first occasion being a 'dummy run' for the gang, who would not carry out the raid, but merely observe the police patrols and other dock activity. On the second occasion, however, the raid would actually take place.

I carried out my patrols on the first Thursday and saw nothing untoward. I did not have any indications that

I was being observed. I carried out my ten o'clock patrol the following week, after making my examination of the premises, which appeared secure; I drove away and stayed out of sight as instructed. A few hours later, all hell broke loose and I returned to the NDLB. There were police officers all over the place including two BTP dog handlers. I was a young, keen officer at the time and eager to know whether the operation had been a success. In essence, the operation had been a great success. The gang had broken into the safe, stolen the money and had all been successfully taken into custody.

One hitch that did take place involved the two dog handlers. As the gang left the premises after the raid, police officers quickly intervened. One of the dog handlers let go of his dog and sent it in pursuit of one of the gang members. Almost simultaneously, the other handler did the same thing and, instead of the dogs going in pursuit of the suspects, they turned on each other, while the two handlers struggled to separate them. Meanwhile, all the gang members were arrested by officers on foot.

This incident, serious as it was, left the two dog handlers very red-faced and blaming each other for the incident, but it caused a great deal of amusement to the many officers who witnessed it. I am unable to name the dog handlers involved, as I am not 100 per cent sure who they were. I do have an idea but the incident occurred almost fifty years ago, and as such I cannot say with any certainty.

Gil Tyler was a former Dog Handler and retired as a Detective Sergeant at Cardiff. In 1967 PC Gil Tyler went on a ten-week dog training course at Elstree and was the dog handler at Barry Docks until 1973. His shift patterns then changed as he worked opposite the station Detective Constable. He enjoyed his time at Barry Docks with police dog 'Chan'. A large part of the Barry Dock estate was taken up with one hundred scrapped steam locomotives and was known throughout the country as the 'Steam Graveyard'. This was owned by a local Barry businessman and the site was a haven for the local thieves. Shortly after finishing the dog course, he was supplied with a transit van with a cage in the back for the dog.

In 1967 the Right Honourable Mrs Barbara Castle visited Newport Docks and met police dog 'Rex'. The Minister of Transport was very interested in police dogs and, as she was about to leave, 'Rex' started to bark. She asked the handler, Police Constable J. Perry, whether the dog was talking to her or barking at her, and the non-committal answer from Police Constable Perry was, 'He doesn't want you to leave him.'

At the British Transport Police Sports Meeting in 1967 the results of the Inter Area Police Dog Competition were: 1st, PC Murphy with dog 'Chance'; 2nd, PC Foot with Dog 'Rinty'; and 3rd, PC Baker with Dog 'Tosca'.

Pete Hempton further recalls that,

1969 was a good year for 'Boss' and, during that year, we chalked up about twenty arrests including two men caught stripping 400 feet of copper wire from cables with a hacksaw on the electrified sections of track between Crewe and Chelford. One of the men attempted a getaway by running over a field, but 'Boss' stopped him in his tracks. One of the men accused me in court of hitting him with my truncheon at the time of the arrest. He was given a three-year Borstal training sentence. The other man was given a conditional discharge for twelve months.

Harold Philbin, an ex-British-Transport-Police-Dog-Handler from Manchester, wrote a book entitled *Rail Revelations* about his exploits with his dog 'Storm'. The dog became something of a legend in the Manchester area, after starting life as a stray and then becoming a BTP dog in 1965. Numerous arrests were attributed to 'Storm' and the following are just a few examples.

In the mid-sixties, PC Harold Philbin was directed to go to the scene of a bullion theft at Adswood sidings, Stockport. On arrival, information from the rail staff established that more than a dozen police officers had already walked around the area and restricted opportunities to do a decent track. The bullion van that had been broken into had been resealed, and sent on its way. Nevertheless he decided to give it a try.

First he put the tracking harness on 'Storm' and began where the track may have started; this was the empty space where the violated rail-van had been standing. Their efforts drew a blank and Harold removed the tracking harness to let 'Storm' run free. Harold then decided upon a different approach and shouted, 'Fetch it son' to the dog.

'Storm' went into the middle of the sidings and, within seconds, he was barking furiously. Harold found him, barking furiously at a large twenty-ton hopper wagon of a type especially built to carry loads of minerals from the quarries. It had a short ladder at the back and a trap door underneath it. Harold climbed the ladder and looked inside the steel wagon. Right on top of the trap door were the missing bags of bullion, and a couple of cartons of wine as well. Leaving 'Storm' with the bullion, Harold went back to his van and radioed into control. The bullion consisted of cloth bags, which were full of the brand new fifty pence pieces, not yet in circulation.

On another occasion it was established that the railway authorities were having a lot of parcels stolen from Clegg Street Parcels Depot at Oldham, even though there was full-time police cover. The yard, warehouses, and trains were loaded with mail-order parcels worth a fortune and easily disposed of in the local pubs. Oldham therefore moved to the top of Harold and 'Storm's' list of priorities and they commenced observations. 'Storm' and Harold were lying in the darkness on the grass, when they saw two suspects nearby. They must have been expecting company, because one of them peered out into the night and whispered in Harold's direction, 'Is that you, Sid?' Harold whispered back, 'Yes.' But he was not having any of that, and they both turned and ran, but to no avail as 'Storm' caught them both.

In the mid-sixties there were rumours circulating the local police stations regarding a gang of thieves, about eight in number, that were reputed to carry a shotgun in their car boot. Most members of this gang were well known to the British Transport Police, and usually operated in a permutation of only two or three at a time. The shotgun rumour did ensure that many policemen gave the deserted sidings a wide berth at night.

The thieves had a way of finding good-quality clothing that could be easily sold to market traders, and they seldom opened the ones with heavy machinery inside. In a siding containing hundreds, sometimes thousands, of identical-looking vans, they accomplished the impossible, and homed in on the higher-value textiles.

Deciding to concentrate on these sidings, 'Storm' and Harold paid a flying visit to Brewery sidings, Manchester, just after midnight one Saturday night. The very first time that Harold looked in the same direction as 'Storm,' he could see a man. He was right at the top of the sidings, and already there was a van door open. Harold and 'Storm' just edged a little bit nearer to him as soon as he jumped up into the van, and disappeared from their sight.

Out of the doorway and onto the ground came a parcel, followed by one or two more in quick succession. Harold released 'Storm' and soon there was furious barking from the dog and a squeal of pain from the man, as he shouted, 'Get him off.' Harold got to him very quickly, and soon established that the man had attempted to run off but, fortunately for him, he had not made the very serious mistake of attacking 'Storm'. The man was only bruised, and a glance at him confirmed Harold's suspicions – this one really was a 'hard case' and needed handling with great care. Also there were most probably one or two offenders still somewhere in the area. It was a case of getting to Willert Street Police Station with him as quickly as possible, so it was on with the handcuffs and away they went.

Standing behind the charge desk a little while later, the desk sergeant informed Harold that the prisoner was wanted on warrant. He was very uncooperative and did not speak except to give his name as 'Andy'. After Harold had charged him, and just before he put him in a cell for the night, 'Andy' did, however, prove that he had a sense of humour. He said to Harold very quietly, 'Here you are, you will definitely need these again,' and handed to Harold his latest American-style handcuffs. How he had got them off, Harold would never know!

Again in the mid-sixties, Mayfield station, Manchester, had suffered from the attention of thieves, and quite a lot of passenger parcels were being stolen during the night. Harold commenced observations with 'Storm' and, at about 3 a.m. one morning, a small van drove by with two men in it, and it went straight up the station approach. Having noted the details of the vehicle, Harold settled down for a short wait and radioed the information to control. A short while later, the van was seen to drive out of the station with parcels loaded to the roof. As the van reached the bottom of the approach road, Harold just tagged on behind it, expecting to be joined by a mobile team, but it just did not happen. Harold decided to continue following.

Approaching the junction at Ardwick Green, the back doors of the van opened, and then it gathered speed as it headed towards Oxford Road. None of the exposed parcels fell out of the van, but the man in the passenger seat moved into the back of the vehicle, and he started to throw parcels in front of Harold's van. As fast as he threw them out, Harold just drove round them and carried on exactly at their speed. Soon there was a trail of valuable parcels scattered for about a mile behind his van. Harold just radioed control to inform them where they were, and advised them of his own ever-changing position. Harold heaved a sigh of relief as he shot through Moss Side and out of the other end towards Fallowfield, and Wilmslow Road.

When Harold eventually drew alongside the van, it slowed down and stopped and, at just the right time, Sergeant Jackson from the BTP arrived in the Mobile Patrol car from the opposite direction, and he blocked them in. Still very wary of these two obviously very successful villains, Harold let 'Storm' out of the van to make the arrest, and then he took the keys out of the thieves' van and put the handcuffs on them both.

'Storm' went in the front passenger seat, while their prisoners went into the dog's cage and away they went. Having retraced his drive all the way back to Mayfield station, there was not a single parcel to be found anywhere, and a radio message to and from our control revealed that no one else had recovered any of them either. Harold took the two thieves back to the train from which they had stolen the parcels. On the ground nearby were two parcels that they had dropped. Harold established that they had stolen the two parcels earlier. They all went straight down to Whitworth Street Police Station, and Harold charged them both with the theft of the two parcels only. The following Monday morning they both pleaded guilty to stealing them and were sentenced to three months' imprisonment.

The following article – 'A quiet weekend' by DI Ben Senior (BTP Journal No. 80 1968) – outlines the activities of 'Storm' still further:

At 8.25 p.m. on Friday, 26 January 1968, information was received at the British Transport Police Control Room, New Bridge Street, Manchester, that a 'block' failure had occurred between Castleton East signal box and Middleton Junction signal box.

This indicated that copper wire thieves were at work, and officers, accompanied by a British Transport Police dog handler with his dog, 'Storm', went to the area. On arrival they searched the line and at Mills Hill, Middleton, they found the 'block', or communication wires, had been cut down, and some pieces partly rolled up. It was evident the thieves had been disturbed.

The handler then met a farmer and learned the thieves had cut a power line to his lineside farmhouse. The farmer had been out checking this line when he saw two men on the Railway. About the same time he saw the flashing lights of the Civil Police cars coming to the railway, and the two men ran into a field. The handler and dog searched the fields and, after about an hour, they discovered a man, up to his waist in water, hiding in a culvert under the railway. He was arrested and dealt with by the CID.

At 10.30 p.m. the same night, certain information was received about a wire theft and, as a result, the British Transport Police CID contacted the Lancashire County CID.

After a conference, observations were set up in the Middleton area. One set of CID officers took up a position, the same handler and his dog took up another, and another set of CID officers maintained liaison with an informant. All were in contact, using Lancashire County personal radios.

At 2.15 a.m. on Saturday, 27 January 1968, a car radio message was received by the officers on observations that intruders had been seen in the Moston railway sidings, Manchester, and that officers had gone to the scene. Shortly afterwards, those officers found a motor car abandoned, with the ignition key still in it, adjacent to the sidings. The observation officers were advised of progress, via radio. A request was made for the dog handler to go to the sidings, but in view of the nature of the observations, he remained at Middleton.

About 3.30 a.m. it was learned that the wire theft was not going to take place and immediately the officers on observations went to Moston sidings. The Lancashire County CID returned to their base.

The handler led the way in a dog van, as he was going to one end of the sidings to do a sweep through them, and the CID were going to the opposite end. Leading from the main road was a minor road, running past some houses to a point near the sidings. As the handler and other officers were passing down the main road, they saw four men, casually walking down the minor road in the direction of the main road. It was realised immediately that these men might be the intruders and both vehicles turned around to intercept them. The handler was quicker and had his dog out of the van and after the men, who had run along a footpath. The CID followed and were just in time to receive a 'present' of one of the men, while the handler and his dog went after the others.

The area at this point is a maze of waste land and railway sidings, and the three men got away. While the arrested man was being questioned, a full-scale search was set up by the other officers. It was found that several vans in the sidings had been opened and two parcels of cloth were found on the edge of the sidings near where the car had been left. The arrested man admitted the car was his and that he had stolen the cloth. He told a specious tale about the other men, stating he did not know them and they had forced him to drive them. His home was searched without tracing any further stolen property.

At 5.50 a.m. the same morning, while he was being charged, a report was received at the Police Control Room of a 'block' failure at Brindle Heath Junction, near Irlam carriage sidings. The handler and his dog, accompanied by other officers, went to the area. The handler went down the line in one direction and officers walked towards him from the opposite end. The handler saw two men near where the communication wires were cut and when the men started to run away, after a warning, he sent his dog after them. The dog caught one, and the other, realising discretion was the better part of valour, literally held up his hands and gave himself up to the handler. The two men were arrested and charged with theft of wire.

The handler then went to Middleton to take up observations with CID officers in regard to the previous information of wire theft. Once again, this theft did not transpire, but eventually the thief was arrested on the Monday following, as a result of enquiries.

On Sunday, 28 January 1968, because of raids on Moston sidings, special observations were set up to cover a period from 5 p.m. to 5 a.m. on Monday. This involved the use of CID officers, dog handlers and portable radios. Due to the nature of the terrain of the district and the apparent *modus operandi* of the thieves, one CID officer and a dog handler went into the sidings and maintained radio contact with other officers, who were to be well away from the sidings in a vehicle, ready to block the road leading from the sidings. The dog handler, as hitherto, and a CID officer went into the sidings about 5.20 p.m. and within minutes realised that thieves were at work.

The handler sent his dog forward to 'find' and within seconds 'Storm' caught and held a man. A number of vans were found open and there was a large amount of goods on the lines nearby. The CID took charge of the man while the handler searched the area, because it was thought another man was involved. The man was questioned and said he had been in the sidings with his brother and admitted stealing the goods found in the sidings. Subsequently, he also admitted having been in the sidings before and cleared up three previous thefts of whisky and carpets.

His house was searched and some property was recovered. Enquiries were continued and details of the missing brother were circulated. His home and various relatives' houses were visited and it was established that he had absconded. On the following Wednesday he was arrested and admitted the offences.

Two receivers of railway property were also detected; one was the husband of a licensee of a public house and the other a working colleague of one of the brothers. This led to the detection of larcenies, not connected to the British Railways Board. At the time of writing all the offenders were awaiting trial.

The wire mentioned is copper wire, similar to telephone wire, and carries the communications of the signal 'block' system between signal boxes. The wires are strung on the telegraph posts alongside the railway and, when the wires are cut or broken, the 'block' indicators in the signal boxes show a 'failure' in the system.

This tale illustrates the exceptionally good work performed by one dog, but the writer was personally involved in the episode, and endorses what he was told years ago by a senior officer of another force, who was in charge of dogs: 'Show me the dog, and I'll tell you what the man is like.'

The dog handler involved was PC Harold Philbin.

Finals day for 1969 was held on Wednesday, 27 August at the London Transport (Metropolitan Railway) Sports Ground. Once again the Dog Competition was very popular; the regulars of the Southern Area (Southampton Docks) won all the trophies, the Big Ben Cup being won yet again by PC Murphy with his hard-worked dog 'Chance'. However, it was good to see the 'Dice Band' of the Scottish officers taking part in the final with their dogs. Police Constable Boughton, Southern Area, with his dog 'Timber' and Police Constable Murphy with his dog 'Chance' won the John William Morrell Trophy.

By 1970 the British Transport Police had a Dog Section of some seventy handlers and dogs. On 3 November 1970 Constable J. Warner, who was based at Euston, together with police dog 'Hobo', received a commendation for 'Good work resulting in the arrest of a known local thief, and his conviction for attempted theft from a National Carriers Limited Depot'.

In 1970 the following article appeared in the *Crewe Chronicle*:

'Boss', the four-year-old Alsatian attached to the British Transport Police at Crewe, earned his third commendation after the Borough magistrates had heard how he 'chalked up' the twentieth arrest in his crime-busting career.

Only weeks after his initial period of training, 'Boss' got his first commendation when three men interfering with mail bags put aside ideas of escape when cornered by the 84-lb dog. Many a thief, vandal and soccer-rowdy can vouch that 'Boss' and his handler, and constant companion, Constable Peter Hempton, form a formidable crime squad, for together they have made more than seventy arrests.

Peter, a Transport Police officer for the past ten years, and 'Boss' – the dog nobody wanted – will be paying extra special attention to the marshalling yards at Crewe where wagons offer juicy targets for lawbreakers. 'Boss' has also been commended for 'scenting out' a time sheet, discarded at the scene of a crime, that prompted enquiries that eventually led to the arrest of a gang of metal thieves responsible for extensive thefts from railway property in the Crewe area.

The Alsatian, which is one of seven out of eighty or so Transport Police dogs to have passed advanced field examinations, and which formed one of the team that beat the best dogs in Scotland in a recent trophy competition, is on duty at Crewe station on alternate Saturdays to welcome the soccer 'specials', where he is a calming influence.

A 'gift dog', he was born at a public house at Tunbridge Wells, Kent. It was 'Hobson's Choice' for Peter when he visited the kennels, for only six-month-old 'Boss' remained. He was a 'barker', and obviously not used to company, and none of the other officers had liked the look of him. They started the initial six-week course one week later than the others and came out top.

Peter's beat includes Wellington, in Shropshire, and parts of the Potteries. Because they are so successful in combatting crime and vandalism on the railways, the number of dogs in the force has been considerably built up in recent years'.

In the *BTP Journal* (Summer Quarter 1970) the following article appeared:

In February 1970 a 'Good Citizen of the Month Award', sponsored by the *Leeds Evening Post*, was presented to Police Constable 192 Douglas Rochford, of the British Transport Police Leeds, and Mr Christopher Wright, also of Leeds. The officers' three-year-old Alsatian police dog 'Anzac' also received a special award of an inscribed collar.

The citation read, 'Late on the night of 22 December Mrs Jean Wrigg was walking her dog on spare land adjoining Welbeck Road. Suddenly a man appeared near to her. When Mrs Wrigg turned round to call her dog the man jumped upon her and pushed her to the ground. He fell on top of her, placed an arm around her neck and his hand over her mouth. Mrs Wrigg screamed and the man said to her, "Keep quiet then I'll not hurt you." At this time Mr Christopher Wright was walking along Welbeck Road when he heard the screams of the attacked woman coming from the darkness. He searched for her and, as he found her, the assailant leapt from the ground and ran away, and was chased by Mr Wright. At this time Mr Douglas Rochford, an off-duty railway police constable, was in his home, and upon hearing the screams of Mrs Wrigg ran from his home with his dog in time to see the pursuit taking place. Mr Rochford joined the chase and his dog jumped at the assailant. With the assistance of Mr Wright the person was detained and the Leeds police were informed. While being held, the assailant said, 'If you hadn't caught me I might have killed her,' and it transpired that he had already attacked two other women that day.'

The second part of the eighth British Transport Police Dog Trials were held at the BTP Training School, Tadworth on Monday 4 October 1971, the first part of the Trials having been held at the Dog Training School, Elstree, Herts. The Chief Constable Mr W. O. Gay QPM was in attendance, together with a number of other senior officers, which included Mr R. E. Kerr, Assistant Chief Constable (Operations and Dogs). The Western Area won the John William Morrell Trophy and PC Murphy with dog 'Chance' won the Big Ben Trophy for the highest-scoring dog in the final. This partnership had won the trophy six times previously, also placing second once and third once. 'Chance' was due to retire early in 1972.

The winner of the Diligence Trophy in 1971 was PC Lambert with his dog 'Kellie', who was born on 6 January 1968 and joined the force on 5 February 1969. He served all his service at Newport Docks. The winner of the John William Morrell Trophy was PC Harrop from Manchester and his dog 'Ferdl'.

On 5 June 1971 the Sub-divisional Headquarters for BTP in Manchester moved to the Tower Block, Piccadilly railway station. Police dog kennels were located on the fourth floor of the building.

In 1971 Michael Layton was a probationer PC at Birmingham and this is his recollection relating to former Dog Handler Ron Woollaston, now deceased:

Ron was always immaculate, and prided himself on having the 'best pair of bulled boots' on New Street station – you could literally see your face in them. As an ex-serviceman he stood ramrod straight in uniform and was a calming influence on his younger colleagues. Ron kept his temper even when goaded by the array of anti-social individuals who frequented the railway, whether they be Saturday night drunks, or crowds of football hooligans gaining courage in numbers. That said, when someone crossed that 'invisible line', his right arm would suddenly appear to grow by at 6 inches as he would grip them in a vice-like grip around the back of the neck and march them off unceremoniously to the police office.

You certainly knew when Ron meant business, as indeed did his police dog. As I recall he was a very large and powerful Alsatian, but Ron took no truck from him and there was no confusion as to who was in charge. When Ron said 'sit', he sat and when Ron said 'go', you got out of the way quickly.

Bill Rogerson, co-author, who retired as Officer in Charge at Bangor in September 2001, but is still working as a volunteer for the force, recalls working with Ron:

I remember one occasion in the early 1970s when I was part of a football train escort to Brighton from Birmingham. It was not usual, but not unheard of, to take a dog handler and dog on a train escort. On this occasion Ron Woollaston and his dog 'Brutus' came with us. After dispersing the fans at Brighton we travelled in the empty stock to the sidings. Bearing in mind my recent training at Tadworth in relation to the third electrified rail *in situ* in the area that we were travelling on, south of London, I was mindful of the fatal consequences if I stepped on them, so naturally I took extra care when alighting from the train in the sidings. Ron took his dog for a walk in the sidings and couldn't understand why it kept yelping. He hadn't realised we were in third rail territory and the dog kept touching the live rail. He was very lucky.

PC Ron Woollaston was based at Birmingham for all of his service in the British Transport Police, the majority of which was as a dog handler. Ron and his faithful canine companion 'Brutus', when they were not doing football duties, were tied up with more conventional policing with their colleagues, spending many an hour on observations.

During the course of his research Bill Rogerson came up with this case that Ron and 'Brutus' were involved in during the early 1970s. Lawley Street freight depot on the edge of Birmingham's city centre was no exception for the attention of thieves. For quite a number of months, night raids on the freight wagons in the sidings at Lawley Street were common place. Therefore the CID decided to keep observations on the sidings with uniformed colleagues, who included PC Ron Woollaston and 'Brutus'.

One night soon after midnight they saw two men from the Nechells area of the city cross the railway lines towards the vans. Then they heard the sound of locks being forced. When they were challenged both men ran off and PC Woollaston gave the command of 'fetch' to 'Brutus', which he did by taking hold of one of them. The second man was arrested shortly afterwards.

The shoes belonging to one of the criminals, the one caught by 'Brutus' were examined and found to match with marks and impressions found on the vans, which had been broken into on two previous occasions. This man told the detectives during his interview, 'I am not talking to you. You are only railway police.' When asked what he got out of it, he replied, 'I had £50 each time.' They subsequently appeared at Birmingham Quarter Sessions, where one of them admitted stealing from the wagons on different dates. The second man pleaded guilty to thefts on one occasion. Goods stolen included shoes, blankets, dresses and underwear.

Upon being sentenced by the recorder, Mr M. V. Argyle, QC, he commented, 'You were two of a greater number of thieves who have played your part in stealing from British Rail. This is not the first of big railway theft cases in the city.

A lamentable picture has been revealed.' The thief caught by 'Brutus' was sentenced to four years' imprisonment and the second man was imprisoned for two years.

A story widely covered by the media was about Midland war hero and retired Birmingham BTP Officer Ron Woollaston, who served in Malaysia as a soldier in 1950:

> A medal was presented to Ron in 1950, which unfortunately had been lost. But miraculously, it made its way back to his widow, Mamie, almost fifty-seven years after it vanished! When Andrew, Mamie's son, logged on to eBay, looking for tyres for his car, he was surprised when he saw his father's prized possession pop up on the screen. Andrew decided he wouldn't let it slip away from the family again. Ron served in the army for five years before returning to Birmingham. He then served as a BTP officer for 30 years and sadly passed away in 1995, not long after his retirement. He told his family that his medal had gone missing just weeks after he received it.

John Harrison recalls his introduction to the 'Guvnor' on his thirteen-week dog-training course at Elstree, in September 1971. He led by example, and was well respected:

> One day we were on a training exercise known as 'the search' for the hidden criminal. We were in woodland when my dog, who was working loose about 70 yards ahead, indicated a 'find' by barking. I raised my hand to the kennel staff instructor and went forward to join my dog and 'arrest' the criminal. On reaching my dog I initially could not see what my dog was barking at, and so wrongly assumed that the dog had got distracted and sent a squirrel up a tree.
>
> Somewhat annoyed I bent down to take my dog by the scruff of the neck to chastise him for taking me on a false

trail, when I was hit over the head, knocking me off balance. As I recovered I looked up to see 'The Guvnor' dropping out of the tree, imparting words of advice that in future I should trust the dog, and that the stick he had hit me with could have been an iron bar. From that day on I trusted my dog implicitly – well, most of the time!

When I was on my initial dog-training course in 1971 at Elstree, one of the guys on that course, Alec Gibb, was to become the first police dog handler at Immingham Docks. He was not a happy bunny was Alec, as he reckoned that there was too much work for just one handler and he wanted more dog handlers to be trained/deployed there.

I do know that Terry Shelton was offered redundancy at one stage, but turned it down when Elstree closed, and then the job offered him an office at FHQ at Park Royal, North London. He had a roving commission to go around the country to ensure training standards were up to scratch, as most of us had started training with local home office forces wherever we were located. Bear in mind that there were only twenty-four of us retained as handlers around the UK.

Terry remained very good friends with Harold Philbin – one of the best dog handlers I ever met in the 1970s. The reason Harold left the BTP was because he and other ex-handlers had a problem getting our dog-food allowance paid, as we had to claim it on our time sheets, which kept 'going missing' and were late in getting to Derby for input into the computer system. So one day, Harold took his dog 'Storm' up to Manchester Divisional Headquarters, and demanded monies owed to him to be paid out of the petty cash. Words were exchanged between him and the person to which he spoke. Other DHQ staff heard the debate, and it ended up with Harold leaving his dog in DHQ for them to feed the dog. Every time this certain person moved, the dog growled and it took quite a while for the senior officer to reach the telephone and make a few calls to get Harold to go back and get his dog. One of those calls was to Terry Shelton!

Unfortunately, there was only going to be one winner, and Harold subsequently left the force. In a way it did Harold a favour because he set himself up with his own security firm and got a big contract with British Rail at Manchester looking after a huge container depot up there.

Pete Hempton further recalls,

At 11.15 p.m. on Friday 15 January 1971 a black man was viciously attacked and robbed in Mill Street, Crewe. The local police were informed and enquiries were commenced. The initial enquiries extended to 5 a.m. on 16 January, during which time many of the local travelling fraternity were found and taken into custody. Throughout this period the Cheshire Constabulary officers were rendered valuable assistance from me and 'Boss', along with one of our detective constables.

Eventually one of the arrested men was charged and received a term of five years' imprisonment. For this assistance I received a letter from the local chief superintendent, thanking myself and 'Boss' for our assistance.

Bill Rogerson recalls some more of his memories of the Dog Section:

Although I was never a dog handler, I took an interest in their work and at one stage thought seriously about joining the Dog Section. When I joined the British Transport Police in April 1971 I was stationed at Birmingham New Street.

I was informed that I would have to wait at least six weeks before I went to a District Police Training School. This was then the normal practice for BTP officers.

As part of my duties during those six weeks, Sergeant Fred Taylor, who was the general-purpose sergeant looking after vehicles, radios and the Dog Section at Birmingham, seconded me to the Dog Section each Tuesday to be 'their criminal' while they trained their dogs. This entailed me wearing an old 'dog-proof' coat and a leather 'arm sleeve'; I would then run away from 'the scene of the crime', carrying a large stick – I wasn't trusted with a starting pistol!

I had to hide in bushes, trees or anywhere else that was available. The dog would then come and find me, and try to tear my arm off while growling and foaming at the mouth. Fortunately, having previous experience of working with an Alsatian, I escaped unscathed. It was great fun while it lasted.

The dog handlers I came into contact with were: PC Ivor Kerslake, with police dog 'Tex'; PC Frank Street, with police dog 'Rebel'; PC Ron Woollaston with police dog 'Brutus' of Birmingham, and PC Don Hughes of Wolverhampton with police dog 'Pip'. Naturally I tried to befriend the dogs by talking to them, obviously while their handlers were present. I was talking to Don's dog 'Pip' in my broad North Lancashire accent, and Don said, 'He doesn't understand you. He can only understand the Black Country dialect,' – one of the most distinctive of all the regional accents, which of course Don spoke very fluently.

Paul Majster retired as a detective constable with the BTP, based in Birmingham, and recalls one particular incident:

On 31 December 1971 I was on duty, together with two other officers, in Washwood Heath Sidings in Birmingham.

I remember it well due to the embarrassing sequence of events that followed. There was myself, DC Ron Wyllie, and PC Frank Street, together with his dog 'Rebel'. Washwood Heath Sidings is a massive place and had been suffering from wagons being attacked and 'catalogue' deliveries being stolen. We had been doing observations for weeks without any luck and there should have been more of us on duty to cover the area but, because it was New Year's Eve, we couldn't get any more staff.

It was a really foggy night but, through all the mist, we suddenly became aware of three people in the distance trying to break into some wagons. Frank shouted to them to stand still or he would let the dog go. They all started to run off and, without thinking, I ran after them into the fog. At the same time Frank had released 'Rebel' and next thing is the dog had hold of my police 'Gannex' raincoat and was biting me on the backside and refusing to let go. The thieves got away.

The next day I had to attend to see the Detective Inspector 'Nobbie' Clark and got a right 'telling off' for getting in the way.

Bill Rogerson further recalls,

In 1972 the Birmingham Division took possession of a fawn-coloured Commer Karrier mini-bus – call sign 'Bravo 54'. This vehicle was to be used as a general purpose one, mainly transporting officers to and from incidents, and also for the Dog Section to use. For this purpose one of the constables, a time-served carpenter, made a dog kennel for the rear of the mini-bus.

It was usually parked on the station approach road at Birmingham New Street. The procedure was that the duty dog handler, on commencing duty, would either arrive from his home by train, or by personal vehicle, and put the dog in the kennel while he went to sign on duty, as each one had a personal key for the vehicle. One particular afternoon the duty dog handler duly arrived for duty and placed his dog in the rear while he went to book on duty and had a cup of tea. Unknown to him one of the beat officers took the vehicle out to an incident in the Bromsgrove area. He didn't realise the dog was in the back until he arrived at his destination. The dog handler got a shock when he went back to the station approach road, only to find that the vehicle was no longer there. He was parted from the dog for about five hours. Needless to say the procedure was tightened up.

Shortly after delivery of the above vehicle I was about halfway through a late-turn tour of duty at Birmingham New Street, when I was called in to see one of the duty sergeants, Norman Plover. He informed me that three of us and PC Street with dog 'Rebel' were going to Stourport, Worcestershire, to remove some travellers who had illegally camped on some railway land. The West Mercia Police had no luck in moving them on and stated that there may be trouble from them.

We went in 'Bravo 54' with 'Rebel' enjoying his brand new mobile kennel. On arrival at Stourport a contingent of West Mercia Police were waiting as back up to assist us. Norman and I saw that there were about six or seven caravans, all occupied. We approached the traveller in charge of the camp and he was informed that we were from the British Transport Police, that they were illegally camped and that they should remove themselves forthwith.

The travellers took one look at our helmet plates and said, 'Yes, sir, we are going no problem – you're the British Transport Police and you're okay.' The West Mercia Police officers just stood there in amazement. Within a few hours the travellers had left.

8

'NIKKI' TAKES THE PIE – AMONG THE FOOTBALL HOOLIGANS

John Harrison recollects,

On 4 March 1972, if my memory serves me correctly, together with my dog 'Nikki' I was part of a serial of officers that included myself, a sergeant and four constables. We were escorting a train of about 480 soccer fans from Stoke City to Wembley, for the League Cup Final against Chelsea.

On this occasion there was little trouble, plenty of banter with the fans, and the day was going well. As we were approaching Wembley I proceeded to walk the length of the train as usual, so as to be in the front coach ready for disembarkation. My well-trained police dog was walking through the Tourist Second Open (TSO) coach, which had an aisle and four seat tables on either side. The fans were allowed to drink alcohol in those days and many of them were drinking and eating at the tables.

We were about halfway along one coach and I noticed my dog lift his head, as a chap was holding this pork pie in his hand, with his elbow on the armrest, and his arm dangling out towards the aisle. He had his back to the dog and it was one of those moments where everything went into 'slow motion' and, before I could shout, 'Leave!', the pork pie was gratefully received by one hungry dog. The coach erupted, at my expense, and my 'red face' must have told it all as I attempted to apologise to the owner of the pork pie, who fortunately took it in good part. One unforgettable football special – but, for me, for the wrong reason!

John Harrison further recalls,

I think it was in 1972, while myself and 'Nikki' were coming to the end of a fourteen-hour night tour of duty guarding the Royal train in sidings in mid-Cheshire, the window of one of the carriages opened. A senior member of the Royal family leaned out and asked if the dog had been up all night. I nodded 'yes', and the enquirer smiled and closed the window.

Bill Rogerson further recalls,

One Sunday afternoon in the spring of 1973, due to the theft of components from brand-new road vehicles, which were on freight wagons ready to go to various destinations in Britain, I was asked to go on observations with a dog handler to Washwood Heath Freight Sidings, which are adjacent to the main Birmingham to Derby railway line, on the outskirts of Birmingham City Centre. We found a brake van, where we took up residence, keeping an eye on the wagons in the sidings. After a few hours our patience was rewarded – a youth suddenly appeared on a wagon a few hundred yards away from us. We went towards him. On seeing us he started to run away from us. The dog handler shouted, 'Stop or I'll let the dog go.' He took no notice of this command and continued running. The handler let his dog loose with the instructions to 'fetch,' and for me to remain where I was for a few minutes and then follow.

The dog ran off, 'like a greyhound out of a trap in the 2.30', followed by the handler in pursuit of the youth. A matter of seconds later the dog stopped, turned round and started chasing his handler. Needless to say, the youth made his getaway, while the handler had to fight his dog off. It was embarrassing to say the least.

I believe it was in the summer of 1973 that there was an arsonist on the loose in the town centre of Sutton Coldfield and neighbouring villages. It was feared that he would strike at the railway stations in the area. So one night I found myself on night turn at Blake Street railway station on the Birmingham to Lichfield railway line, along with Don Hughes and his dog, 'Pip', from Wolverhampton. Don's dog was the biggest and hairiest Alsatian I have ever seen. It was a fearsome brute and would probably give the Hound of the Baskervilles a run for its money.

Don and I, along with his dog, duly settled down for the night in the glass waiting shelter on the Lichfield-bound platform. This shelter was very similar to the bus shelters that are in use on our streets. Don and I had to sit upright all night, but the dog laid down at Don's feet, snoring very loudly and giving the odd twitch, indicating that he was dreaming about what dogs dream about, and only surfacing when he smelt our sandwiches – needless to say, he didn't get anything. Fortunately the arsonist didn't strike on the railway.

Bill Rogerson went on,

The Lawley Street freight depot in Birmingham was one of the largest in the Midlands and handled heavy freight from all over the country. In the late 1960s and early 1970s it was managed by National Carriers Ltd (NCL). A lot of the goods, including food, spirits, cigarettes, washing machines, furniture, greenhouses, etc., destined for the businesses and households, especially in the Birmingham area, would be sorted in the warehouse and taken by road transport. Inevitably, with such a large concentration of merchandise, it became a haven for the local thieves and, in an effort to deter and catch them, a presence of CID officers, one detective sergeant and, I believe, two detective constables were permanently attached to the depot. A twenty-four-hour uniform presence was provided by the constables from Birmingham New Street on a rota basis.

I think it was sometime towards the end of 1973 when NCL gave notice that they did not require the services of the British Transport Police at the depot. The uniform presence was withdrawn almost immediately and they were replaced by staff from a well-known security firm of the period. Due to contractual arrangements, the CID remained for a few months longer. One day, the depot manager approached the detective sergeant in charge, Cyril Ball, and informed him that there was an unusual theft taking place, that of dog food. This had been previously unheard of – yes, cartons of cigarettes, cases of whisky, lawnmowers and the like, but dog food! Puzzled by this, Cyril arranged for observations using his officers and, as dog food was involved, he arranged for our dog handlers from Birmingham New Street to be involved as well.

After a couple of nights, the culprits were identified. It was the officers from the security firm stealing the cartons of dog food for their dogs.

In 1973 Southampton PC 'Spud' Murphy trained his 'general purpose' dog to detect cannabis, which was being imported into the country, often among goods and freight. The superintendent was impressed and obtained a dog specifically for this purpose. 'Cap' (named after a ship's captain who donated him) was multi-handled by four officers. On one occasion PC Boughton was with 'Cap' when he put the dog into the back of a lorry. The dog gave an indication by somersaulting backwards in his excitement. Several sacks of cannabis were found in the lorry, with a street value of many thousands of pounds.

Pete Hempton recalls the following article being written in the *Crewe Chronicle*, in respect of his dog 'Boss', dated 2 August 1973:

BOSS, 200 ARRESTS IN LINE FOR TITLE – A Crewe-based railway police dog is among the top three for an award as the best criminal dog in the country. Nine-year-old 'Boss,' who has more than two hundred arrests to his credit, has been commended ten times during eight and half years' service, including twice this year. He is challenging for the Diligence trophy, presented each year by the British Transport Police.

His handler since he was six months old is Constable Peter Hempton, aged thirty-six, who says that the winner from the seventy-five dogs eligible in this nationwide competition will be known about September. 'If 'Boss' doesn't win, he should be at least second or third', he added.

'Boss', who is kept at Constable Hempton's home in Crewe, has been with the British Transport Police demonstration team throughout the country. He is the senior of two railway police dogs covering the Crewe–Potteries–Shrewsbury area in work involving patrolling marshalling yards, football trains, vandalism patrols, tracking from a crime scene and chasing and apprehending criminals.

Northern and Western Area dog teams fought it out at Tadworth on Monday October 8 1973 for the John William Morrell Trophy. In their nine-year existence the trials had greatly improved the standard of dog performance through team work. Each area nominated two dogs and handlers and, after knock-outs, the two winning teams met in the final. The Northern Area again won with six points against the Western Area's four. Individual markings were: PC Ablard (Preston) with dog 'Ben' – 360 points; PC Boughton (Southampton) with dog 'Timber' – 332.5 points; PC Harrop (Manchester) with dog 'Ferdl' with 273.5 points, and PC Lambert (Newport) with dog 'Kellie' – 258 points. PC Ablard (Preston) won the Big Ben Trophy. The Assistant Chief Constable (Operations) Mr R. E. Kerr presented the Diligence Trophy for the most meritorious work during 1972 to PC R. L. Farmer (Liverpool) with dog 'Rinty'. Runners-up were PC Hempton (Crewe) with dog 'Boss' and PC Coulby (Derby) with dog 'Panther'.

Here is one example of tracking, as recalled by John Harrison,

One November night in 1974 a BTP dog and its handler had cause to assist the CID at Mold Junction North Wales, when thieves had been disturbed raiding some parcels vans stored over the weekend in a British Railways marshalling yard. The dog set off on the scent where they had last been seen minutes earlier, crossed the railway junction and the main Chester to Holyhead railway line, and cleared the railway boundary fence. He then went across a nearby field towards a public footpath, where it suddenly stopped and indicated to its handler. In the shrubbery nearby, two boxes of spirits and other items that had been stolen earlier were recovered. Unfortunately, in the ongoing search, the track led to a row of terraced houses and a van parked nearby, which drove away as the dog and police officers arrived.

John Harrison recollects,

Crewe was, and still is, the meeting point for a number of railway lines connecting various parts of the country. It therefore made sense in 1974, when rumours started to circulate that Elstree was closing, for us to try and establish a dog-training establishment there. It started off as an unofficial thing, as the hierarchy was not too keen, but the Dog Section managed to build one in the freight sidings at Basford Hall, on the southern outskirts of Crewe. The portable buildings that were used were redundant from the railway and donated by various departments. This was an ideal facility for dog handlers from Crewe, Birmingham, Preston, Liverpool, and Manchester to meet for training sessions, as the farmer in the adjacent field would allow the dogs in when there was no livestock. We also left our dogs there when handlers went on leave, rather than taking them to Elstree. In the 1980s the training establishment was officially recognised and a civilian kennel man was employed. A few years later, however, it was closed down and all training was carried out at Tadworth.

On 4 July 1974 PC Don Gordon and his dog 'Jim' caught a man stealing cable at Grand Terminus Junction in Glasgow. The offender slashed the officer around the face and stabbed the dog before escaping. The officer with his dog gave chase and, despite receiving further injuries, tackled the offender again. The officer required thirty-eight stitches to his wounds and both he and 'Jim' were subsequently awarded the Whitbread Shield for brave conduct, which was an internal BTP award.

Colin Sinclair, a member of the BTP History Group, and the researcher into the recipients of the Whitbread Shield, expands the above story with the below-mentioned discovery of a BTP Journal:

The Chief Constable has announced the award of the shield to PC Donald Gordon, Glasgow, for meritorious police work. The thirty-six-year-old officer gained it for his work at Grand Terminus Junction, Glasgow, on July 4, 1974. With his dog 'Jim', Don caught a man stealing cable, but when he attempted to arrest him, the man slashed him over the eye with a knife. 'Jim' also tackled him but was extensively slashed about the face and body.

The man made off, but Don and his dog chased and caught him as he was trying to get through a gate. When the constable tackled him the man again slashed his face and was able to make good his escape.

Despite his injuries Don got to a telephone and alerted his colleagues. He needed thirty-eight stitches in his wound and his dog needed treatment by a vet.

The assailant was eventually traced and sentenced to seven years' imprisonment. Both PC Gordon and his faithful canine friend were soon back on duty, none the worse for their wounds. Despite their ordeals both are as active as ever and always ready to have a go.

Biographical Note – Colin's personal note:

Don served with the Royal Air Force Police before joining BTP at Glasgow in 1966 at the age of 27. He served in Glasgow and Dalmuir and spent many years as a dog-handler before retiring in 1996. Don is a member of NARBTPO (National Association of Retired British Transport Police Officers).

On Saturday July 6 1974, the Ryton Rugby Club, in the county of Durham, held their Annual Gala Day in aid of local charities. A request was made to the Newcastle Divisional Commander for the British Transport Police to give a display. A programme was devised by the dog-handlers concerned – Police Constable Brown and 'Fritz', Police Constable Card and 'Sabre' of Newcastle, Police Constable Bell and 'Sabba', and Police Constable Horton and 'Simba' of the Darlington District. Inspector E. T. Locke was responsible for a running commentary throughout the display, which lasted thirty minutes.

The display included obedience exercises, agility tests and incidents of criminal work. A crowd of over 2,000 adults and children enjoyed the show, which was described as excellent. The applause throughout the display showed how much the crowd appreciated it, and the handlers were able to answer numerous questions afterwards.

Between 1973 and 1974, arrests by BTP dog handlers rose from 738 to 908 but this did not sufficiently impress the new Chief Constable Eric Haslam, who joined the force from Kent. He subsequently reduced the Dog Section to just twenty-four dogs.

Fred Keeler, who was in a senior civilian management position with the force when he retired, recalls the following:

In the early 1970s as secretary to the police conference I was occasionally invited out to see what it was like at the 'sharp end'. One such invitation was from Chief Inspector Shelton, then head of the Force Dog Section, to visit the Dog Training School at Elstree, Hertfordshire. This I was pleased to accept and, on arrival at the school on 4 March 1975, I was told the only way I could see what happened was to be out with the handlers and their dogs; I met PC George Hinselwood, who invited me to select the wellington boots I would need from the store. The smallest size available was size eleven; however, with the aid of a few *Daily Mirrors*, we solved that problem!

After meeting a few of the handlers and their dogs I went out to watch, I thought, the training in progress, and very quickly declined the chance to run across a field with a sack over my arm to see how a dog could stop me. This was an easy decision to make as running in those boots was out of the question and the four-legged fellow standing beside me looked hungry. I did, however, accept the invitation to hide in the woods adjacent to the training school in any one of the filing cabinets that were scattered about, knowing there was a rope on the inside of the cabinet door to enable me to keep the door closed!

I remember hearing a handler give some commands to his dog some distance away from where I was, and all was quiet until I first heard a dog sniffing at the bottom of the cabinet. Then, when he started to sniff at the small gap between the doors of the cabinet, he began to bark like I have never heard a dog bark before. I knew I was safe, of course, as I had the rope to hang on to but, believe me, by the time the handler had put the dog back on the lead and said it was safe for me to let go of the rope my knuckles were white.

I did have the pleasure of observing more of the training that day, and indeed learned a lot – but, forty years on from the day as I write this, 'hanging on for dear life' only seems like yesterday!

On 6 November 1975, as a result of a decision to reduce the strength of police dogs in the BTP from seventy-two to twenty-four, dog handlers across the force were notified as to whether or not they had 'avoided the axe'.

The review affected dogs operating within the rail jurisdiction of the force and on this date PC Harrison and PC Howell were notified that they were to remain at Crewe with their dogs. In contrast, PC Senior based at Gloucester with 'Duke', PC Freeman at Birmingham with 'Ricky', PC Payne at Leicester with 'Sheba', and PC Hughes at Birmingham with 'Pip' were somewhat summarily given until 21 December 1975 to return to ordinary duties. They were, however, given approval to be allowed to retain their dogs as personal pets without payment.

What follows is the story of the legend 'Ginger' Ablard. From 1969, 'Ginger' Ablard was a dog handler at Preston and in October 1979 he was promoted to uniform sergeant overseeing the Dog Section. The section had been reduced in 1975 and the morale of the dog handlers was at an all-time low. Ginger's appointment was to bring a new sense of direction to the Dog Section.

Although Ginger is a native of Derbyshire he joined the British Transport Police at Preston in 1968. Towards the end of his probation he joined the Dog Section under the instruction of Terry Shelton. After successfully completing the initial course he returned to Preston. Sadly his first dog went blind after a year and Ginger then took on 'Ben', an Alsatian.

Ginger is a unique person within the British Transport Police, in that there is nowhere on the railway system within Great Britain that he hasn't served, and that includes Belfast, Northern Ireland. He was one of the few officers to hold a dual warrant card, one for England/Wales and Scotland.

In the early 1970s, while stationed at Preston, Ginger was regularly called upon with 'Ben', along with Gerry Baines and his dog from Heysham Harbour, together with colleagues from Heysham, Preston, Liverpool and Manchester, to travel on the three British Railways ships that plied between Heysham and Belfast: the *Duke of Lancaster*, the *Duke of Rothesay* and the *Duke of Argyll*. A police presence was necessary on these ships at the weekends, as there were large numbers of Belfast-based Manchester United supporters travelling on them to see their hometown hero George Best.

Ginger recalls several occasions when he was called, in full British uniform, with 'Ben' to supervise the fans at Belfast Donegall Quay, both disembarking and embarking. He recalls being on the quay at Belfast sorting out the supporters, with members of the Royal Ulster Constabulary and the British Army, to a background of bombs, bullets and buildings being blown up. On one occasion there was a pitched battle on the quay, between the fans of differing religious denominations. He said, 'It was like a scene from the film *Zulu* – all we needed was Ivor Emmanuel singing "Men of Harlech".'

Even on the ships during the eight-hour crossing, while other officers were taking a well-earned break, Ginger was gainfully employed patrolling the ships, with 'Ben' monitoring out the supporters, which could number up to 1,000 and many of which had been consuming alcohol. He recalls travelling as an escort on the *Duke of Lancaster*, across the Irish Sea, on a particular crossing, when he was informed that his nearest back up was a Royal Navy frigate on manoeuvres in the North of Scotland. Fortunately they were not needed as 'Ben' proved his worth.

On another journey to Heysham there was a fight between fans in the forward bar of the *Duke of Rothesay*. He reveals that seven or eight of them were arrested under the Merchant Shipping Act and duly appeared at Morecambe Magistrates' Court, where they were dealt with by the presiding bench.

Being based at Preston, a regular duty for Ginger was at Blackpool, the brash and cheerful Lancashire resort. With the coming of the railways in 1846, visitors went in their millions, especially from the northern mill towns, and in the early 1970s more and more southerners left their traditional south-coast resorts to visit this English tradition.

Ginger, along with his faithful companion 'Ben', regularly attended the town's North station for football duties. In those days Blackpool Football Club was in the old first division and attracted supporters from all over England, who would make a weekend of their visit trying to pick fights with the local inhabitants. Also Blackpool supporters would come to North station to try and fight with the visitors. Although the Bloomfield Road ground is nearer to Blackpool South station, the majority of the football traffic takes place at North station, as this is the larger of the two stations. Ginger and 'Ben' had their work cut out keeping rival factions apart.

He was also gainfully employed keeping law and order at Blackpool North station on Saturday mornings and afternoons during August on the occasion of the 'Glasgow Fortnight', when a number of Glaswegians would use the special excursion trains that ran between Glasgow and Blackpool, during which they consumed large amounts of alcohol and then wanted to fight with anyone in sight. The famous Blackpool Illuminations and bank holiday weekends at Blackpool saw no rest for Ginger and 'Ben'; they would be employed maintaining law and order between the numerous crowds returning on the excursion trains.

Ginger was frequently called upon to patrol Fleetwood Docks, some 7 miles to the north of Blackpool, which handled large amounts of freight traffic between the port and Belfast. They were also to be seen at Morecambe Promenade station assisting colleagues from Heysham harbour keeping law and order, in relation to the persons travelling from Leeds and Bradford on bank holidays.

In the summer months in the mid-1970s, Ginger and 'Ben', were involved in almost permanent observations for three months at Blea Moor, between Ribblehead Viaduct and Dent, one of the remotest places in England on the railway network, being some three-quarters of a mile from the nearest road, on the Settle to Carlisle railway line. This was due to the theft of cable from the lineside. His nearest back up was miles away. Ginger remembers these observations well, as it appeared that false information was being fed to the force, and it transpired that railway employees were actually involved. They were caught red-handed in the 2,629-yard Blea Moor Tunnel.

Another incident on the Settle to Carlisle line Ginger remembers dealing with was that of a dangerous dog at Dent railway station in the bleak Yorkshire Dales. Dent is one of the most remote railway stations in England, being some 4 miles from the village of Dent. Ginger and 'Ben' dealt with the incident to the satisfaction of the complainant.

In 1975 Ginger and 'Ben' were invited to take part in a demonstration at a large fête, in Rhyl, North Wales. While setting up for the display, a lady reported to Ginger the theft of her purse and contents. As no North Wales police officers were around, Ginger and 'Ben' made some initial enquiries, which led them to a set of portable toilets. The lady's purse minus the contents was located in a toilet cistern. Three local youths were questioned by Ginger and were arrested and charged with the theft. Ginger and 'Ben' later received a commendation for their work.

Ginger and 'Ben' were the last team to win the John William Morrell Trophy and the Big Ben Trophy. They say that dogs have a sixth sense. 'Ben' certainly did at the force Dog Trials in 1975. Ginger and 'Ben' were the proud recipients of the John William Morrell Trophy. Going forward to receive the trophy from Eric Haslam, the then chief constable, Ginger put 'Ben' in the sit position facing the chief constable. However, as Ginger was walking towards Mr Haslam, 'Ben' immediately turned round and sat with his back to the chief constable, and wouldn't budge. The next day it was announced that Elstree was to be closed and the Dog Section would be drastically reduced.

When the Dog Section in the north-west was reduced in strength in 1975, Ginger found himself, on a daily basis, covering an area from Carlisle to Warrington as the other dog handlers from Carlisle, Heysham, Wigan, Manchester and Liverpool had either been made redundant or reduced in establishment. On occasions he was called on to cover further afield.

Another duty took Ginger and 'Ben' to the British Transport Docks at Barrow in Furness, as Fiat motor cars were being imported through the docks – the interior fittings, mainly the radios, were the subject of thefts. Working alongside officers from Heysham harbour, a number of arrests from within the local community were made.

Ginger also acknowledges the sterling efforts, determination and enthusiasm of Mr Stanley Peck, the Chief Constable Kenneth Ogram and Assistant Chief Constable, Area Commander (Scotland) George Smith-Leach, in bringing the Dog Section back up to strength and the subsequent opening of a dog-training centre at Tadworth.

Over the years working with a strong commitment in partnership with 'Ben', Ginger achieved positive results that dramatically reduced the amount of incidents of crime on the railways, docks and harbours. During his twenty-eight and a half years' service in the Dog Section he performed duties in connection with Royal visits, thefts, football duties, public disorder and vandalism. In 1988 Sergeant 'Ginger' Ablard was awarded the British Empire Medal in the Queen's New Year Honours List for his services to the BTP Dog Section.

A couple more memories from Bill Rogerson:

One particularly wet Sunday afternoon in the winter of 1975 I went to Northampton as part of my patrol. This post consisted of two offices and did not have a cleaner; therefore it was up to the duty officer to make sure the offices were kept clean and tidy. On this occasion I duly mopped the two rooms and generally cleaned them. I then made myself a coffee prior to returning to Coventry, when the door opened and in walked a very wet London-based dog handler and an equally wet dog. They lived in Northampton, and were on their way to work by train. The dog suddenly gave an almighty shake and all the rain that had soaked into his fur was unleashed all over the one of the offices, covering the papers, furniture and the floor. A few choice words were spoken before I cleaned the mess up from the canine culprit.

When I first went to Leicester in February 1976 one of the officers I met was Police Constable Alan Payne and his Alsatian dog, which unusually was a bitch, called 'Sheba'. Up to Alan having his dog, all the dogs on the force had been male.

In 1976 while I was serving in the CID at Leicester I had an Old English Sheepdog as a pet and on occasions I would take him on the train when visiting the family in Lancashire. One day I had a laugh with one of the railway staff, who shall we say was a little gullible. He saw me on the train with my dog. He said that it was unusual to see me on the train with a dog. I told him that, as I was a CID officer, this was an Alsatian in disguise and we were off on a case. He seemed to believe me and often asked if I still used the dog for duty.

During the long hot summer of 1976 the railway authorities decided to take all the copper telephone wire on the wooden telegraph poles down between Kettering and Bedford, replacing it with new cable that ran along the track. The copper wire was subject to numerous thefts and my colleagues and I kept observations during the long summer nights.

As we were keeping observations for about a month, our locations were changed to relieve the boredom. One night I was teamed up with a dog handler in his van. It wasn't a very pleasant experience as the dog kept on emitting foul odours from its rear orifice and the nights were particularly hot. However, as we were about to call it a night, we had a call from a colleague to the effect that suspects had been seen on the railway line. We made our way across a potato field; this was one of the roughest rides I've ever experienced. I was bounced from side to side going over the rows of potatoes and this didn't help the dog's flatulence one little bit.

By the time we got to the scene the suspects had made good their escape, although they were caught a couple of nights later. The unofficial ploughing of the farmer's field invited a public complaint from him about his ruined crops.

The following is a recollection from Paul Robb, who retired as an assistant chief constable with BTP:

When I joined in 1976 the Euston Division did not have a dog handler. In those days on nights there were certain functions that were undertaken on a 'Pan London' basis and the night duty dog handler was a shared resource from the divisions that had one. A few of the handlers were 'characters', to say the least.

Force HQ Control, known as 'BX', put out a call for the night-duty dog handler to attend a location – I think it was to go to King's Cross depot at the request of one of the duty officers. The call was acknowledged and the handler duly reported to the supervisor as requested. He explained to the dog handler that suspects had been seen in the depot but that they had officers covering the perimeter so he wanted a dog to go in to 'flush' them out. The handler looked somewhat puzzled and then explained that, as the request had been for a 'dog handler', he had not brought the dog with him!

In another incident involving the same officer, again on nights, a call for urgent assistance to Bricklayers' Arms depot was put over the radio as there were suspects on site. Bricklayers' Arms was a large depot in south east London near the Old Kent Road. It was a magnet for the local thieves of that part of London and beyond. The night-duty dog handler was mobile in central London in Chelsea when he received the call, and began racing down the King's Road when he saw a Metropolitan Police officer on foot patrol. He stopped his van and shouted to the officer that there was an urgent assistance call.

Without hesitation the young Met officer jumped in the van and off they sped. The police vehicle left the King's Road and sped across the river and headed away from Chelsea to the incident, which was over 4 miles and three Metropolitan Police divisions away from the officer's beat. On arrival at Bricklayers' Arms a slightly panic-stricken Met officer enquired as to how he was going to explain his whereabouts to his sergeant!

In 1977 Sergeant Thomas Park retired from the BTP based in Nottingham, at the age of fifty-seven years. He was a self-taught cartoonist and produced many brilliant examples of cartoons for the *BTP Police Journal*, which took a wry look at police topics. Among these was the subject of police dogs.

Bill Rogerson recalls,

In the 1970s when Ginger Ablard was on holiday, his dog van was never idle, as it was used as a spare vehicle and, on one particular occasion in late May 1978, it was at

Heysham harbour, where I was based. I remember it well. It was a very warm spring evening at about 19.00, with the sun shining and not a cloud in the sky. I had just finished my meal break, and was about to go for a walk in shirt sleeve order around the Harbour, when I received a telephone call from the signalman at Carnforth East Junction signal box. He informed me that he believed that intruders were in the signal box at Wennington, situated on the Carnforth to Skipton railway line, on the borders of Lancashire and North Yorkshire, and some 17 miles from Heysham.

I immediately jumped into Ginger's dog van and made my way to Wennington. The smell of 'Ben' assaulted my nostrils there and back. Ginger would have been used to the smell. On arrival the most amazing sight appeared before my eyes. There was about an eighth of an inch of snow on the ground, which had been caused by a freak snowfall. The staff from the local Signal & Telegraph department joined me and confirmed that the freak weather conditions had caused the block instruments to ring by themselves.

Bill continues,

Saturday 20 May 1978 was memorable for a certain dog handler from Preston, but for all the wrong reasons. It wasn't unusual for us to go on mutual aid to other stations for football duty in the north west and further afield. This particular day Scotland was playing England in an international football match at Hampden Park, Glasgow. I and a contingent of officers from Heysham, Lancaster, Preston, Liverpool and Manchester went on secondment to Glasgow to assist our Scotland-based colleagues in dealing with the crowds using Glasgow Central station. We all travelled up on an early morning train to Glasgow for the afternoon kick-off. Ginger Ablard and his dog 'Ben' travelled on the train with us.

On arrival at Glasgow we were given a briefing and assigned to a Scottish officer. All went well dealing with the supporters on the outward leg of their journeys to Hampden Park station. On the return I, along with some other England-based officers, was assigned to the main concourse with some of our Scotland-based officers. The returning supporters were quite high after indulging rather heavily in whisky, beer and lager. Thankfully due to our tact and tolerance with them they gave us no trouble. However, unknown to us on the concourse, a disturbance was taking place between the Scottish and English supporters in Hope Street near to a side entrance of the station.

I then saw some officers coming from the direction of the disturbance, laughing their heads off. It transpired that 'Ginger' Ablard and 'Ben' had been assisting in dispersing the crowd, along with PC Don Gordon, a Glasgow-based officer and police dog 'Jim'. A senior officer was also assisting in dispersing the crowd but, due to his position, 'Ben' bit him under the top of his left arm as he was in 'Ben's' 'line of sight.' The crowd dispersed and the senior officer had to receive treatment for his wound, which included having a tetanus injection, the only snag being that he had a phobia about needles.

Shortly afterwards it was time to catch our train home south of the border. While we were on the train dealing with some of the English supporters, two Scottish officers, one of whom was another senior officer, came running along the platform looking for Ginger, who by now thought he was in trouble. The officers shook him warmly by the hand and asked if his dog was all right. Ginger breathed a huge sigh of relief.

Richard Stacpoole-Ryding, who retired as a Sergeant from London Victoria and is the author of the book, *The British Transport Police: An Illustrated History* recalls an incident when he had to call on a dog handler to assist him:

I do recall when I was a Sergeant at Victoria, in 1978 asking for support from the London Transport Area, as it was then, for a dog handler to deal with a 'mad' dog that was tethered outside the ladies' toilets located near No. 1 platform.

The owner was inside and was one of the 'binners' who frequented the station and had to be constantly moved on. John Reynolds was the handler – the first LT area dog handler – and he took control of the dog and removed it to the RSPCA at Chiswick. A female PC took control of the female 'binner' who was causing absolute mayhem and soliciting the attention of the travelling public during the rush hour. The female was eventually arrested and charged with assault on police, breach of the peace and one or two by-law offences. I recall that the magistrate was concerned about the dog's welfare and asked that the RSPCA be made aware of the female's lifestyle when considering releasing the dog back to the owner. I had to go to Chiswick and liaise with the RSPCA, who took over the case with a view to prosecuting the female for animal neglect – the dog was in a manky condition and out of control. I can't remember what happened, except that the female was jailed for thirty days – so what happened about the dog, I have no idea.

I suppose the interesting part is the fact that John Reynolds was the first appointed dog handler on the LT Area, and proved his worth time and time again. I think he was commended on one or two occasions and received a Royal Humane Society (RHS) award for assisting a person under a tube train.

The incident stuck in my mind as it was unusual and I had to look up good old 'Moriarty' for legislation regarding dogs, in case the matter escalated. I do recall that the duty senior officer was not too happy about the issue; probably because it was rather a nuisance and a time-consuming incident and not one you would normally encounter on a railway station.

The following article, entitled 'Our Four-Legged Policemen' and by BONZO, appeared in issue number 121 of *BTP Journal,* dated autumn 1978:

Some three years ago, due to the economic climate prevailing at the time, the Force Dog Training School had to be closed. The exceptionally high standard of training and enthusiasm of Chief Inspector Shelton, since retired, and his deputy, Sergeant Peter Hempton, now stationed at Crewe, was, without fear of contradiction, the finest in the country.

It is a fair comment to say that 'dedicated' handlers have only just about recovered from the blow. Good dogs, some young and some in their prime, were forced into premature retirement overnight. In many a division in the force, particularly during the football season, they were sadly missed. A good many dogs were kept by handlers as family pets. Ex-handlers will tell you, though, that when they leave home for duty at their various stations, even after three years of being stood down, the whines and frenzied barking of 'please take me with you' still resound around many a policeman's home. On a happier note, some dogs have been taken back on duty.

One station that did not lose its four-legged policemen was Crewe in the Midlands Division. There, Constable Eddie Howell with dog 'Rick', and Constable David Tucker with dog 'Zac', have more than kept the flag flying. They are fortunate because Sergeant Peter Hempton is also stationed at Crewe and he has never lost his love and enthusiasm for canine training – a job he has undertaken to do in addition his patrol duties. To see both officers and dogs being put through the most vigorous training is indeed a pleasing and rewarding sight.

At Crewe, these officers have the use of three fields, a small wood, brook, disused building, railway sidings, jumps, ladders and everything else that was provided at Elstree. Most dogs and handlers today receive their basic and refresher training at civil police training schools, but at Crewe, Peter Hempton is justifiably proud that the training of 'Rick' and 'Zac' is in the best tradition of the British Transport Police. Although the dogs are based at Crewe, they are available for work throughout the Midlands Division.

Constable Eddie Howell joined the force in December 1963 and became a handler at Crewe in April 1975. His dog 'Rick' is five years of age and between them they have several good arrests and detections over the years. 'Rick' is renowned for his tracking ability and has 'sniffed out' numerous items of stolen property and criminals in hiding – a very keen dog that thrives on work and is always eager to have a go.

Constable David Tucker joined the force in November 1974 and only became a handler in December 1977. His dog 'Zac' at one and a half years of age is still learning his trade, but events have shown that he must be a star pupil.

What two well-trained dogs and two competent and enthusiastic handlers can achieve is revealed in the following remarkable figures for the first four and a half months of 1978: Arrests – thirteen, Detections/Summary Offences – forty-two. In addition, both dogs have been involved in over a dozen serious incidents involving large crowds of football hooligans.

A few of the cases and incidents in which the dogs have been involved are as follows:

Parcel thefts, Birmingham – As a result of persistent parcel thefts from Curzon Street parcels depot in Birmingham, the divisional detective chief inspector organised special observations at the depot. The CID officers keeping watch were accompanied by Constable Tucker and 'Zac'.

At about 6 p.m. on Sunday 30 April 1978, three youths entered the depot and began to pick up parcels. Constable Tucker shouted to them, 'Police, stand still or I will release the dog.' The youths ran away from the officer, who sent the dog to give chase. On seeing the dog approaching, one youth stood still and was arrested.

A second youth was then observed running from the entrance to the warehouse. The officer again sent in the dog but this youth ignored his warning for him to stand still and he was detained by the dog, who got hold of him by the right arm. The third youth then ran from the warehouse entrance towards the side of the depot towards where Constable Tucker was situated. This youth dropped a parcel as he tried to escape but he was arrested by Constable Tucker and dog 'Zac'. Property to the value of £282 was later recovered and all three youths appeared before the court. The youths also admitted being in the depot on previous occasions.

Attempting to steal a vehicle at Crewe – While on mobile patrol duties, constables Howell and Tucker with police dogs 'Rick' and 'Zac', as a result of a radio message received from Cheshire Constabulary Panda Control, attended the rear of the British Rail car park, Pedley Street, Crewe.

On arrival they saw three male persons run from the car park across the North Junction and towards Uphill Sidings, followed by two county police officers. Both handlers and dogs then joined in the chase. Constable Howell shouted to the two police officers to fall back to enable them to release the dogs. He then shouted to the three men, 'Stand still or we will release the dogs.' The men continued running. The handlers released their dogs simultaneously and commanded the dogs to 'Stop them'.

At this time there were several trains running into Crewe and the driver of a train shouted to the two handlers that he was stopping to allow the dogs to continue the chase. The dogs were directed through the sidings, up an embankment, over a wire fence and, after a chase up a busy main road, the dogs apprehended the men. Later, both handlers returned to the car park and after examination of the vehicles thereon, found an Austin 1800 Saloon had been entered from the front passenger's door and the ignition wires had been connected under the steering column and dashboard. All three men, all with previous convictions, duly appeared at court.

Criminal damage, Crewe – At 2.15 a.m. on Sunday 14 May 1978, Constable Tucker with police dog 'Zac' and Constable Price of this force went to Crewe station entrance, where they found several people who had been causing a disturbance at the station entrance, on the main road and in a nearby hotel. As the officers approached the group, one of them put his fist through a large glass window at the station front during a fit of temper. All of these people had been drinking and were in a very aggressive mood. On seeing the officers approaching, the group of youths began to move away. Constable Tucker shouted to the youth who had broken the window to stand still. He was arrested by the officers with dog 'Zac'. Constable Tucker and the dog then moved the crowd away from the station area. Cheshire Constabulary was advised of the possible disturbance in the main road outside the hotel and they attended. This man appeared at Crewe and Nantwich Magistrates' Court on a charge of criminal damage.

Handling stolen property – On Thursday, 16 February 1978, Constable Tucker was on duty with police dog 'Zac' and Detective Constable Brookshaw, keeping observations on the British Rail car park, Pedley Street, Crewe, when a man was seen walking across the car park from the direction of the station, carrying two cartons. Constable Tucker left his place of concealment and shouted to the person, 'Stand still.' This he did immediately upon seeing the dog; he was later interviewed by Detective Constable Brookshaw and arrested for handling stolen property.

Theft of parcels in transit – On Sunday 21 May 1978, CID officers and Constable Howell with police dog 'Rick' were on special observations at Curzon Street parcels depot, Birmingham. At 7.15 p.m. on that date, a thirty-one-year-old man was seen to enter the shed and steal three parcels. As he left the shed, Constable Howell shouted, 'Police, stand still or I will release the dog.' On seeing the dog approach, the man dropped the parcels, put his hands in the air and shouted, 'Don't send the dog in, I'm not a violent man.'

This man was then charged by the detectives with the theft of parcels in transit to the value of £389.62. He asked for three further crimes to be taken into consideration.

These are just a few brief details of the excellent work being carried out by the handlers and dogs of the Midlands Division.

Liaison between Cheshire Constabulary and this force has always been first class, particularly among dog handlers. When an incident occurs in Crewe and the local Police require the assistance of a dog and their own are not available, over the years they have always called upon

Alan Morecock with
explosive-search dog, 'Max'.

Alan Morecock with
general-purpose dog 'Jazz'.

Above: 'Ginger' Ablard, together with an unknown handler, and John Harrison and 'Spud' Murphy at Tadworth Dog Trials with two judges.

Below: Eddie Howell with police dog 'Rick', Pete Hempton, and Dave Tucker with police dog 'Zac'.

Above: Pete Hempton acting as a 'criminal' while training with a dog at Crewe.

Below: Three unidentified dog handlers with dogs at a parcels depot.

Above: John Harrison, with Colin Sladden and police dog, at Leeds railway station.

Below: Andy Fidgett's drugs dog 'Ozzie' with general-purpose dog 'Ned'.

Dave Tucker, Alan Morecock, Mel Harris, and 'Ginger' Ablard at Crewe *c.* 1970s with two dogs.

Police officer on a train with a 'muzzled' dog *c.* 1920s–1930s.

Above: Six police officers at Hull Docks with Airedale dogs – dated 26 March 1938.

Below: Police Sergeant with two senior officers and police dog at Hull – dated post-1939.

Above: Four dog handlers and dogs from LMS Railway Police. The picture was taken during the Second World War and the officers are carrying shoulder-holstered pistols.

Below: Dogs lined up on parade at Tadworth. The handlers include Alan Morecock and Mel Harris.

Above: Five dog handlers with dogs at Cardiff Docks in 1968.

Left: Ron Woollaston with police dog 'Brutus' at Birmingham New Street station in 1968.

Sergeant Allinson with Airedale police dog 'Jim' at NE Railway Docks Hull c. 1909.

John Mellor with police dog 'Chas' on their last patrol at Cardiff Docks in April 1985.

Above: Terry Shelton, with an Alsatian dog, in a classroom at Police Dog Training School.

Below: Police dog in training at Elstree.

Above: Eleven police dogs on parade with handlers and senior officers in a wood yard at Alexandra Dock Hull *c.* 1960. The picture includes Sergeant Wreathall (front row, far right).

Right: Mick Kinirey with police dog 'Tazz' and trophies.

Above: BTP officers outside Llanelli railway station, including a dog handler with his dog during a 'Q train' exercise.

Below: Ron Woollaston with police dog 'Brutus' standing next to a hoard of stolen property taken from Lawley Street goods yard in Birmingham *c*. 1968.

Above: Mel Harris with police dog 'Sabre' at Staffordshire Police Dog Training Centre (Back row – third from left).

Right: New recruit – Labrador 'Oscar' while being puppy-minded with an adult dog.

Above: Mel Harris with 'Sabre' and other officers, prior to a Royal visit at Birmingham New Street station.

Left: Picture card photo of explosive-search dog 'Perdy'.

Above: Police dog 'Fred' and drugs dog 'Lucky' outside Tadworth Dog Training School in 2009, just before it closed.

Below: Cartoon by 'Ward' from *Railnews* – relating to BTP dogs.

"Oh and this is our undercover team — they're in disguise."

"WATCH THIS 'ARRY – I'VE JUST TOLD HIM HE'S WANTED AT THE BOTTOM!"

Above: Cartoon by 'Park' from *BTP Journals* – relating to BTP dogs.

Left: PC David Coleman with police dog 'Vinnie' at PDSA investiture.

the British Transport Police if they are on duty. Two such incidents are worthwhile noting:

Arrest for other forces, attempted burglary – At midnight on Tuesday 9 May 1978, as a result of a request made by the Cheshire Constabulary, Constable Tucker and police dog 'Zac' attended the Co-operative Stores, Buxton Avenue, Crewe. There, the duty inspector informed him that his own dog handler was not immediately available and that he was of the opinion that there were intruders on the premises. Constable Tucker and 'Zac' commenced a search in the rear yard of the building and 'Zac' flushed out a man hiding in an outhouse. He was arrested for the crime of attempted burglary. Also recovered from the scene were housebreaking implements.

Arrest for other forces, burglary – At about 12.30 a.m. on Thursday 11 May 1978, as a result of an automatic burglar alarm being activated in a building adjacent to Crewe railway station, PCs Howell and Tucker, with dogs 'Rick' and 'Zac', attended and two men were seen in the vicinity making good their escape along a railway embankment. They were chased and both men gained entrance into Crewe Alexandra football ground. A search of the ground by the dogs resulted in both men being arrested. They were subsequently charged with burglary.

In the summer of this year (1978), with the permission of the Area Commander (Western Area), they will give demonstrations for charity at fêtes in and around Crewe. Their performance, as always, will be of a very high standard indeed. Although 'Rick' and 'Zac' are always keen and eager to deal with thugs, hooligans and criminals, they also have a gentler side and many a child will pat their noble heads.

In this violent society in which policemen must carry out their duty, it is comforting to see, in some places of our jurisdiction, the ever-ready and well-trained Alsatian, whose very presence is always a deterrent to the thug and football hooligan.

The British Transport Police, although now much fewer in number, each year make a most valuable contribution to the maintenance of law and order. Statistics reveal that many a criminal has just cause to curse these 'canine coppers'.

Bill Rogerson recalls further,

One Tuesday in June 1979, while stationed at Heysham harbour, I was asked if I would like to work my rest day on the next day to assist in the removal of travellers from the railway yard at Haslingden on the long-closed Accrington to Ramsbottom railway line.

Early the following day I went with colleague Gerry Baines, an ex-dog handler himself, to Preston, where we met up with Sergeant Madge Dowling and Ginger Ablard with his dog 'Ben'. We went off in Ginger's vehicle, which was a Ford Escort estate car, painted bright yellow. On arrival at Haslingden we found that the travellers had left. While discussing our next course of action, we were approached by officers of the Lancashire Constabulary who were looking for thieves who had robbed a nearby jeweller.

Ginger offered assistance with his dog and started tracking through the disued railway tunnel. The thieves were later apprehended in a nearby field. By this time it was time for lunch and we went to the town of Padiham near Burnley and the four of us purchased a meat-and-potato pie each from a local pie shop. We sat in the car to eat our pies.

Madge and Ginger were in the front while Gerry and I were in the rear seats, with 'Ben', Ginger's dog in the rear portion of the vehicle. Gerry took a bite out of his pie and was chewing it slowly, obviously enjoying this Lancashire delicacy, when all of a sudden 'Ben' lurched forward licking his lips and snatched the rest of the pie from the hand of a mesmerised Gerry. The three of us couldn't eat our pies for laughing. Gerry's face was an absolute picture.

On being promoted to Crewe in 1979 I quickly established that we had a very good working relationship with the Cheshire Constabulary and in particular their Dog Section. Handlers from both forces used to help each other out on mutual aid. Sometimes I was asked if I could supply a dog handler if a Cheshire one wasn't available and vice versa.

I soon got to know the characteristics of the officers. Each and every one was unique in his or her own way. The retired officers, and probably a few serving officers, will remember the CRO 74 form (Modus Operandi and Descriptive Form), which was to be filled in when a person had been arrested. One of the sections to be completed was 'How criminal left the premises.' This could be answered simply such as 'egress as ingress', 'via an open door', 'by forcing the back door open', etc. However, we had one officer, who was not a dog handler, but fancied himself as a comedian. On one occasion, when he made an arrest in conjunction with one of the Crewe dog handlers, he wrote in the CRO 74 in respect of his prisoner: 'In handcuffs, in a compartment in the rear cage of the dog van, with the dog in the other'. It was never queried. Someone at New Scotland Yard no doubt had a good laugh.

Up until the 1960s, there was a dedicated establishment of British Transport Police at Bolton's Trinity Street station, but these were cut back and Bolton was covered from the police establishment at Manchester Victoria and Manchester Piccadilly.

Around 1978/1979, the Post Office investigation department realised that several mail bags were being stolen from the parcels depot on a regular basis and reported the matter to the force. Tony Parkinson, a Manchester-based dog handler, takes up the story:

I had a dog called 'Bruce', who in 1977 had been trained at the Lancashire Constabulary Dog Training School, Preston. The CID from Manchester had arranged for observations to be carried out on the depot on this particular Saturday night and they asked 'Bruce' and me to be part of the team. The observation point was on the opposite side of Bolton station to where the mail bags were in the warehouse yard.

At around midnight, several bodies appeared on the top of the wall and dropped down, making their way into the warehouse. A few minutes later, we crept through the road wagons and trailers to where the miscreants had entered the building through a loading bay. I shouted for them to come out or I would send the dog in. No response was forthcoming, so I sent 'Bruce' onto the loading bay and into the building.

He wasn't away long before he came back, trying to run past me and the CID. I stopped him and sent him back in – the same result. Not away long, he came back and tried to run past us. I sent him in again. This time he didn't go into the building but ran to the trailer behind us and dragged two men out from under it. Several cartons were recovered and they were charged with burglary and duly dealt with at court. The moral of the story is that you should believe your dog.

9

'MAJOR' DOES A RUNNER AND THE LOCKERBIE DISASTER

In 1976 Steve Gardner joined the British Transport Police in Leeds and was allocated collar number 'N 149'. Prior to that date, the Dog Section had just had its handlers reduced greatly in number. Leeds was one of the posts that had all its handlers removed. Apart from the handlers at the docks, the only handlers based at mainline stations were as follows: Scotland – three or four, Manchester – one, Preston – one, Crewe – two, Birmingham – two, Cardiff – one and Newport – one.

Either in 1976 or 1977 there were four posts advertised in the London area. The Dog School at Elstree had closed and handlers now attended the Home Office Dog Schools for their training courses.

In 1980 vacancies occurred at both Liverpool and Preston for handlers so Steve Gardener applied for both vacancies and was given Liverpool. In January 1981 he attended the Lancashire Constabulary Training School at Hutton, Preston for his basic course. With police dog 'Tushka' he came top of the course. Because 'Tushka' was classed as a stray and had been handed into Preston Police Station, Lancashire

Constabulary decided it would make a good news story for the local newspaper. Steve, along with the training staff, was interviewed by the local paper and duly appeared on the front page.

At this time there was also a change of collar numbers within the force and he became PC 1725. During Steve's and 'Tushka's' time at Liverpool there were the following handlers in and around the north-west of England: PC Jimmy Harvey based at Liverpool; PC Tony Parkinson at Manchester; PC Adrian Wells at Preston; PCs Dave Tucker and Eddie Howell at Crewe; PCs Alan Morecock and Mel Harris at Birmingham.

In the summer of 1982 Steve left the Dog Section at Liverpool and returned to Leeds as a patrol police constable; at this time Leeds had decided to restart its Dog Section and appointed PC John (Corky) Hawkins and PC Ian Harrison. 'Corky' attended the West Yorkshire Police Dog School with police dog 'Santos', while Ian attended the Lancashire Constabulary School with police dog 'Zac'.

About three years later, PC Nigel Cox transferred to BTP Sheffield and became their only handler. This lasted a short while when in 1985 he resigned and the post was transferred to Leeds. Steve successfully applied and attended the BTP Dog School at Tadworth in January 1986. He returned operationally to Leeds with police dog 'Khan' in April 1986. By now the Dog Section had grown immensely under Chief Inspector John Lloyd's leadership with handlers based at: Newcastle (PCs John Foster, Bob McMullen, later replaced by Alan Gunn), London (Handlers at both mainline stations and London Underground), Southampton (PC Steve Chalk) and Bristol (PC Dave Spencer) who was with the Dog Section until 1994.

Steve Gardner recollects some incidents while working with 'Tushka' and 'Khan' in Liverpool and Leeds respectively:

Up to the 1980s Garston Docks was the only remaining dock in Liverpool that was under the control of the British Transport Docks Board and as such was policed by BTP. The dock contained compounds where containers were stored after arriving by train from various parts of the UK before being loaded onto departure by ship and vice versa. The dock had four beat 'bobbies' that covered the twenty-four hours. In the absence of the beat bobby for whatever reason I was detailed to give visits during my tour of duty. It was during one of these visits in the early hours that control advised me that intruders had been spotted by security guards in one of these compounds.

I made my way to the compound and met up with one of the security guards, who advised me that a colleague and himself had seen two men loitering around the containers and, when challenged, they had climbed onto the dock wall and made off behind the containers. His colleague had made his way to the far end of the containers hoping to catch them when they climbed down the dock wall.

By now both security guards were stationed at either end of the wall and the containers. To their disbelief neither man could be seen. The containers were tight up against the dock wall and the only way out was over the dock wall. It was then that I noticed that the river was only a few feet below the dock wall. I harnessed police dog 'Tushka' and carefully lifted him onto the dock wall. Keeping a short tracking line, I too climbed up onto the wall.

'Tushka' soon picked up the scent and we made our way along the dock wall, which would have been about 3 feet wide. 'Tushka' carefully made his way along the wall, nose to the ground, tail in the air – always a good sign that the dog is tracking well.

The containers were tight up against the wall and, as we approached the last of three containers, 'Tushka' lifted his head and his tail went down again – this is a sure sign that the dog is having problems detecting the scent. I cast him about again but he still could not detect any scent past this point. We made our way back to the start of the track and again spoke to both the security guards, who repeated the story again just as they had before.

By this time the duty sergeant had arrived from Lime Street station and all the facts were relayed to him. He then asked me what my thoughts on the incident were. I said the only conclusion was that the two men had left the wall at the point where the dog had lost the scent, as the only way out for them was to climb over and onto the exterior of the wall, but as the tide was up then they must have ended up in the river. We searched the best way we could, with torches, but no one was seen.

The security guards were adamant as to what had happened so we had no evidence to the contrary but to believe their story. The duty sergeant advised that BTP Lime Street control would advise Merseyside Police regarding the incident just in case they had any missing persons reported to them. With low tide at first light the sergeant asked me to stay in the area and search the nearby foreshore for any sign of the two men. As a result of this search of the foreshore, no evidence of the two men was found.

Strange to relate, about two or three weeks later, while on half-nights again, BTP received a call from Merseyside Police to advise them that a body had been seen floating in the river earlier that day, and the river authorities advised that it was expected that the body would come ashore near to Garston Docks. Again I was despatched to search the foreshore at first light – again nothing was found.

Returning the call to Merseyside Police, they advised that if the body had missed Garston then the next landfall for it would be on the North Wales coast. Nothing further was ever heard regarding the two 'missing males' – could it be that the lone body was one of them? No missing persons were reported, but I still believe police dog 'Tushka' had tracked them to the dock wall edge from where they had disappeared into the Mersey.

One afternoon I received a call to assist Liverpool-based Mobile Support Unit (MSU) officers, who were dealing with an assault on a member of rail staff at Sandhills station, which is in the northern part of the city. Another Liverpool-based MSU officer accompanied me to the scene.

An update from officers at the scene now advised that the alleged offenders had made their way across open land and were now on the canal towpath that runs parallel to the railway lines. On our arrival at the location, the two alleged offenders could be seen on the canal footpath making their way away from the area. A check of the access gate showed it to be well and truly secure; the MSU officer decided to climb over the adjacent wall and as he went over the top he then found out that although the wall was 4 feet high on the roadside it was something like 10 feet on the other side. No way was I going to put the dog over that wall.

On checking the next access point, the gate there was locked. Despite a challenge from me telling them to stand still or the dog would be released, along with a few barks from police dog 'Tushka', more in hope than anything else, they continued to make their way along the towpath. What would have been a 'straight chase' for the dog had been thwarted.

I went back to the original location, to find the MSU officer standing on the canal towpath with the two alleged offenders now swimming across the canal towards a three-storey industrial building that stood adjacent to the canal with no access from the road. Once across the canal they climbed out of the water and using the drainpipe managed to gain access to the roof. It was while they were doing this that I noticed that they were only clad in their underpants.

Despite repeated calls for them to come they stated that they would stay where they were, to which came our reply that we would be there as long as it takes. A few barks from 'Tushka' showed how strong our intention was. Just then the duty inspector arrived and requested that the fire service attend to get the two down. Once down and informed that they were under arrest, we set about reuniting them with their clothes and one of the two stated that they had undressed and left their clothes on the canal towpath. A quick search of the area failed to locate any clothing, to which the other male stated that he was aware that police dogs could sniff someone's clothes and follow their scent – a fallacy. Obviously someone had been watching too many second-rate drama films. So, where were the clothes – he advised us that he had thrown them into the canal and sunk them, so the dog could not get any scent from them.

At this point the first screamed that not only was his wallet in his jeans pocket, but so were his house keys. Someone quickly provided two pairs of scruffy overalls for them to wear, to save them some embarrassment on their arrival at the Main Bridewell in Liverpool.

Hunts Cross railway station is some 7 or 8 miles south of Liverpool city centre. Working half-nights I was requested to attend the station as a neighbour had reported the sounds of loud banging noises coming from the station buildings. On approaching the buildings, which were at road level, I noticed that a house across the road from the station had an upstairs light showing. This was probably where the call originated from, but because of the lateness of the hour any enquiries that had to be made could be made during daylight hours, not at 1 a.m. in the morning.

On checking the access doors to the building they were heavy old-fashioned wood doors that were securely fastened, a check of the property to the side of doors revealed a tall wooden gate that was overgrown and appeared to not have been used from many a year. With police dog 'Tushka', I began to search for some form of access and found an entrance down onto the platform. By this time 'Tushka' had his nose to the ground, having found some scent and from there I had to negotiate another two sets of stairs from another platform and finally reached the small foyer that contained the booking office. The wall opposite the booking office had three or four gothic arched-style windows that were all intact so the alleged intruders must have entered the same way as we had.

On checking the booking office window security shutters, I found that they had been pulled off and the booking office window smashed, with all the glass scattered on the booking office counter and floor – too dangerous to put the dog in. So, placing my anorak onto the counter, I managed to lean as far as possible to check that no one was in there and also check to see if the safe was secure. All appeared in order so I set about securing the shutters in the best way I could. 'Tushka' was now laid down behind me on the foyer floor when all of a sudden he started barking. When I looked round, I found him on all four legs, barking furiously at one of the large gothic windows, through which I could now see the apparition of an elderly woman with her pale complexion dressed in what appeared to be a full-length white cotton night dress and a white mop cap, just like something out of the Victorian days. She was beckoning me towards her; quickly I grabbed 'Tushka's' lead and retraced our steps back out to the front of the station.

I checked the access to the location where I had seen the apparition, only to get to the overgrown gate at the side of the booking office. 'Tushka' showed no signs of detecting any scent on this side of the gate. I made my way back to the booking office window and secured it best I could. Another search outside failed to give any clues as to this woman's identity or location. A radio call to control advised me that the railway would not be sending anyone out to check the safe/office or repair the window until staff commenced duty later that morning. I advised them of what actions I had taken but omitted any detail re the 'apparition'.

Throughout the next few days the incident kept puzzling me but I decided to keep the details of the apparition to myself, as I was aware of 'scouse' humour, especially concerning taking the mickey out of me, a 'woolly back'. The mystery surrounding the apparition was solved a few days later when an older end PC and I were discussing the incident, and he asked had I seen the informant at all. I advised him that I hadn't seen anybody and had only secured the premises. He could understand the informant not coming to see me on the night, as she was the old station master's widow in her late eighties or early nineties and living above the booking office.

Then all became apparent – the call had come from the widow, not from the house opposite the station and obviously she came down to see what was going on while

I was making a noise securing the shutters. Just for the record, nothing had been stolen from the station – only my pride had been dented.

On the York side of Leeds stands Neville Hill motive power depot, with a branch running down a slight incline in a cutting to Hunslet oil terminal. Regular rail traffic along this branch consisted of train-hauled petrol tankers, both full and empty. One afternoon railway control advised that fires at been lit on the lineside and, as such, all rail traffic was suspended until the fires and alleged offenders were dealt with.

On arriving at Neville Hill with police dog 'Khan' I set off down the branch line. It was not long before I saw the culprits who, on seeing the dog and me, ran off into nearby streets. Just then an adult male appeared out of the undergrowth on the opposite side to the fires and began to walk down the centre of the single track. Knowing that all rail traffic was suspended, I challenged him, warning him to stand still or the dog would be released. At this point he began to run down the track. I released 'Khan', who soon caught up with the male, who then decided to stand still, with 'Khan' circling the best way he could on the track and barking at him. Suddenly the male set off running but didn't get very far before 'Khan' took hold of his right arm in his mouth, causing the male to stop.

Upon questioning him I asked him why he decided to run from the dog when he had previously stopped. He replied that he thought the dog was playing and that he could run away and the dog wouldn't follow him. How wrong he was. He also denied being involved in the fires but still got reported for trespass.

I was called from home one Sunday afternoon to rendezvous with a York-based DC who had been advised that a section of cut railway cable had been located by railway staff in the Castleford area. As I was in a marked police van, I left the van parked in the local police station yard. This served two purposes; one, the vehicle was safe in a secure yard, and the other was that the duty sergeant at Castleford knew where we were in case we needed any assistance.

I located the DC who showed me where the cable was and we then made our way under a nearby bridge where, after a short while, we heard the sound of something being dragged along the sleepers on the track. Lo and behold, there appeared a male dragging a length of cable. I challenged him, warning that unless he stood still the dog would be released; the male on hearing this then ran off along the track with police dog 'Khan' in pursuit. The DC ran towards the exit gate on the railway banking; the male then changed direction and headed towards the gate, with the result that the male, the DC and the dog all met up at the same time.

I called the dog off while the DC arrested and handcuffed the male. We retrieved the length of cable but now had a problem – one prisoner, two officers, one dog and a length of cable, but no vehicle as the DC had left his vehicle at Castleford railway station, which, although close to the police station, was some 2 miles away.

After a quick consultation the DC contacted West Yorkshire Police (BTP had just started using multi-channel radios) and arranged for a car to collect him and the prisoner, convey them to Castleford railway station to collect the CID car and then come back for the dog and me. Unfortunately Castleford Police Station was not a designated police station and we would have to go to Normanton Police Station, which is some 5 miles the other side of Castleford.

On the DC's return with the Maxi car, the prisoner sat in the front passenger seat. I sat in the rear seats with the dog beside me and behind the driver, and the cable went in the boot.

As we were driving along I suddenly heard the sound of a zip being opened, followed by a popping noise, and looked down to see 'Khan' with the remains of a tomato skin hanging from his mouth. I then became aware that not only had 'Khan' unzipped the DC's bag but had managed to open the plastic lunch box and remove a sandwich, which now was being consumed by the dog. The prisoner now was doubled up with laughter, to which the DC made this comment: he didn't mind getting into a tussle with the prisoner and the dog, he didn't mind the dog sitting on the back seat of the CID car, but he drew the line at the dog eating his sandwich. I apologised profusely and promised to replace the sandwich!

A few months later the same DC and I were on observations in the York area for mechanical plant thefts. We had managed to obtain the key for a location that overlooked the railway. The evening was uneventful and, once the railway staff had arrived at the site, we stood down and were joined by the uniformed officers from York.

While talking to the uniformed officers, both the DC and myself related the previous incident at Castleford – in fact, we had both been laughing about it during the observations. Suddenly the DC asked where the dog was, and I replied that it was in the back of the CID car. 'The rest of my sandwiches are in my bag,' said the DC. With that, we both ran to the car just as 'Khan' was sticking his nose in the DC's bag.

Who says lighting doesn't strike the same place twice!

In 1980 PC Tony Parkinson, in Manchester, became the first BTP officer to undergo training for detecting explosives when he and his dog attended a course in Cheshire. PC Tony Parkinson recalls,

> Owing to the increase of activity by the IRA on the UK mainland, police forces began training dogs to indicate the presence of explosives during high-level security searches. The BTP were no exception and, as a course to train dogs for that purpose became available at Cheshire Constabulary, I was enrolled with police dog 'Bruce' and successfully completed it.
>
> So much for the official version – now this is what really happened! I was on a training day at Crewe when the Cheshire dog sergeant said that he was going to run a course with a couple of his lads. He said that he could handle a couple of us as well if we wanted to attend at no cost. I approached a senior person within the division with the idea and he 'umm-ed and ahh-ed' to begin with but, when I said it was free, he agreed – although I later found out that the Cheshire sergeant got a 'bollocking' from his boss for agreeing to this.
>
> I did the course with another BTP officer but he didn't get through. The first that Force Headquarters knew about it was when the course reports landed on their desks, at which point they thought that it was a good idea!
>
> My first operational search was the opening of the Britannia road bridge, 130 feet over the Menai Straits in North Wales. In those days all we used to do before was a cursory walk along the tracks, so I had to show the inspector from Holyhead what to do with me.

John 'Corky' Hawkins retired as a dog handler at Leeds. He joined the British Transport Police as a constable in December 1977 and joined the Dog Section in late 1982, serving until he retired in May 2011. He served his entire career in Leeds. Upon joining the force there were no dogs in the North Eastern Area other than the dogs based on the docks at Hull. This was due to the Dog Section being 'chopped' in the early 1970s. John and his police dog 'Riot' were the first ever BTP team to compete in the National Police Dog Trials in 2008. John takes up his story:

I was interviewed in 1982 as part of the re-build of the Dog Section for the two vacancies at Leeds. The other applicant was PC Ian Harrison who had to pass his driving test within six weeks to get the job. We were interviewed by Inspector John Lloyd, who was new from the Metropolitan Police and PS 'Ginger' Ablard. 'Ginger' sat slightly behind Inspector Lloyd and, on every good answer, either winked or gave the 'thumbs up'. We were both successful.

I attended my first basic course with the West Yorkshire Police, due to the fact that the Dog School at Tadworth was still being built, in late December 1982. My uncle was my dog instructor and my father was a Sergeant in the West Yorkshire Police Dog Section. So there was no real pressure then!

My first dog was 'Santos'. With 'Santos' I competed in two force dog trials, coming last in both. I should point out that my, and PC Harrison's, first dog vehicle was a Hillman Avenger estate in blue with no dog cages – just a dog guard. Luckily our dogs got on with each other.

During the early 1980s I was on duty at Leeds railway station with 'Santos', awaiting the hooligan element of Birmingham City 'Zulu Warriors'. They arrived, stormed the ticket barriers and ran out of the station. I ran to stop them with my dog but slipped on some oil. I went down and 'Santos' grabbed me by the arm and started shaking me about; he then realised whom he was biting and let go. By this time the 'Zulus' had stopped to watch. I got up and went towards them and they all ran back to the station – they probably thought that the dog was mad!

Around about the same time with 'Santos' I was talking to a member of the Leeds hooligan element, the 'Service Crew', when 'Santos' suddenly leapt up, and took him to the floor by the arm. Two West Yorkshire police officers ran up, picked him up and put him in the back of the prison van. About an hour later, they asked, 'What did you lock him up for?' I replied, 'I didn't lock him up – you did.' We went to the van, spoke to the lad and sent him on his way. No complaint, no problem – maybe different today.

'Santos' looked like a Timber Wolf, one good ear and one floppy ear. This one particular evening, in the early 1980s, I was dropping Steve Gardner and his dog 'Khan' off at their home. At Steve's house, his dog got out, spun round and launched himself at the cage of my van, where an ear of 'Santos' was stuck out of the cage. Subsequently 'Khan' bit about an inch or so off the end of Santos's' ear. Yes, it was his good ear. A trip had to be made to the vet's.

I was on protection duties for a forthcoming Royal visit at an overnight stabling point in Newark. During the early morning, either myself or Ian Harrison would be required to make a fry up for everyone – as we were the best at it. This time it was my turn. Inspector Tony Clift, who later became a superintendent, was in charge and, at about 5 a.m., decided to put a music cassette tape on in the music system of the control vehicle 'Charlie 99'. He didn't realise that the tannoy was on and the sound of The Three Degrees singing, 'When will I see you again' went out all over the site. Luckily it was His Royal Highness Prince Charles on the train and The Three Degrees were his favourite group. No one helped to turn it off.

After a Royal visit at Wakefield we had to drop off Superintendent Derek Ley of Leeds, who was always immaculate. When we left him he was completely covered in dog hairs.

I then went on to have a dog named 'Zico', with whom I got a second, third, fourth and two fifth placings in the force dog trials. I then re-handled a dog for one year called 'Zen', who died of an illness.

Alan Morecock joined the British Transport Police in 1969 and was based at Birmingham New Street station. He became a dog handler in 1979 and did his initial training at Tadworth, under the supervision of 'Ginger' Ablard. His first dog was sixteen-month-old short-haired Alsatian 'Jazz', whose name was taken from the song 'The Jazz Singer'. Alan recalls,

He was a great dog and we got involved in all sorts of jobs together. I did a lot of work with Brian Preece, who was stationed at Wolverhampton for a time. One day in the early 1980s Brian and I went out to Codsall to set up an observations point for youths stealing from cars loaded onto trains, which were being attacked while stationary at signals. We found a spot in the daytime and then went back when it was dark and waited. Russ Brown, the detective sergeant, was in another observations point and suddenly shouted over the radio that people were attacking a train. Brian and I started running, and I shouted in the dark for them to stand still. I let 'Jazz' go and he went off and was soon barking.

As I ran, I suddenly fell over some track that had been left lineside following our earlier visit, and I finished up in agony on the floor. By the time I got to 'Jazz' he was holding one offender, who was shouting to be released, and three others were detained by the other officers.

Alan went on,

> Brian Preece and I used to do a lot of observations in Oxley
> Sidings, in Wolverhampton, and we were always making
> arrests. I always used to have a plastic sheet to lie on in the
> bushes and we would put the dog in between us to keep
> warm. On one occasion we were in Codsall again when a
> security officer spotted us lying down in the dark and asked
> us what we were doing. We were so scruffy we had to show
> our warrant cards to stop him phoning for the police!
>
> 'Jazz' did well in the Force Dog Trials and won awards in
> 1983 and the following year. In December 1983 I did a 'CS
> Gas Course' at No. 3 Regional Police Dog Training Centre
> in Staffordshire. As part of the course 'Jazz' and I were put
> into a chamber full of CS gas. It has no effect on dogs but it
> certainly had an effect on me. The Instructor Chief Inspector
> Bryn Phillips did a 'spoof' certificate for me confirming that
> I had passed the course and said, 'It must be noted that police
> dog 'Jazz' is the one with the hair and is the intelligent part
> of the team.'
>
> I had 'Jazz' for eight years before he was retired. I kept
> him at home for twelve months, and then Inspector Derek
> Hackett had him as a pet at his home in Sutton Coldfield.
> After a year Derek found 'Jazz' dead at the bottom of the
> stairs one morning when he woke up. I was really upset
> when he told me. I loved all of my dogs – some people used
> to say that I loved them more than my wife.

Mike Morris, who retired as an Inspector with BTP, recalls
some lighter moments in the history of the Dog Section:

> I remember an incident in 1980 when I, and a number of
> other handlers, were turned out to capture what numerous

sightings had reported was an escaped crocodile, or possibly an alligator. The potential dangers of cornering such an animal may well be imagined, but what was an additional concern to me was the 'specialist equipment' I had been issued with to restrain the beast, which consisted of the standard pole and noose used to capture errant dogs and convey them into a vehicle.

No-one explained what I should do with the alligator, if we were sufficiently lucky enough to get the noose on it. Fortunately, no alligator, or crocodile, was found, and it must therefore join the ranks of the 'Beast of Bodmin', and the 'Loch Ness Monster'.

Any dog owner will know that a critically important part of a dog's training is 'house-training'. All police dogs are of course taught how to behave in polite society. There are occasions, however, when 'man's best friend' can let him down. One day a handler, who shall remain anonymous, was out with his dog on the London Underground system. While rattling along, a very attractive young lady caught the handler's eye. She smiled at him, and the handler smiled back. Her smile became larger, his smile became larger.

It was at this point of hope that a familiar, but unpleasant, odour began to assail his nostrils and he looked down to discover, to his horror, that his dog simply could not wait until the next stop, and was doing what comes naturally. The handler later explained, it was not clearing the 'spillage', or the embarrassment, that was the worst aspect; it was the malevolent looks directed at the pair by all the other passengers, trapped as they were with the resultant effluvium.

On his very first deployment as what is officially titled a Passive Drug Detection Dog, the Border Collie – not a dog generally known for its aggression – promptly bit the hand of the first person he was introduced to – unfortunately a visiting American female tourist. As the handler says, following first aid, many apologies, and dog bite procedure, Border Collie temperament tests were undertaken.

In another instance a rather well-endowed female tourist bent down to fuss one of the 'search' dogs, who promptly took a liking to her scarf and tugged it away, unfortunately freeing her ample bosom, from what the handler describes as her 'anchorage.' No words were exchanged.

Without wishing to be too biased, among the range of stories from various handlers, there was one individual who seemed to stand out among all the others.

This unfortunate experience with what we shall term 'doggy doo' does suggest that things always happen in threes. On dropping his lead one night in a park, the handler recovered it, only to find it covered in 'doo' from some previous passing animal. In an attempt to clean up, he found some tissues in a litter bin; it was while he was trying to use these, that he discovered that they contained the result of what we may term someone's 'romantic encounter', and he was then covered in that as well.

While exercising his dog, in company with another handler, he bent to pick up some dog mess, when his legs were taken from under him by the other handler's dog. Unfortunately he managed to land in the middle of it.

While deployed for potential football disorder, this handler was clearing up after his dog. Unfortunately he got some residue on his hand, and scratched his nose. His partner was somewhat surprised to see the handler walking with his arms outstretched, and a funny look on his face. He then said, 'I've got dog shit up my nose.' A situation that, as his partner said, was not something he could immediately assist with as he was dealing with some 400 mixed Millwall and West Ham fans.

One night, one particular handler sent his dog after a running thief, and they both soon disappeared into the darkness. Having temporarily lost the dog, the handler called out repeatedly for him. He was rewarded with one single bark. When he traced the dog, as a result of the bark, he found him holding on to the leg of the thief, who himself was hanging from an 8-foot chain-link fence. It later transpired that the dog had taken the thief on the arm, as he was trained to do, and was holding him. When his 'Dad' shouted for him, the dog released his hold to supply the one bark. Taking his chance the thief attempted to scale the fence, whereupon the dog seized his leg, and hung on till 'Dad' arrived.

Mick Morris reflects on two other stories, which explain how complex it is to find an ideal working police dog:

While donated dogs are always welcome, there must invariably be the question: why is this person donating this dog? Does the dog possess character traits or physical problems that mean it is going to be a potential danger to either the public or its handler, or will it be incapable of physically undertaking police duties?

A brief example of two instances known to me are my own first police dog named 'Steel' who, while the size of a small Shetland pony, and sufficiently fierce-looking to put the fear of God into anyone, actually possessed such a kind nature that he was incapable of biting. He eventually went to a loving family, who had the most relaxed and friendly German Shepherd they had ever seen.

Sadly the second instance was of a dog that appeared perfectly normal, until he defecated. At this point he would attack anyone near him, including his potential handler. It became plain that in an attempt to 'house-train' him, his previous owner had beaten the dog every time it 'messed'. Attempts to eradicate this behaviour failed, and the dog, which was incapable of being re-homed with such a savage trait, had to be put down. The ultimate result of bad treatment and a poor attempt at 'training'.

PC John Mellor and 'Chas' worked at Cardiff in the 1980s and sometimes travelled on the 'Q' trains to catch trespassers and vandals. 'Chas' and John had some success catching the offenders. Malcolm Clegg further recalls the following incident:

This occurred around 1981 while I was a uniform sergeant at Swansea Docks. I was on duty in the main police station at Swansea Docks when a report was received of intruders within the premises of the West Glamorgan Timber & Plywood Company. I immediately sent Police Constable Phillip Williams (Dog Handler Swansea Docks) to the scene, and then contacted Police Constable John Worley (transit van patrol officer) via the radio and directed him to the scene to liaise with PC Williams.

After about ten or fifteen minutes, and unable to contact the officer by radio, I drove to the scene. Upon arrival I found the Ford Escort hatchback (dog handler's car with grille in the back) parked on the roadway. The transit van was parked a couple of yards behind.

As I got out of the car I saw PC Williams sitting on the pavement with his dog licking the officer's face. PC Worley was sitting alongside him with his head in his hands. After speaking to the officers, I was able to find out what had happened.

Police Constable Williams was the first officer to arrive on the scene just in time to witness two youths climbing over the fence from the timber company. PC Williams jumped out of his vehicle, ran around the back and quickly lifted the tailgate to get his dog out of the vehicle. The tailgate, however, did not stay open as it should have done, but crashed back down with considerable force, striking PC Williams on the head causing him to slump to the ground.

The dog managed to alight from the car and started to lick PC Williams on the face. It was at this point that PC Worley arrived and jumped out of the transit van. He saw the two intruders running away from the scene, and he assumed that PC Williams had been assaulted by the youths.

PC Worley then pushed up the tailgate of the escort with a view to putting the dog back inside the car while he pursued the youths, but history repeated itself and PC Worley was struck on the head rendering him semi-conscious. The youths were never apprehended.

Although the above incident will be seen by many as being highly amusing, it could have caused serious injury to one or both officers. The Ford Motor Company later admitted liability in respect of a defective tail gate. PC Williams left the force shortly after this incident. He was allowed to keep his dog but was never replaced as a dog handler. He was therefore the last dog handler ever to serve at Swansea Docks.

Bill Rogerson further recalls,

Crewe was, and still is, the centre of the universe as far as railway junctions are concerned. It goes without saying that during the football season supporters from all over the country would change trains at Crewe and therefore it was necessary to have a uniformed police presence and, if possible, dogs and their handlers on the platforms to quell any potential disorder.

In 1981 the three emergency services, along with the British Transport Police at Crewe and the staff at Leighton Hospital, Crewe, entered teams into an *It's a Knockout* style competition at Leighton Hospital to raise funds for the kidney unit. Our dog handlers entered against the Cheshire Constabulary dog handlers. I can't remember who won, but we had a cracking day. The dogs were the centre of attraction from the public.

One particular evening on a Saturday in November 1981, I was on duty on the station platforms when I was called to a small disturbance between two sets of supporters who were in the process of changing trains. That evening, I had a dog and handler on duty with me. They accompanied me to the disturbance and we set about to split them up. The dog suddenly flew at a man who was particularly noisy and waving his arms around in the air, like a windmill at full speed. The dog took hold of his arm and the handler brought the situation under control as he was trained to do. The man then complained that the dog had torn the sleeve of his brand new leather jacket. The dog handler very unsympathetically said to him, 'Your fault – go to the hardware shop and buy some vinyl weld.' The man was arrested for disorderly conduct.

While stationed at Crewe, which was in the Midlands division, it was normal practice for us on a Saturday to go on mutual aid to places such as Wolverhampton, Birmingham New Street, and Smethwick Rolfe Street, for West Bromwich Albion's ground. These duties were usually covered by overtime. We usually returned on the 18.05 Birmingham New Street to Glasgow Central InterCity train, which conveyed a buffet car. It usually arrived in Crewe at 19.05.

More often than not football supporters from the northwest of England, who had been watching their team playing in the Midlands, would usually return on this train escorted by the returning officers to Crewe. However, there were occasions when there were no police officers on the train and the supporters took advantage of this fact, stealing whatever they could from the buffet when the steward's attention was distracted. We would usually end up recording the crime at Crewe, which was not too good for our figures.

One Saturday evening in the winter months of 1982, after performing duty in the Midlands I returned on this train with a couple of officers and a dog handler along with his trusty companion. There were some north-west-based supporters, who were travelling on the train and changing at Crewe.

Sticking my neck out, as the dog was supposed to travel in the brake van, I put the dog and handler to work in the buffet. The dog just sat on the floor opposite the counter, no doubt thinking about the meat pies on display. The supporters got a shock when they saw the dog sat there. It was a case of 'form an orderly queue, lads'. A few days later I received a telephone call from the British Rail catering manager responsible for the buffet car, thanking me for the initiative and stating that for the first time in ages the buffet actually made a profit that evening.

At twenty-four years of age, WPC Margaret 'Maggy' Lyall, née Kealey, became the first female dog handler in the British Transport Police and was based in Scotland. Maggy and her fourteen-month-old German Shepherd dog 'Denny' completed their fifteen-week training course at the Strathclyde Police Dog Training Centre in Glasgow, and a further week's 'in force' training at Crewe.

Based at Glasgow, and with more than five years' service, her role was to patrol mainly in Glasgow and the West Coast of Scotland, along with three other handlers and their canine companions. With a typically sharp sense of Scottish humour, Maggy recalls her days as the force's first female dog handler:

I was the first female dog handler in the force, and was taken on by the then-new Dog Inspector John Lloyd in November 1982. John Lloyd had come to us from the Met and had distinguished himself, I believe, while in the Met, as being the handler and dog who brought the IRA Balcome Street Siege to a close. He worked with Ginger Ablard, who was a brilliant Sergeant and instructor, who worked out of Crewe.

Tadworth Dog Training School had just been thought about at that time and there was great 'kerfuffle' by the locals, who were against it, but John won them around, promising them that they would have regular dog handler patrols in the area!

I was initially trained by Strathclyde Police in Glasgow and all other training was with John and Ginger Ablard at Crewe or Tadworth. My dog was called 'Denny'; he was kennelled at home. I got a dog van and I worked by myself, on shifts in the Scottish area. We had some great arrests, mainly for metal and cable thefts, as they were the main crime criteria at that time. 'Denny' was a great tracking dog; he could track from here to hell and back. He was great at retrieving, although I recall one night, at 2.00 a.m. in Polmadie Yard in the south side of Glasgow, I was doing observations on the buffet cars that were stabled overnight in the yard. They were full of foodstuffs and drink etc., and they were always being broken into. As I patrolled I found a buffet car door open and I lifted up 'Denny' and threw him in the door. I heard his claws on the lino floor and I heard him growling. I could hear the pulling and pushing movement and I thought, 'Quids in – a body!' I got in the buffet car, and 'Denny' was 'wrestling' and eating two cooked turkeys that were on the floor!

He was 90 lbs in weight, and I taught him a few tricks. If we got to a high wall or fence he was able to jump up on my back and over the wall. It was, however, a bit of a bitch to get him to stand on the other side so I could get over.

He was brilliant at man work – shall I say, very enthusiastic – and I never, ever got a 'standoff' out of him. During initial training he put an instructor in hospital by biting him during a standoff training session on ice one day. It was the sergeant's fault as he had no sleeve on and was a bit of a smart-arse guy. I thought I was going to lose him to the army after that incident, but John Lloyd was called up from London. He and Ginger had a look at him and it was decided that he was not a problem; just that he didn't need any more man work!

He was a hard, hard dog and was used for football and crowd-control duties at that time; scary son of a bitch was 'Denny'. I worked on jobs with dog handlers from our home office forces as we all got to know each other through the initial training and dog work was accepted in any 'jurisdiction' at that time. I learned a lot from them.

I recall during my dog service that the command for 'hold him' was changed to 'stop him', as 'hold him' indicated you were encouraging the dog to assault the perpetrator ... strange old world, eh?

I had 'Denny' for seven working years, until he developed severe hip displasia and had to retire. I was fortunate as the ACC Scotland at that time gifted me 'Denny' at the end of his service – just as well, or I would have stolen him anyway!

I didn't take on another dog as by then I was married and the thoughts of a family were looming, and I knew the hard work of having a dog, a child, and a husband to look after would be too much. My dog-handling years were the best of my service. It was very hard work but also very rewarding.

People used to ask me if I was not scared out at night, myself with only a dog. I was safer with that dog than I was with a shift of men. They were fabulous times that I look back on fondly. I recall being told that, way before my time in the force in the sixties and early seventies, there were six dogs in Scotland, based in Glasgow, and there were kennels at Bellahouston and a PC who was a kennel man.

Maggy was awarded an MBE in the 2005 Birthday Honours List for her services to the British Transport Police.

Viv Head researched the next story as part of his work on the history of policing Cardiff Docks for a book called *Between the Sea & the North Star*, which is yet to be published. The story also includes the account from Allan Beddoe himself:

There can be no better illustration of the effectiveness of a well-trained dog than the incident that led to PC Allan Beddoe and his dog 'Major' featuring in the national news.

Early in 1983, British Transport Police CID officers at Cardiff were investigating a burglary and the unlawful taking of a motor vehicle. A small engineering works in Collingdon Road had been attacked and the safe stolen. Entry had been gained to the premises through a hole in the wall made when a forklift truck had been used to smash through the brickwork.

Acting on information that came from an unlikely source, one of the well-known prostitutes who frequented the docks, the unopened safe was discovered in a disused quarry at Leckwith on the outskirts of Cardiff. Believing that the suspects would return to try to retrieve the contents, Detective Inspector Vic Miller and a number of other officers set themselves up to lie in wait.

Among the officers were two dog handlers, PC John Mellor with his dog, 'Chas', and PC Allan Beddoe with his four-year-old German shepherd dog, 'Major'. Darkness was falling when, to the astonishment of the officers, two men dropped down the quarry face on a rope and began to attack the back of the safe with a hammer and crowbar.

The waiting officers moved in to make the arrest, but in the darkness and confusion one of the men escaped. The other was arrested by PC John Mellor and his dog. PC Beddoe's dog 'Major' set off in pursuit of the fleeing figure. Using the rope, the suspect scaled the 120-foot quarry face, ran crashing through dense woodland in the dark and swam across a nearby river.

PC Beddoe tried in vain to recall 'Major' but he did not respond. Then came the sound of a gunshot, subsequently found to be unconnected, but nevertheless, fearing for the safety of his dog, the handler and other officers made a sustained but fruitless search for the dog and, of course, for the suspect. The officers were eventually forced to abandon the search, with the intention of returning at daybreak.

As a matter of routine, the absence of the police dog was reported to the South Wales Police. Later that evening, a young woman rang the local police station to report that an Alsatian dog was sitting on the pavement in Penarth Road in the Grangetown area of Cardiff. Seeing that the dog appeared to be exhausted, but was refusing to move, she had given it some food and water, which had been gratefully received.

Wondering whether it was the missing police dog, the local officers telephoned the BTP control room and asked them to attend. The first officer on the scene was Inspector Tony Kitts, who had been at the quarry earlier, but who was now in the process of going off duty. He was able to confirm that it was indeed 'Major' sitting on the pavement. It was now some four hours since the dog had gone missing in the quarry, nearly 5 miles distant from where he was now sitting.

Inspector Kitts tried to persuade the dog to go with him but he steadfastly refused to budge. He was sitting outside the front door of a house and wasn't going to move for anyone. PC Beddoe and the CID officers were called to the scene and it was clear that 'Major' was very interested in this one particular house. Hoping the dog was still on the case, entry was gained to the premises by CID officers led by DI Vic Miller. 'Major', now back under the control of his handler PC Beddoe, went to the rear of the premises to prevent any possibility of a rapid escape through the back garden. Information was given that the suspect might be hiding in a basement flat and it was thoroughly searched, but there was no sign of anyone. The informant was positive that the suspect was still in the flat and 'Major' still wasn't prepared to leave. The flat was searched for a second time but again there was no sign of any occupants.

Eventually, it dawned on DI Miller that the one sure way of finding the suspect if indeed he was in the flat, was to let 'Major' in to finish the job. In the interests of safety, everyone was ordered out of the house, and several families were crowded together outside on the pavement while the dog got what he had wanted all along. In one of the bedrooms, 'Major' began barking at a wardrobe and would not be distracted.

The wardrobe had already twice been opened and searched without revealing anybody, but the dog was insistent. But then, triggered by the sound of the dog, there came muffled cries and suddenly the whole wardrobe came crashing forward with the suspect tumbling forward with it. Ian Augustus Jones had been hiding in a tiny space behind a specially built false panel at the back. You could almost see the grin on the dog's face!

Two days later Jones pleaded guilty to several criminal offences at Cardiff Magistrates' Court and was sent to prison for six months. 'Major' had pulled off a truly remarkable track, through the quarry and adjacent woods, across a river and along busy arterial roads, for a distance of 5 miles, all without any guidance or assistance from his handler. And when he could go no further, having been confronted by a locked door, he simply sat down and waited patiently for the 'cavalry to arrive'.

When he was interviewed, Jones complained about the pesky dog's persistence, explaining that he had swum across the Ely River in an attempt to shake his pursuer off but the dog had simply waded in and swum after him.

'An outstanding piece of police work by any estimation' – Major's story was reported in both the local and national press, including the front page of the *Daily Express*. The handler and his dog were both later commended by the Chief Constable.

The Chief Constable's Commendation citation reads as follows:

I am pleased to commend Constable A. G. Beddoe and his police dog 'Major' for their initiative, and the particular determination and resolve of police dog 'Major', who on 8 March 1983, tracked a suspect, while unsupervised, for 5 miles and remained in the vicinity of the suspect's residence for three and half hours until officers arrived and the man was arrested. He was subsequently sentenced to six months' imprisonment at Cardiff City Magistrates' Court on 10 March 1983 for offences of criminal damage and taking and driving away a motor vehicle.

'There's just no escaping Major' – by John Christopher from the *Daily Express*, dated Monday March 14 1983:

> To escape a police ambush, an agile criminal scaled a 120 foot quarry face, crashed through dense woodland, and swam a river. But he failed to shake off one of his pursuers – Police Alsatian 'Major'. The four-year-old German Shepherd dog swam the river after him, nipping him on the ankle and leg. Pausing to shake the water from his coat, 'Major' padded behind the fleeing criminal for 6 miles in darkness across country and along a busy street. His handler, British Transport policeman, Allan Beddoe, thirty-six years, and other officers had been waiting at the quarry at Llandough, near Cardiff, for a gang to collect a stolen safe that had been dumped there. '"Major" did not respond to my recall and I thought he had been killed,' PC Beddoe said. One man was arrested in the quarry. The search for the other was called off until dawn. But four hours later an Inspector on his way home stopped at a red traffic light in Penarth Road, Cardiff and spotted 'Major' sitting on a door step ... forty arrests already.'

It is worth remembering that dogs have 220 million scent receptors whereas a human has about 5 million.

The official opening of the new Dog Training Wing at the Training Centre, Tadworth took place on Friday 30 March 1984. After an absence of nearly eight years, the force once again had its own Dog Training Wing. Performing the opening ceremony was James G. Urquhart, Esq., CVO, Chairman of the Police Committee, who was introduced by the Chief Constable Kenneth H. Ogram, Esq., QPM.

The Chief Constable in his address made reference to how much the Chairman and the Police Committee were doing to ensure that the officers of the force were able to carry out their day-to-day duties with the most up-to-date equipment and that, in these days of terrorism and public order situations, dogs would have the best possible training and be available to back up the officers controlling such situations. A lot of planning had gone into the construction of the new Dog Wing and was regarded as one of the best in the country.

Mr Urquhart in his address said that the Chief Constable's need for the force to have its own dog Training Wing had been supported by Stanley E. Peck, Esq., CBE, BEM, QPM, DL, former HM Inspector of Constabulary and now a member of the Police Committee, who had prevailed on the Police Committee that trained dogs were an essential part of the modern police service. It was a department that needed to be expanded and, in doing so, it was necessary for it to have its own Training Wing.

The project had taken two years to complete. It gave him much pleasure in opening the new Dog Training Wing. Afterwards, Mr Urquhart unveiled a commemorative plaque; a demonstration of the work that could be done by the dogs followed.

The force then had thirty-nine dogs, which included two 'sniffer' dogs used for the detection of explosives. When attending the Training Wing, the dogs and handlers would be able to train on some 2,500 acres of farmland near the centre. Only two years before, the force's dog-handling branch had been allowed to run down to just twenty-four animals of all shapes and sizes. Then Inspector John Lloyd had been brought in from the Metropolitan Police to re-organise and transform the operation, assisted by two Sergeants: George Ablard, based at Crewe, and Alan Jackson in London.

Previously the dogs were quartered overnight in kennels but now they would be considered as part of the handler's family, living with him at home. 'We know the dogs prefer it,' said Inspector Lloyd. 'It helps to build up a special relationship with their handler.'

Since the dogs were brought back, police arrests had soared and public order had improved. Typical of how useful the dogs could be came after a football match at Blackpool when 1,000 visiting Manchester City supporters ran amok in the railway station. The local police were overrun but within two minutes two police dogs had restored order. They shepherded the fans into an orderly queue and onto waiting trains, peacefully and quickly.

As well as the German Shepherds, the force had specialist dogs also trained by Inspector Lloyd to 'sniff out' explosives. One of these, 'Ben', a young Labrador, had been working non-stop with his handler PC Denis Young of London – often up to fourteen hours a day – attending bomb scares at stations and Royal visits. Together they had given valuable assistance to the Met. Police in incidents such as the Harrods car bombing the previous Christmas.

Constable John Mellor, based at Cardiff with his dog 'Chas', who had responsibility for policing the South Wales area, commented on the facilities: 'Everything here is done with a professional touch. Each time we attend we seem to master something new to make us more proficient.'

The British Transport Police Dog Trials took place in 1984 at the Force Training Centre, Tadworth between 29 and 31 May in the presence of the Chief Constable, Kenneth H. Ogram Esq., QPM. Ten officers and their dogs took part in the finals and the results were as follows: 1st, Constable Harrison, Leeds, with police dog 'Zac'; 2nd, Constable Moore, London Transport, with police dog 'Karl'; 3rd, Constable Reynolds, London Transport, with police dog 'Rebel'; 4th Constable Mellor, South Wales, with police dog 'Chas';

5th, Constable Eggleton, Hull Docks, with police dog 'Tushka'; 6th Constable Murray, Southampton, with police dog 'Major'; 7th, Constable Beddoe, South Wales, with police dog 'Major'; 8th, Constable Morecock, Birmingham with police dog 'Jazz'; 9th Constable Slade, Southampton, with police dog 'Ace', and 10th, Constable Stroud, London Transport, with police dog 'Rex'.

The Ogram Challenge Cup, donated by the Chief Constable, was awarded to the overall winner of the Trials, namely PC Harrison and police dog 'Zac' from Leeds. The Stanley Peck Trophy donated by S. E. Peck, Esq., CBE, BEM, QPM, DL was awarded to the dog and handler obtaining the highest marks in tracking, namely PC Moore and police dog 'Karl' from London Transport Division. The Grantham Trophy, donated by A. GRANTHAM Ltd, was awarded to the dog and handler obtaining the highest marks in 'man work', namely PC Beddoe and police dog 'Major' from South Wales. The Obedience Shield, which was donated by ex-Police Constable T. Murphy, was awarded to the dog and handler obtaining the highest marks in the exercise, and was won by PC Harrison and police dog 'Zac' from Leeds. Finally the Lloyd Shield, donated by Inspector J. Lloyd, was awarded to the dog and handler who performed the most outstanding police dog action of 1983. Fittingly, this was won by PC Beddoe and police dog 'Major' from South Wales.

Bill Rogerson further recalls,

During the month of June 1984, copper telephone wire was being stolen from the telegraph poles situated alongside the Chester to Shrewsbury railway line, in the Gobowen area of Shropshire. The CID from Crewe naturally took charge of the case and arranged observations during the forthcoming nights.

One night I was part of the observations team, which also consisted of a dog handler from Birmingham. One of the team spotted two thieves on the embankment. The order was given to release the dog to chase them. The dog ran for a few yards and decided to cock its leg up against a telegraph pole and relieve itself for what seemed an eternity, much to the annoyance of the handler and the CID officers. By the time the dog had finished, the thieves made their getaway in a Ford Transit van. They were caught a few weeks later.

At the height of the miners' strike in 1984 I was stationed at Crewe. One morning during the strike I was on early turn at Crewe, when I was informed via Divisional Headquarters in Birmingham that intelligence had been received to the effect that large numbers of pickets would be attending Ironbridge Colliery in Shropshire to try and blockade a coal train that was leaving later in the day. A Mobile Support Unit (MSU) in full riot gear was a being sent to the scene.

Due to the fact that a majority of our officers were engaged in picket duty in Yorkshire, I was to form a hastily arranged back up serial to the MSU, with two PCs from Crewe and PC Eddie Howell and his dog 'Rick', along with a couple of officers from Shrewsbury. All we had was our wooden truncheons as protection. The senior officer, who briefed me, as the serial commander, informed me that our location was to be on a car park of a public house some 2 miles away from the Colliery Railhead. Fortunately the pickets never materialised and our services were not required.

While I was on a twelve-hour night duty one Saturday night at Crewe in November 1984, after all the football traffic had died down I received a request from the duty inspector at Crewe Police Station for assistance to search for armed robbers who had attacked the landlord of a public house in Nantwich, while he was cashing up at about 2.00. It was believed that the suspects had made their way onto the Crewe to Chester main railway line.

After a briefing by the inspector, the dog handlers from the two forces made their way onto the line. I and one of my constables followed on foot. Upon reaching a village with the grand name of Aston-Juxta-Mondrum, near Nantwich, the search was called off and we went onto a dark unlit country lane. As I was walking along the lane I lost my footing and fell into a ditch. This was one of the several occasions during my career that I had been in the proverbial 'shit'.

One night during the early 1980s, while stationed at Crewe, I was on twelve-hour nights when myself and a PC, who shall we say was really too nice and polite to be a police officer, were called to one of the platforms at around 9.30 p.m., due to a drunk making a complete nuisance of himself. It turned out that he was a Scotsman from Glasgow, who was well and truly inebriated. He wanted to fight the world and was arrested for being drunk and disorderly.

On the way to the police office he started struggling violently with the two of us. We managed to get him into the office and began to search him. However, at this point, the duty dog handler, Eddie Howell, and his dog 'Rick', walked in for their meal break. The prisoner became more violent and Eddie put his dog in the 'down' position to come and assist us. As we were restraining the prisoner, he lashed out with his feet kicking 'Rick' in the side.

The PC who had assisted me initially went red in the face with rage and it seemed to swell up to twice its size, and he screamed at the prisoner, 'You've hit a dog, you've hit a dog', and I could see that he was so incensed that I had to restrain him as well as the prisoner!

Tony Parkinson recalls a couple of incidents around 1983/84 that he was involved in:

It was one evening I was on mobile patrol with 'Bruce' and DC Steve Partridge. We had gone past a Jaguar car parked on a back street a couple of times during the night.

As we approached it again, a figure ran away from it and we noticed that one of the windows was smashed. The man ran round the buildings very close to the Mancunian Way, which was a major road, so there was no chance of sending the dog. I sent Steve (Budgie) Partridge instead and drove round to try and cut him off.

With a gasping, 'He's gone down there,' I followed Steve's directions and drove into a side street that ended with an open gate onto the bank of the River Irwell. Once through the gate and onto the river bank, I sent the dog in. He was away for a couple of minutes before coming back to try and slip past me. I sent 'Bruce' in again, with the same result. This time he ran past me onto a patch of wasteland. He dragged the car thief from out of the bushes with a 'Dad knows nothing' look.

Around about the same period a loaded Freightliner train was shunted out of the Freightliner depot and put into Trafford Park sidings for an hour or so before leaving at its scheduled time. The local villains became aware of this procedure and began forcing open the doors while it was in the sidings.

The CID wanted observations on the train, so with 'Bruce' a DS and three DCs we went to the sidings one evening. The train arrived from the depot and, after about half an hour, 'Bruce's' ears pricked up and he looked across the sidings. Three men were creeping across towards the train.

We lay in wait for them to come out from the rear of the train. 'Bruce' jumped up, leapt over me and the CID, and ran towards the perimeter fence. The detectives were in the process of passing some comments about the useless dog, when they saw him rounding up the three men, stopping them going any further. They had come away from the train unseen by anyone until the dog decided that 'Dad and the detectives know nothing. I'd better stop 'em before they get away'. With these incidents, 'Bruce' certainly earned his meat and biscuits.

The following amusing article, entitled 'One Dog and His Man', was written by Paul Mulville from Liverpool, who sadly is no longer with us. The article appeared in a *BTP Journal* in 1986:

I joined the British Transport Police in 1984 after an uneventful birth and a bit of upbringing, and was given to a man to train as a police dog handler. Now, this is all very well and I'm as willing as the next dog to pull my weight but really, some of the men they give you to train are damned hard work. I mean – they just haven't got a clue.

Anyway, to cut a long story short, I managed to knock him into some sort of shape to get him through the Initial Training Course and then they dropped the bomb-shell – I was sent with him to Liverpool. 'Go and sort the place out, lad,' they said, so off we went with the good wishes of the Chief Inspector ringing in our ears and the smirks of the other dogs and handlers imprinted on our minds.

Well, we did manage to pull a few decent jobs out of the hat and I let it be known that the man was under my control, so nobody better mess about with him or me. Funny really, most humans seemed to like him yet they seemed to give me a wide berth. Mind you, that's the way I like it. Respect for the coat and authority and all that, but it didn't turn my head.

Talking about heads, we were out one night at the Freightliner depot when I saw one of the local yobs having a go at a whisky wagon. He spots us and legs it, so, as there's no chance of my man catching him, I thought, 'It's down to you, my son', and gives chase. I catches up with him and he turns around and hits me on the head with a shunting pole he just happened to be carrying – Christ, did I see stars! I thought that Halley's Comet had reached earth. So, when I come to my senses, he's had it away on his toes and shins over this 10-feet-high wire fence like an Olympic athlete.

Now, brave I may be – stupid, I ain't – so I sits down and waits for the cavalry. Up comes super-cop, all puffing and panting, sympathy oozing from every pore of his body and he says to me, 'You all right, boy?' Ask yourself, someone nearly splits you in half and you're sitting there with your paw on your head trying to hold your brains in, and some berk asks if you're 'All right'. It's lucky he can't speak canine, I'll tell you. Mind you, he's not bad is my man. Let me tell you about him.

His human name is Paul and he pretends to be a police constable at Liverpool. (God knows how he survived without me at Tadworth). He lives in the grounds of my one-bedroomed pad at Liverpool with a female human. I feel a bit sorry for him sometimes because he has to share his bedroom with this female human, whereas I have my place to myself, still beggars can't be choosers I suppose.

He seems to quite like fetching and carrying for me, so to make it up to him I take him out on lots of 'walkies' and give him plenty of exercise. He only gets excited about once a month when he gets a bit of white paper with numbers on it.

Sometimes he jumps up and down and says rude words, which I pretend not to understand. I suppose it's because the police don't pay him in food and biscuits like they pay me – just bits of paper he gets. Catch me standing for that!

The best of times of all are when we have to do football duties and I can strut about, all important like, and bark for a lot. I do a lot of barking to keep things in order and sometimes if the yobs don't do as they're told, they get the sharp edge of my tongue – and teeth too if I get the chance of a nip.

One Saturday, we're sorting out this gang of football yobs and one of them kicks me in the teeth. Was I happy? – I was not. It turns out that he's broken one of my best gnashers and when I go to the quack, he says that I've got to have some dental work done by a proper dentist. Well, everybody is very impressed by this and suddenly I'm a star. All the newspapers want my picture so I call a photo session and invite Paul along just to keep order. He has a smashing time and I let him be in a few of the pictures. Then Radio Merseyside want me to give an interview and some female human appears with a little black box and a microphone.

So I give her what she needs and, when she's finished, she twiddles a few knobs and the black box starts barking back at me. You could have knocked me down with a 'Bonio'.

So now you know. When you humans say, 'It's a dog's life', just remember who does the fetching and carrying, who feeds whom, and who gets the rollicking when things go wrong. I'd rather have my job than yours – any day.

By the way, remember the yob who kicked me in the teeth? My man Paul tells me that some judge might give him a one-bedroomed pad for a while. There just ain't any justice.

Now I must leave you to get ready for nights. The female human will probably say as usual – 'Got your sandwiches?' She doesn't ask me what I've got – she knows the answer:

'Nothing'. But she does say, 'Look after our man'. I give her a wink 'cause I know what she means.

See you soon, 'Sabre'.

From late 1985 the British Railways Board were engaged in the electrification of the East Coast Main Line between London and Edinburgh. No problems were experienced in the North East Division until 1 April 1986, at which time an amount of aluminium return conductor wire was stolen from a location called 'Gamston', which is north of Newark. A further thirteen incidents were reported between Newark and Wakefield during the period 1 April 1986 to 7 December 1987. Until this date there were no detections made in relation to any offence committed.

The thefts and attempted thefts became more serious because, on occasions where the wire was cut by the thieves, it recoiled and got tangled up in passing trains, which caused delays and disruptions to the services. Such was the problem that it was decided at the North-East Divisional Headquarters that a special squad should be formed solely to deal with the theft/damage in relation to the electrification project. The squad consisted of a mixture of CID and uniformed officers, which included PC John Hawkins and police dog 'Santos'. As a result of this squad, a number of arrests were made by the team.

The Force Dog Trials were held at the Force Training Centre, Tadworth on 14 and 15 October 1987 and the final placings were: 1st, PC Harrison, Leeds, with 'Zak'; 2nd, PS Jackson, London, with 'Rocky'; 3rd, PC Wright, Preston, with 'Duke'; 4th, PC Standford, London Underground, with 'Toby'; 5th, PC Hucks, London, with 'Zero'; 6th, PC Campbell, Glasgow, with 'Zak'; 7th, PC Glendenning, Birmingham, with 'Raef'; 8th, PC Moore, London Underground, with 'Major'; 9th, PC

Mellor, Cardiff, with 'Chas'; 10th, PC Hawkins, Leeds, with 'Santos'.

The Ogram Challenge Cup, which was donated by the Chief Constable, was awarded to the overall winner, PC Harrison and police dog 'Zak'. The Stanley Peck Trophy was awarded to the handler and dog obtaining the highest marks in tracking – joint winners were PC Campbell and police dog 'Zak' and PC Glendenning and police dog 'Raef'. The Grantham Trophy was awarded to the handler and dog obtaining the highest marks in 'man work', namely PC Harrison and police dog 'Zak', Leeds. The Obedience Shield was awarded to the handler and dog obtaining the highest marks in the obedience exercise, namely PC Harrison and police dog 'Zak'. The Lloyd Shield was awarded to the handler and dog who performed the most outstanding police dog action of 1986/7, namely PC Leonard and police dog 'Thunder' from Force Headquarters.

Bill Rogerson further recalls,

We have all heard about people impersonating police officers, but a Labrador impersonating a police dog? During the summer of 1988, while stationed at Holyhead, I was on duty on late turn on the station, when I was approached by officers from HM Revenue & Customs, from Liverpool, who out of courtesy informed me that they were carrying out a drugs-related operation with their passive drugs dog, a black Labrador.

The boat train from London Euston arrived on platform one and a number of passengers alighted and made their way to the embarkation hall, where the customs team and I were on duty. However, there was a large group of particularly noisy Irish youths, who were drunk. The customs officer with the dog looked at me and said, 'These may be a problem,

Sarge, but "Max" can impersonate a BTP dog and sort them out.' Sure enough, the handler commanded 'Max' to let out a couple of barks, which was enough to sober the youths up pretty quickly.

In March 1987 PC Alan Morecock, based in Birmingham, started training with his new dog – eighteen-month-old 'Conan', who was a long-haired Alsatian with a long mane that gave it the appearance of being a lion. His name came from the film *Conan the Barbarian*.

Alan takes up the story:

I did a fair bit of public order work with 'Conan' on football match days all over the West and East Midlands. On one occasion I was with some officers at the top of the service road leading from Hill Street up into New Street station when a horde of Birmingham City's 'Zulu' warrior hooligans came charging up the road. I always used to tell officers not to get in front of the dog but, on this occasion, as we moved forward to confront them, the superintendent got in front of me to get under a barrier and, as he did so, 'Conan' bit him on the backside.

We also used to take the dogs on football special trains. On one particular one I was again with Brian Preece coming back from Norwich with either Birmingham City or Villa fans. The fans were wrecking the train and throwing the toilets out of the windows. It was getting out of control and I shouted that I was going to let the dog go. All you could hear was a series of coach doors being slammed shut down the train as they locked themselves in. On another occasion at Hereford when Birmingham fans were visiting, I literally found myself with the dog standing between the two sets of supporters trying to keep them apart.

Alan continued,

I remember three jobs in particular working with 'Conan'. The first one was when, following a visit to Dudley Freightliner depot, we discovered that a container had been broken into and decided to set up some observations involving eight officers and 'Conan'. I parked the dog van in an empty 40-foot container and sat in there with Brian Preece and the dog. After four or five hours we heard some voices in the dark and saw a woman on the tracks directing three children what to steal from an open container. I remember they were excited about beans and Newcastle Brown Ales. That night we arrested twenty-two people in the depot; they just kept coming and every time I threatened to let 'Conan' go they all just froze in their tracks.

On another occasion Brian and I were in Oxley Sidings again, keeping observations on the buffet cars that were being broken into. We were lying on a sheet again and it was so cold that I couldn't open my mouth, even though I was lying next to the dog. Eventually two people came along and 'Conan' duly detained them. When we went into the custody block with our prisoners, the custody sergeant assumed I was one of those arrested because I was so scruffy.

The third job related to two seventeen-year-olds, whom I found firing air rifles at trains in Castle Vale. They spotted me and 'Conan' and ran off and jumped into the nearby river Tame. They started swimming across like how you see in the films, with the rifles over their heads. I shouted for them to stop or I would send the dog in to get them. They thought better of it and came back soaking wet. I took them back to New Street for the CID to deal with them and when we got there one of them queried whether I would really have let the dog go into the river. I said, 'Don't be daft – my dog can't swim.' I don't think he saw the funny side of it.

Alan went on,

> I had 'Conan' for six years before he developed a severe ear
> problem and, although the force spent £2,000 on vet's bills
> trying to sort it out, they eventually decided to retire him.
> I had a friend who was a caravan owner in Wales and he
> took him as a guard dog on the site. He lived for another
> six years and it was always emotional when I went down to
> see him.

Things did not, however, always go to plan when selecting
new dogs for training, which Alan found out to his cost when
he took on his next dog 'Jason', who took his name from the
film *Jason and the Argonauts*. Alan recalls,

> He was a short-haired Alsatian, very powerfully built, whom
> anyone would have been proud to handle. I started training
> with him and, after the first six weeks, took him home for
> the weekend. Families play a big part in the life of a dog
> handler and it was important for the dog to bond with them
> as well. However, with 'Jason', the minute my wife started
> to try and feed him he started growling at her. She said she
> didn't like him because his eyes were too close to his nose,
> so it wasn't a good start! I took him back to Training Centre
> and on Monday had a fantastic training session with him;
> things were going really well. On the Tuesday, however,
> we were doing an exercise called 'Search for Persons', and
> the idea was for the dog to find 'Ginger' Ablard up a tree.
> We duly found 'Ginger' but, each time the dog approached
> the tree, he just peed on it and then came back to me.
>
> After the third attempt I ordered 'Jason' to sit, at which
> point he grabbed me by my left arm and bit me all the way
> up it. After that, he started on my left leg and I finished up

being kept in overnight at Epsom General Hospital in Surrey. I was determined to get back into training so, even though my arm was heavily bandaged, I went back to the kennels the next day and took 'Jason' out for a walk.

From the moment I put his lead on, he kept looking at me and growling and, as we were walking in the fields next to the Training Centre, I sensed that he was about to attack me again. I finished up having to throw his lead over a strong tree branch to apply some leverage to control the dog while I called for help. Two officers eventually came with dog-catcher poles to control him and the decision was made that he was not suited for police work. He finished up being sent to a military establishment at Melton Mowbray where I understand he bit two more handlers.

Some eight weeks later Alan Morecock started training with his next dog 'Dylan', who was named after the Welsh poet Dylan Thomas. Alan recalls,

He was a short-haired Alsatian and a great dog to work with. I had him with me until I retired in 1998. When policing football fans he showed no fear and, whenever I whispered 'speak' quietly to him, he barked on command. On one occasion I was faced by a crowd of Wolverhampton hooligans known as the 'Subway Army' who were trying to get at some opposing fans on the stairs leading to the platforms. I shouted for them to keep back but they kept coming so I put the dog on a long lead and, after a few got bitten, they backed off.

In 1990 Alan Morecock also took on a short-haired German Pointer called 'Max' after the film *Mad Max*. He was trained at the Police Dog Training Centre in Durham as an explosives sniffer dog. 'Max' got on well with 'Dylan', but had a strong temperament, and Alan confesses that 'Max' was the only dog that he was actually afraid of. Alan concludes his story:

When I retired, I kept both dogs as pets. 'Max' died of cancer about six months after he retired and 'Dylan' died in the same year after he got a condition called 'colitis' and I had to have him put down. I was with him at the end and was devastated.

Passive Alert Detection (PAD) dogs were first used by the Customs and Excise and the Prison Service but, in 1988, the use of such dogs were brought to the attention of BTP Detective Chief Superintendent Peter Whent. As a result PC Judy Bailey attended a Home Office course on Passive Alert Detection with dog 'Benji' and became one of the first female dog handlers in London. In the following two years the BTP were used as a pilot force for this aspect of policing with dogs and the experiment was highly successful, with this partnership carrying out 4,000 searches that resulted in 1,546 arrests for drugs. Other forces then followed the lead of the BTP in training and using 'PAD' dogs.

Malcolm Clegg recalls a further incident in 1989:

While employed as detective sergeant at Swansea, I called upon the assistance of the divisional dog handlers, either PC John Mellor or PC Allan Beddoe, on a number of occasions, usually to assist in observations. One quite persistent problem during the late 1980s involved the theft of wagon bearings from wagons berthed in sidings at various locations within the Swansea area. One such set of sidings was Burrows Sidings, about 2 or 3 miles east of Swansea. We had established that the thefts seemed to take place after dark but before midnight.

PC John Mellor was the divisional dog handler who came to assist and we parked our vehicles about one mile away from the sidings so as not to be disturbed. During our walk to the sidings we had to walk along a grass footpath that passed through some woods for a distance of about half a mile.

PC Mellor insisted that he walk at the front with his dog to lead the way. He often told people that he had 'cat's eyes' due to his experience in jungle warfare while serving in the army in Malaya during the 1950s conflicts. As we walked through the woods in semi-darkness, he would keep saying things like 'watch this tree' or 'duck your head, lads'. All of a sudden I heard a loud 'whack' and PC Mellor slumped to the floor, having walked into the branch of a tree that was overhanging the footpath.

Fortunately, he was unhurt, but his pride had taken a nasty dent. We did reach the sidings a short while later, only to find that the wagons had already been jacked up and a large quantity of bearings stolen. We never did catch the persons responsible; I must say, however, that PC Mellor was a friend of mine and in my opinion was an extremely efficient and dedicated dog handler.

In 1989 trouble erupted at Cardiff railway station as skirmishes took place between Cardiff City football fans and Welsh rugby fans. Retired Superintendent Tony Thompson recalled the event:

We escorted 500 soccer supporters back from Bath on a specially organised train after Cardiff City's match against Bristol Rovers. As the supporters were being escorted along the subway and out of the station, some of them turned around and went up to the platform where there were rugby supporters waiting to catch trains to Swansea. We had to draw truncheons and deploy PC Allan Beddoe with his dog to break up the confrontations. Eight people were arrested for public order offences.

The Lockerbie Disaster

On 21 December 1989 a terrorist bomb exploded on board Pan Am Flight 103, a passenger jet, causing it to crash on the town of Lockerbie, in Scotland. Two BTP dog handlers, Davy Connell and Alistair Campbell, were soon on the scene and went on to perform a thirty-three-hour tour of duty, during which they recovered a grim total of twenty-three bodies.

PCs Callum Weir and Neil Russell later attended the scene and remained on site for the next four weeks. They subsequently gave evidence at the court case in Holland, some eleven years later. An article by Eddie Toal from *Railnews*, entitled 'Grim role for BT Police at Lockerbie', describes events as they unfolded:

Glasgow-based BT Police dog-handling teams discovered evidence of particular interest to scientists trying to discover why a jumbo jet plunged out of the night sky and onto the town of Lockerbie last December.

And the railway police, who sent four dog teams and five constables to assist at the accident scene for a fortnight, received a special thank-you from Dumfries and Galloway Constabulary.

The important find occurred on Christmas Eve, four days after 259 passengers and eleven townspeople had died in Britain's worst ever air crash.

PCs David Connell and Alistair Campbell together with their German Shepherds 'Rebel' and 'Zac' were among 2,000 police, soldiers, and civilians scouring the area along the doomed airliner's flight path.

In dense forest undergrowth some 8 miles south east of the crash site, the dogs' sensitive noses sniffed out two items that their handlers immediately recognised would be of particular interest to the air accident investigation team.

'As the investigation is still under way, we're not at liberty to say exactly what they were,' PC Connell told *Railnews*. 'But we can confirm that they were sent south for thorough forensic examination.'

Later a statement from the Department of Transport declared that Pan Am's fatal flight 103 crashed as a result of a mid-air explosion soon after it crossed the Scottish border.

PCs Connell and Campbell will never forget the night that hell engulfed peaceful Sherwood Crescent at the south end of Lockerbie.

'A call for assistance had gone out and we arrived at the crash,' said PC Campbell. 'I've never seen anything like it. A couple of houses had been completely obliterated, several others were in flames, a petrol station on the nearby motorway was on fire, and the streets were littered with wreckage and bodies. It was horrific. The intense heat, together with the fumes, handicapped the dogs in the search for victims. Sometime around midnight the plane's cockpit was located on a farm 3 miles away so we were despatched along with a local mountain rescue team to search that area for bodies and, hopefully, survivors.

But it soon became apparent that there would be no survivors. With the dogs running free off the leash, the party had located seventeen bodies by dawn. Two of them were still strapped to their seats. One was a little girl of about eight years old. Our railway experience had prepared us for what was likely to be in store.

PC Campbell observed grimly, 'Having seen rail suicide victims and witnessed other accidents we knew what to expect.' In obedience to investigators' instructions, the bodies were left where they lay and their positions plotted on the map.

After a half-hour break the two policemen and their dogs were out again, combing the hills around Fulford Bridge about 10 miles away. This time the hunt was for wreckage, personal property and cargo. 'With their acute sense of smell – forty times more sensitive than that of humans – the dogs have no difficulty in detecting new scents,' explained Constable Connell. 'They are also trained to differentiate between people and property, so you can concentrate on one or the other.'

When the two officers returned to the temporary police information centre in Lockerbie Academy at lunchtime, they were ushered into a room to meet two VIP visitors – the Prime Minister and Prince Andrew. 'They'd already been shown around the crash scene and were obviously affected,' said PC Connell. 'Over a cup of tea we told them what we'd been doing. Mrs Thatcher was visibly upset. She told us, "All you can do is just carry on."'

And so they did. Now joined by BT constables Neil Russell and Callum Weir, and their dogs 'Storm' and 'Karl', PCs Connell and Campbell took 'Rebel' and 'Zac' back to the hills.

They formed part of a search team, which was airlifted by RAF Chinook helicopter to Midhill near Langholm.

Set down at the summit, nearly 3,000 feet up, the team scoured the entire hill in the course of the next few hours, finding some seats, light wreckage and mail. Then they trudged back up to the top again to pick up the return helicopter. But gale-force winds prevented the Chinook getting through so the team had to scramble back down again and walk a further 4 miles into Langholm. It was just after 23.00 when weary PCs Connell and Campbell booked off. They had been on duty for thirty-one hours.

In the next fortnight their search activity took them as far south as the border, for on the night the airliner plummeted to the earth the headwind had been 115 mph at 30,000 feet and accident investigators reckoned that debris could be scattered along a wide and lengthy corridor.

The four railway police-dog teams found hundreds of pieces of wreckage, mail, and heartrending items of personal property including suitcases, jewellery and passports.

Meanwhile, these very items of property were the prime concern of another BT Police team working in Lockerbie.

Acting Sergeant Angus Turner, WPC Karen Ringrose, and PCs Paul Steven, Bill Park and Mike McEwan had the task of examining everything recovered by the search parties so that each article could be indexed and collected for return to the airline or to relatives.

'When we reported to Lockerbie on the morning after the crash, the Dumfries & Galloway police decided our experience in dealing with vast amounts of personal property strewn around in the aftermath of train crashes would be of particular use,' said Acting Sergeant Turner. 'Under the command of one of their senior officers we commandeered a warehouse and began indexing items, which were beginning to arrive by the lorry load.'

The grisly task had another purpose – to help identify victims and to keep an eye out for anything that might be of interest to the accident investigators. It involved thousands of articles. Throughout their fortnight tour of duty the BT Police wore protective clothing, surgical gloves and face masks as they sifted through clothing, luggage and passports.

Speaking on behalf of Dumfries & Galloway Constabulary, Inspector Mike Deas told *Railnews*: 'The initial plea for assistance was answered by police forces from as far away as Grampian and Northumberland. The BT Police were part of a major operation and they did a very valuable job. We are extremely grateful for their help and co-operation.'

10

'SABRE'S' STORY

PC Mel Harris was stationed with the British Transport Police at Birmingham New Street and has provided a detailed account of his period of service as a dog handler. It is informative but above all else tells the 'human' story of man's relationships with dogs. For the authors it was a most humbling experience to read as the retired officer tells it 'just how it was'. He recalls,

In December 1979 I collected police dog 'Sabre' from Lancashire Police Dog Training Centre. He was eleven months old at the time. This was in preparation for a ten-week dog course to commence at Staffordshire Police Dog Training Centre on 7 January 1980. I will never forget our first meeting; the Police Dog Sergeant took me to where 'Sabre' was kennelled, where I found him running up and down barking loudly. The Sergeant said simply, 'This is your dog', opened the kennel door and ushered me inside. I was apprehensive and sweating profusely and was under the impression that the sergeant was 'testing my mettle' by assessing my reaction to his instruction. I entered the kennel and, to my overwhelming relief, 'Sabre' stopped barking and rushed up to me wagging his tail. He had found someone to love him – one hurdle over but many more to follow.

I kennelled 'Sabre' at home for a month, before the start of my course, which enabled my family, namely my wife Lyn and our two daughters, Rebecca, aged seven years, and Emma, three years old, to build up a relationship with 'Sabre'.

I duly attended the training course in Staffordshire, which included four dogs and their handlers from the West Midlands Police, three from West Mercia Police, and four from Staffordshire Police, as well as me and 'Sabre'. The course consisted of a number of aspects including obedience, agility, tracking, criminal work, searching, and a test for courage.

I found the course to be both physically and mentally challenging, not just for myself but also for 'Sabre'. He was still a young dog and needed to mature. He had a pleasing demeanour and showed a willing attitude to the training, and I was determined that we would both succeed, no matter what the course threw at us.

On the second half of the course we both made significant progress and a good all-round standard was achieved, after which we duly passed out of the Dog Training Centre on 3 April 1980. While I was away my wife related an incident to me when the dustman came to empty our bin one day. My three-year-old, Emma, was playing in the side entrance to the house when he enquired, somewhat apprehensively, 'Is the dog there', to which she replied, 'No, he's gone to school with my dad.'

After completing the initial course it was continuous training for me and 'Sabre'. We attended the training area at Basford Hall, Crewe on Tuesdays of each week, under the watchful of Dog Sergeant 'Ginger' Ablard. If, for any reason, training was not possible at Basford we were welcome to train with West Midlands Police dog handlers.

All the time we were operational, 'Sabre' never ceased to amaze me with his ability to track and recover persons and property. First and foremost I always regarded 'Sabre' as a working dog while on duty and I always discouraged members of the public, in a diplomatic way, from petting him especially in volatile situations such as when controlling football crowds. In the many dangerous situations in which we were involved, 'Sabre' was fearless and utterly dependable; I am convinced that he would have laid down his life for me.

When 'Sabre' was off duty, that was his downtime to relax, and to become our family pet – he came first!

I was based at Birmingham New Street station along with PC Alan Morecock. We covered a large geographical area consisting of the West Midlands, Derby, Nottingham and Leicestershire. Our duties could entail football, observations, terrorist incidents, Royal security duties, serious obstructions, and general patrols; it was never a dull moment. The variety of work was interesting, satisfying, and adrenaline-fuelled, especially when 'Sabre' was involved in a chase and detained someone.

'Sabre' was involved in many incidents and the following are just a sample of his achievements while working with Mel. In July 1981 Mel and 'Sabre' received praise from Chief Constable K. Ogram for being part of a team brought together at short notice to tackle damage being caused to trains travelling from Kensington to Inverness. As a result of their efforts three juveniles were detained.

On 12 October 1981 a man was murdered in Watford and Hertfordshire Constabulary requested that BTP officers conduct a search of a stretch of railway track in Staffordshire to look for the murder weapon. Mel and 'Sabre' were involved in the search on 15 October 1981 when a knife, which was later confirmed as being the murder weapon, was recovered lineside.

In January 1983 Mel Harris was on duty with 'Sabre' with CID officers keeping observations at Birmingham International car park when they disturbed three males acting suspiciously, who it later turned out were in a stolen vehicle. The occupants drove at one of the CID officers and struck him before driving off and abandoning the vehicle on the construction site of the new Birmingham Airport. 'Sabre' tracked the three for more than a mile and a half through boggy conditions, and mud up to the officer's knees in places, before losing the scent.

In the same month they were at the same location with uniformed and CID officers in the early hours of the morning, when two vehicles, each containing two occupants, came onto the car park. They were acting suspiciously and started paying some attention to a vehicle that had been stolen and abandoned on the car park earlier.

CID officers subsequently managed to stop and detain the occupants of one of the vehicles but, as the second was approached, the vehicle was driven at PC Harris who managed to jump clear. In doing so, he threw his torch at the windscreen of the car, which shattered. 'Mel' gave chase in the dog van and eventually managed to block the vehicle in before deploying 'Sabre' to make two further arrests. A search of the home addresses of those arrested revealed a large quantity of stolen car parts.

Just days later Mel was keeping observations at Marston Green railway station on his own, when he observed a vehicle containing three youths enter the station car park. The driver of the vehicle then got out, with a pair of pliers in his hand, and broke into an adjacent vehicle. PC Harris deployed 'Sabre' and, after arresting the first offender and securing him in the dog van, he then detained the other two and locked them in their own vehicle before calling for assistance.

In March 1983 an alarm was activated at the HMRC warehouse at the Inland Port in Landor Street, Birmingham. Mel attended, together with 'Sabre', and discovered that the premises had been broken into. After a search of the area, 'Sabre' discovered the intruder hiding behind some crates. Despite being told to stand still by the officer, the burglar backed away and was bitten on the leg before understanding the error of his ways. A further search of the area led to a pair of bolt-croppers being recovered, which had been used to break into the premises.

In May 1983 he attended the Force Dog Trials held at Tadworth and 'Sabre' was champion dog in winning the Ogram Challenge Cup and the Stanley Peck Trophy for best dog in tracking.

In the run up to Christmas 1983 PC Harris was again on duty with 'Sabre' and CID officers, keeping observations in the Coventry area in relation to thefts from motor vehicles, when he saw two youths cross over the main railway line and break into a stationary vehicle on a car park. Mel challenged the youths and ordered them to stop, at which point they ran off. The officer gave chase and chose to keep 'Sabre' on a long lead. As they went round the blind corner of a hut they were confronted by one of the youths holding a hammer in a threatening manner. 'Sabre' quickly resolved the situation by seizing hold of the offender's left leg and biting him, at which point he dropped the hammer and gave up.

Within twenty-four hours Mel was in action again with 'Sabre' at Coventry railway station when they observed a youth enter the first floor of the car park, who then began trying car doors. He was confronted by 'Sabre' next to a vehicle that had been opened with a strip of plastic binding tape, and gave up without offering any resistance.

PC Jim Rentell recalls a slightly more humorous incident in the early 1980s:

I was working as a beat officer at Birmingham International and during a rail strike I teamed up with Mel and his dog to check station car parks. It was winter and we were doing twelve-hour shifts. The weather was awful and, as I recall, it was so cold I had even put a pair of my wife's tights on underneath my uniform! As we walked around parked vehicles, 'Sabre' started to look more and more like a hedgehog as his long coat literally froze up. Eventually we put the dog back into the warmth of the dog van but, for some reason, he started whining. I climbed into the front seat and, coming out of the cold into the warm, I closed my eyes just for a second. The dog carried on whining and suddenly Mel shouted, 'Cease', which was his command for the dog to be quiet. He was so loud that I nearly wet myself, which would have presented some difficulties with the tights on.

In January 1984, following an assault on a police inspector who had tried to detain persons stealing from cars at Birmingham International, 'Sabre' showed off his search skills when he tracked for three quarters of a mile from the scene of the assault to a grass bank where car keys, and part of a car radio were recovered, and then on to a second location where two further keys were found on open ground.

In February 1984 PC Harris and 'Sabre' found themselves at Hartshill Sidings in Nuneaton keeping observations, with CID officers, in relation to a spate of thefts of steel. A transit van with three men on board subsequently drove into the sidings and the occupants started loading lengths of rail into the back of the van. The officer approached them with 'Sabre' and they were ordered to stand still, which they did. After being arrested they went on to admit nine other similar offences.

In the same month Mel was on patrol in the multi-storey car park at Wolverhampton railway station when 'Sabre' indicated a number of stolen cycle parts, which were the proceeds of a burglary at a local shop.

At the beginning of May 1984 PC Harris carried out observations at Ryecroft Junction in Walsall in relation to thefts of cable, together with CID officers. This location was in the middle of a highly deprived area where levels of criminality were high and police officers were often confronted by criminals. Five youths were observed pushing a wheelbarrow beside the track and started cutting up lengths of copper signalling cable that were loaded into it.

They were challenged to stand still but immediately dispersed. Mel released 'Sabre', who chased and caught one of them. During the course of being detained, the offender was bitten by 'Sabre' on the right knee and subsequently received an anti-tetanus injection. The other four were arrested later at their home addresses.

In June 1984 PC Harris and 'Sabre' were keeping observations in the Wolverhampton area, with DC Brian Preece, when they observed two men walking along the track carrying a quantity of copper piping and wire, which it later transpired had come from premises broken into locally.

In September 1984 Mel was on duty with 'Sabre' at Wolverhampton railway station for a local derby football match with Birmingham City. As a number of visiting fans alighted a train, one of them in particular began shouting and swearing. Despite warnings to desist from Mel he then became abusive to the officer and then proceeded to make disparaging remarks about 'Sabre', which did not go down well with Mel who promptly arrested him for a public order offence.

On the return the officer found himself facing a large number of disorderly fans who broke into Wolverhampton station via one of the exits and stormed across the main lines onto the middle platform. PC Harris placed himself on the platform to prevent further disturbances taking place, while at the same time stones and two-pence pieces were thrown at him and 'Sabre' from the platform opposite.

At the beginning of October 1984 PC Harris was on duty with 'Sabre' on the concourse of New Street station monitoring Manchester United supporters returning from Villa Park. His attention was drawn to a tall youth who was a local. He was shouting and using offensive language but despite being warned he failed to desist. PC Harris took hold of him and was immediately surrounded by up to twenty-five youths who became threatening. The officer hung onto his prisoner while 'Sabre' kept the others at bay until other officers arrived.

Also in October 1984 PC Harris was on duty in Ward End when he observed four youths trespassing on the railway. He challenged them to stop but they immediately started to run up a steep embankment. Mel released 'Sabre', who managed to prevent one of them from escaping through a hole in the fence by blocking his way and barking at him. 'Sabre' then found a second youth hiding in undergrowth and the other two were later traced at their homes.

On 13 October 1984 Mel and his dog showed great courage when confronting a large crowd of some 250 'Zulu Warriors', football hooligans associated with Birmingham City. They had just attacked two BTP officers on New Street station and Mel placed himself in harm's way with 'Sabre' so as to defend them and clear the station. This attack has a place in the book *Hunting the Hooligans*, which describes how the Zulu Warriors were tackled in a covert police operation code named 'Red Card'.

Also in 1984 Mel and 'Sabre', along with PC Dave Tucker and police dog 'Kaison', found themselves covering Swansea Docks performing duties relating to the Miners' Strike.

At the start of 1985 Mel conducted observations with 'Sabre' this time at a railway yard in Walsall during the hours of darkness. During the observations two men were seen carrying stolen car batteries. They were challenged to stand still on threat of releasing 'Sabre' and two more suspects found themselves under arrest.

In the summer of 1985 Mel responded with 'Sabre' to an assistance call at Dudley Freightliner terminal where eight youths were spotted stealing bottles of cider from containers. On being challenged to stand still they ran off in different directions into a wooded area adjacent to the terminal and the car park of nearby Dudley Zoo. Mel released 'Sabre', who detained one youth on the car park, and then discovered another two hiding in undergrowth. A substantial amount of stolen property was also recovered and the five other suspects detained by other officers.

On 25 July 1985 PC Harris and 'Sabre' assisted Regional Crime Squad officers engaged in an operation at Birmingham New Street station, which resulted in the arrest of three men who were found in possession of jewellery stolen from a burglary in Leicester.

On the day that Mel and 'Sabre' received a commendation for their bravery, in relation to the incident involving 'Zulu Warriors', the dangers faced by BTP officers routinely when dealing with football hooligans on the rail network were highlighted when attention was drawn to the recovery of six Stanley knives as Stoke fans arrived at Crewe.

In the autumn of 1985 PC Harris was carrying out observations in Wigston, Leicestershire, together with two CID officers, when they spotted two youths approaching a train, which had come to a halt at signals on the main Birmingham to Leicester railway line. The doors of the rear parcels van were opened and mail bags thrown onto the track as the train moved off. They proceeded to carry three mail bags into an adjacent clearing where they were challenged by the BTP officers and one person was detained. The second ran off into a housing estate followed by Mel and 'Sabre' who tracked him through the estate where he was detained. Seven other youths were later arrested in connection with mailbag thefts, and they went on to admit some thirty burglaries in the Wigston area.

This became something of a favourite pastime for some criminals and it was certainly not the last time Mel and 'Sabre' were to find themselves chasing mailbag thieves. On a separate occasion 'Sabre' detained a man near Wolverhampton who was involved in stealing mailbags from a slow-moving train. He later got sentenced to three months' imprisonment.

At the beginning of 1986 Mel was again out in the Brandon area of Coventry, keeping observations with other officers, when they observed four youths smashing lineside telephones and signalling equipment, on the main railway line to London Euston. The officer challenged them and told them to stand still, otherwise he would release the dog. Two of them did as instructed, and were detained by the officer, while the other two ran off. A search of the area was conducted by 'Sabre' who found a third youth hiding in undergrowth, who was also arrested. Damage estimated at £10,000 was caused. Little did Mel know it at the time, but this would prove to be one of 'Sabre's' last successful cases.

Mel continues the story:

In March 1986 'Sabre' had been showing signs of a hip injury and, as a result of a hip x-ray, my veterinary surgeon diagnosed hip displasia. The vet was of the opinion that 'Sabre' should retire from active duties forthwith. I notified Chief Inspector Lloyd, who was head of the Force Dog School at Tadworth, that I wished to keep 'Sabre' as a family pet, and asked to be transferred from the Dog Section back to normal patrol duties, and both requests were granted.

Once 'Sabre' was retired from police duties, he became a 'house dog'. He settled well into his retirement. His bed was situated in the alcove between the kitchen and our lounge/ dining room. Double doors separated this area. Each night we would close the double doors, but 'Sabre' had worked it out that, if he head-butted the centre of the doors, they would spring open. This gave him access to the lounge and consequently when we came down in the morning he would be fully stretched out on the comfy sofa with a 'Lord of the Manor' look on his face. That was our 'Sabre'. I hated leaving him each time I went on duty, but I knew my wife would be spoiling him big time. No matter what shift I was working he would still get his walk when I got home.

On occasions we would leave 'Sabre' and our girls in the trusted hands of my twin brother Maurice (Mo) and his wife Margaret. At that time they were living in Worksop and Mo was a serving Police Sergeant with the BTP in Sheffield. Both 'Sabre' and the girls were well taken care of and always spoilt rotten. One weekend in particular, after Mo had walked 'Sabre', he bedded him down in the hallway between the garage and the kitchen area. Sometime during the night, at about 3 a.m., 'Sabre' had negotiated his way through all the closed doors downstairs, made his way to their bedroom and begun licking Mo's face. After the shock of 'Sabre's' early morning call, Mo led him back downstairs to his own bed.

Between 1986 and 1989 'Sabre' was in reasonably good health but in the summer of 1989 his hip displasia worsened to the extent that he was in extreme pain, and was finding it difficult to raise himself up, and to walk any distance. The medication he was on did not seem to help, and the vet's advice was that it would be kinder to 'Sabre' and myself for him to be put to sleep.

I just wanted to do the best for him. He had been a loyal and trusted friend and police dog. On my journey with 'Sabre' I had no conception of the close working relationship, and incredible bond and love that would develop between him, me, and my family.

On a Saturday morning in August 1989, while our two daughters Rebecca and Emma were out with friends, I made the hardest decision of my life, and with my wife Lyn I took 'Sabre' to the vet. We were both traumatised and emotionally drained by what was about to take place.

I held 'Sabre' while the injection was administered and took effect. I didn't want to let go of him or leave him in the surgery, and it took me some time to compose myself. We eventually drove home, feeling so empty, and on our return we had to break the devastating news to our girls. We had tried to protect them from the ordeal but in hindsight I got it wrong as my elder daughter Rebecca said, 'I know, Dad, but you didn't give us a chance to say goodbye to "Sabre".'

It still affects me now and I shall carry it to my grave. Losing 'Sabre' was like a family bereavement. I still have his leads, dog collars, tracking harness and trophies. They are very precious to me and a constant reminder of the indelible presence he had in all of our lives.

He wasn't just a police dog; he was one of our family.

II

'JOCK' TACKLES CABLE THIEVES

Former Dog Handler Neil McEwan recalls,

While I was working in the Dog Section at Tadworth, I remember the previous Dog Chief Inspector, back in the 1990s, sitting in his office alone at Tadworth, roaring with laughter. I went in to see if he was okay and he told me about a dog-bite report that had just come in from one of the Scottish handlers, PC Neil Russell and his dog 'Storm' from Glasgow, both now retired. Neil had been driving home from duty and come across a warehouse with the door open and alarm sounding, with a vehicle parked outside.

Suspecting there were suspects on the premises, in the process of a burglary, he called the job in and challenged into the building for the suspects to come out, or else the dog would be released to search. The suspects chose not to show themselves, so 'Storm', who was a quite formidable dog, was released to search for the intruders. Unfortunately, what Neil didn't know was that two Strathclyde CID officers had happened upon the same open door and alarm sounding just a few minutes earlier and had entered the building also. It was their vehicle that was parked, unbeknown to Neil.

Inside the building, 'Storm' searched with vigour and located the two 'suspects' quickly, who began to run from the dog as 'Storm' approached the final phase of the chase and ultimately the attack of a fleeing suspect, as he was trained to do. The detective thinking quickly, pulled out his police warrant card and showed it to the dog shouting, 'Police!', in the obvious hope that it would deter the dog from biting one of 'our own' – it didn't work!

Following the official naming of an InterCity electric locomotive No. 90012 *British Transport Police* at a ceremony on Manchester's Piccadilly station on 16 July 1993, a number of displays were held, one of which was a display by PC Mark Jones and his dog 'Zimba', a German Shepherd.

The naming ceremony also provided an ideal opportunity for the presentation of a cheque for £3,500 to Booth Hall Children's Hospital, with Chief Constable Desmond O'Brien, and two cast members from *The Bill* – Trudie Goodwin (Sergeant June Ackland) and Graham Cole (PC Tony Stamp) to do the honours.

BTP staff in Manchester began collecting money for the Neurological Ward 14, which was threatened with closure, following a visit by children to Manchester Victoria's station. Chairman of the fundraising committee was PC Dave Thomson, together with dog handlers Paul Cliffe and Mark Jones, who had been leading the efforts to raise money for special-needs toys.

For those children who were unable to attend on the day of the naming, a special visit was made to the hospital the following week by police dogs 'Zimba' and 'Roscoe'. 'Just holding the lead can be very therapeutic for these kids,' said PC Jones.

John Hawkins recalls that displays did not always go to plan:

Moving to the early 1990s, Railsafe, a football competition, was held at York as track safety awareness for local schools. The Dog Section part was the usual display. For some reason the North East Division were short of dogs, so PC Charlie Steel from Liverpool came over to assist. My dog at this time was 'Zigo', who was a calm and friendly dog. Just prior to starting the display Charlie's dog kept pestering my dog. I could see he was getting 'cheesed off' and told Charlie, but his dog continued – suddenly there was blood everywhere – yes, 'Zigo' had bitten Charlie's dog's ear. We managed to slow the blood while the display was done. Charlie's dog required seven stitches.

Tony Parkinson further recalls,

It was early November – I think 1994 – and there had been a spate of cable thefts in the Hyde area of Manchester. Following a 'block failure' call, as usual after midnight and pitch black, I attended the area with the dog and located the cut end of the cable.

The dog started to track through a wooded area for about 500 yards before emerging onto a main road where the track stopped. Nothing was found. A couple of nights later, another block failure in the same area resulted in me attending with dog 'Jock'. He began to show signs of picking up scent on the ballast and cable troughing at a point around where he had previously tracked through the woods. Normally, the concrete troughing lids would have been lifted and left, exposing the cables, but, on this occasion, the lids were still in position covering the cables.

Owing to the interest shown by 'Jock', I lifted the lids to find a cut end. From that point, 'Jock' continued tracking and around every 25 yards or so, he showed excessive interest, so the lids were lifted to reveal missing cable. After about 200 yards and more lids being lifted, I found the other cut end.

'Jock' continued to track for another couple of hundred yards before crossing the tracks, up the embankment, to the boundary fence, which was 10-foot chain-link with no way through to the adjacent playing fields. We gained access to the playing fields, and to the point 'Jock' had tracked to, and recommenced the track, which carried on across two football fields and onto rough ground where the track stopped at a building. Laid along the length of the building and covered with the long grass was the cable.

An executive decision was made that, owing to its location, the thieves would not recover the cable in daylight so I made arrangements to get a couple of late/night officers out for observations the following night. Around 8.00 p.m. the following night, four of us were in position in the rough stuff where the cable was laid.

As it was 5 November and Bonfire Night, we were treated to some wonderful firework displays for the next four hours until the dog pricked his ears up and looked in the direction of the railway lines. Silhouetted against the chain link fence were three men. They pushed a pallet over the fence and then scrambled over it themselves and made their way towards the cable and us. Once there, they laid the pallet down, dragged the cable to it and, after coiling it up, laid it on the pallet.

It then became just another bonfire. We approached out of the darkness, 'Jock' first, and arrested them. They were responsible for all the cable thefts in the area and the reason 'Jock' 'lost' the track a couple of nights earlier was because they had bagged up the cable and taken a taxi. The cable thefts in the area stopped after this.

One little thing – while tracking over the troughing, I turned round at one point and saw a ferret stand on its hind legs to find out who was disturbing its sleep. On my way home, driving along the busy A6 through Levenshulme, a ferret came out of a side street, stopped and looked at me. I think the 'jungle telegraph' must have reached the one in Hyde to confirm I was going home.

PC David Jenkins, with police dog 'Zac', were the overall winners of the 1995 Force Dog Trials.

Tony Parkinson further recalls,

About 1996/97 one of the Manchester Football clubs was playing at Goodison Park, Liverpool. After the match, the Manchester supporters, some 600 in number, were put on buses, which formed an escorted convoy to Edge Hill station. Edge Hill station is at the bottom of an approach road, which forms a cul-de-sac bordered by high walls and the station buildings. There is an access gate in each bottom corner onto the platforms.

On arrival at the station, the plan was to allow the passengers of each bus to alight on an individual basis so they could be formed in an orderly queue for them to be admitted onto the platform as the football special trains arrived. That was the plan.

What actually happened was that, when the buses arrived, the passengers disembarked en bloc and charged down the approach, pinning the dozen or so MSU officers under the command of Sergeants Mick Owen and John Milor against the walls and building. The weight of the marauding crowd prevented them from moving and they were being crushed.

With police dog 'Jock', I had been in the centre of the approach about halfway up as they charged past me. With 'Jock' barking and snapping, I got in between the crowd and a wall. The crowd eased back away from us and, one by one, we released the trapped officers and, with the assistance of Merseyside Police officers who had now arrived, managed to form them into an orderly queue.

The only thing that prevented injuries to our officers was the presence of 'Jock' and the ability for him to put fear into the crowd that they might be bitten if they did not back off.

In 1996 it was announced that Peter Heard had taken over at the Tadworth Training Centre as the Force's Dog Training Manager, following the retirement of John Lloyd. With thirty years' experience in the Metropolitan Police to call upon, including eight as a senior home office instructor at the Keston Dog Training School, Peter had mastered all aspects of dog-training, including general duties, drugs, explosives and human remains operations. He had been an operational dog handler in south London for twelve years and had two retired German Shepherd dogs.

Bill Rogerson recalls another couple of incidents:

During my time in North Wales we didn't really have the need for a regular dog handler; anyway, the nearest ones were at Crewe (86 miles away), Liverpool (72 miles away) and Manchester (98 miles away), so we used the North Wales Police dog handlers, with whom I had a very good relationship.

However, whenever there was a Royal visit on our patch in North Wales, our own dog handlers would attend. In the early 1990s a 'triangle' was added to the railway sidings at Valley, the village where I live, near Holyhead, mainly for the purposes of turning the steam locomotives working the thrice-weekly excursion trains along the North Wales Coast.

This extension to the sidings was an ideal opportunity to stable the Royal train when any members of the Royal Family visited the Isle of Anglesey. On the first opportunity of such a visit I, as the local officer in charge at Bangor, was invited to a planning meeting, as naturally I had local knowledge of the area.

During the meeting, the question of searching by an explosives detector dog was discussed. For security reasons, I will not elaborate on the procedure, but suffice to say the dog would be set to work to do its 'sniffing-out' duty. The officer in charge of the meeting asked the dog handler if there were any questions. He stated that he was happy as it seemed to be a routine matter, until I chirped up and informed the meeting about the adders that resided in the adjacent fields and the railway embankment. There was a stunned silence and the search scenario was quickly rewritten.

Access to the mainland side of Robert Stephenson's famous Britannia Bridge, which connects the mainland with the Isle of Anglesey, for a vehicle is via a railway-owned narrow lane, leading from a main road in the Treborth area of Bangor. The area of land immediately underneath the bridge is railway-owned as well. Due to its isolated location, in 1998 it attracted a lot of anti-social behaviour, such as fly-tipping, courting couples and illegal raves, etc. Due to my limited resources at Bangor and the vast area I had to cover, it was virtually impossible to give the area the attention it deserved.

However, Phil Gerard, a North Wales Police general-purpose dog handler for their Western Division, covering the Isle of Anglesey and Gwynedd, and myself came up with a cunning plan to thwart the culprits. Phil and his family had recently moved into a cottage in the lane. He asked if it would be possible to park his dog van in the lane, thus preventing vehicle and pedestrian access to the bridge. In return he would patrol the area with his faithful companion, a German Shepherd, as part of his exercise. The plan was cleared with the local railway management and the anti-social behaviour ceased almost overnight.

I think it was in September 1999, while stationed at Bangor as the officer in charge, that I had occasion to call on the Dog Section to assist with observations on the main Holyhead to Chester Railway Line at a place called Star, approximately one mile to the west of Llanfairpwllgwyngyllgogerychwyrndrobwllllantysiliogogoch, known locally as Llanfair P.G. or Llanfairpwll, on the beautiful Isle of Anglesey. During the early hours of a Monday morning, metal farm gates were being thrown onto the railway lines.

On the night of one of the observations, together with a detective sergeant from Crewe, I decided to keep observations from the railway embankment, each of us tucked up in a separate, large green dustbin liner to keep warm and blend in with the grass. Previously it was agreed that we would call on the assistance of a dog handler from the Liverpool sub-division to assist us. The plan was for him to be parked up in a lay-by on the nearby main road so that he could have easy access to the scene.

After carefully giving him directions we arranged to meet him in the station car park at the said Llanfairpwllgwyngyllgogerychwyrndrobwllllantysiliogogoch at 11.45 p.m. this particular Sunday evening for a briefing. Well, 11.45 p.m. came and went, and still no sign of the dog and handler. We made contact with him via the radio and via Liverpool control, as there were no mobiles in those days.

He assured us that he was in the car park and was awaiting our arrival. We told him that we were there and we could not see him. He was adamant that he was there and that we were in the wrong location. After a bit of detective work I established that he was in fact at Llanfairfechan station some 12 miles to the east of us. He quickly joined us and we settled down to our observations, which proved negative. However we eventually caught the culprit, who was in fact the daughter of a farmer, who suffered from mental health problems.

The impact that dogs could have on law-abiding members of the public are illustrated by Mike Morris, who further recalls that in early 1999,

The London Underground Area Dog Section put on a public display to raise funds for the St Mary's Roman Catholic Primary School, Church Road, Portslade, East Sussex. A total of £2,100 was raised for the school. They also dealt with a missing child and a little dispute as well. The dogs involved were 'Glen', handled by PC John Shelley, and PC Jones with 'Boycie'.

Following the event the chairman of the Parent and Teacher Association wrote a following letter of appreciation.

12

'KLAUS' COMES HOME –
A NEW CENTURY

Police dog 'Klaus' became famous for a few hours in February 2000 after going missing from the Southend home of his handler PC Steve Gould. 'Klaus' chewed through a fence at around teatime in his bid for a few hours of freedom, but was picked up by a council dog warden and reunited with Steve the next day. Public concern for the two-year-old German Shepherd was heightened because he was recovering from a castration operation the week before.

London South Dog Handler Chris Jessup came up trumps for a children's centre in Kent after raising £500 during his training course at Tadworth. PC Jessup managed to raise £350 of the total in a single night. The money was donated to Chalklands Centre in Strood, Kent. The centre was based at Elaine Primary School and catered for eighteen children aged four to eleven with severe emotional or behavioural difficulties.

The money was raised from evening events at Tadworth during Chris's twelve-week dog-training course. 'I wanted to do something that would benefit the kids,' commented Chris. The cheque was handed over by Chris and his German

Shepherd 'Flynn' to the head teacher, Justin Smith, at the school in February 2000.

During the summer of 2000, British Transport Police officers from Bradford worked very closely with the Bradford Youth Offending Team in a bid to reduce trespass and vandalism. In August of that year, eight of the children were invited to force headquarters. PC Steve Gould and his dog 'Sheppey' and Sergeant Tom Goodyear and his dog 'Milo' showed the visitors from Bradford how explosives dogs operate.

Normally the man in the middle, keeping rival football sides apart, is the referee, but when rival fans clashed at Aldgate East Underground station on 26 August 2000, it was two of the force's dog handlers who found themselves caught between the warring factions. The two groups of fans, totalling over 100, were intent on fighting each other and the only thing stopping them was Sergeant Tom Goodyear, and police dog 'Barney', and his colleague Maurice Stanford, with police dog 'Jac'. Showing a great deal of personal courage, the two officers placed themselves between the two rival groups to keep them apart and contain the situation.

Although heavily outnumbered, the two officers and their dogs held the line, despite coming under missile attack until support arrived. They managed to maintain order throughout a very hairy situation, earning them Chief Constable's Commendations as a result, which were presented at a ceremony in the summer of 2001.

In May of 2001 the management of the ScotRail franchise presented BTP drugs dog 'Barney', a Springer Spaniel, with his own first-class 'All ScotRail Stations Rail Pass', valid for duty and leisure purposes.

In 2001 BTP dog handlers raised £960 to support the 'hearing dogs service': hearing dogs for the deaf are trained to identify useful sounds, such as telephones, alarm clocks, door bells and kitchen timers, so that they can alert their deaf partners, usually by leading them to the source of the sound. In case of danger – a fire or smoke alarm for instance – the dog will lie down beside their partner.

The money was raised by quiz nights and raffles down at the Force Training Centre Tadworth and a cheque was handed over by Tom Goodyear and his dog 'Milo' on a visit in July 2001 to the charity's own training centre in Oxfordshire.

'It was a real treat to see these dogs put through their paces,' said Sergeant Goodyear. 'Hearing dogs are selected from a variety of breeds and cross-breeds, many of them being rescue dogs. I saw two dogs there that had been dumped in a plastic bag as puppies.' Tom was shown round the training centre by National Appeals manager Diane Howe and trainer Tom Green.

The following article, entitled 'Playful pet is really an undercover police dog', appeared in the *London Evening Standard* on Monday 6 August 2001:

When dog handler and dog are working in the public eye, it is customary for the dog handler to be in full uniform. However in August 2001 Dick Murray, transport editor of the *London Evening Standard*, met up with PC Mike Lambert-Hope in civilian clothes and his dog 'Leo' in a park in London. On meeting them it would appear that both man and his dog were like any other dog owner, out for 'walkies' in the park.

Four-year-old 'Leo' was out for walkies with his loving owner. He may have been leaping for a ball and enjoying himself but this German Shepherd with a 'pink hippo' hanging from his collar is really an undercover police dog. What seems an innocent game rapidly changes as 'Leo' and his British Transport Police handler, Mike Lambert-Hope, edge closer to the vandals they have seen hurling stones at trains.

The next moment the vandals are having their names and addresses taken or being escorted to the station to await their parents or guardians. For 'Leo' and his handler are the latest weapon used by London Underground to stop the increase in vandals hurling rocks and other missiles at passing trains.

With tracks going through open parkland in east London, a uniformed policeman would stand out a mile. PC Lambert-Hope, aged forty-nine years, said: 'It is certainly paying dividends. I have been able to get really close to the vandals before they realise who I am.'

Don't let the fluffy toy and tennis ball fool anyone. On command 'Leo' drops the ball and immediately turns into a 'working' police dog. 'Everyone knows what a police dog can do and they really are a deterrent,' said PC Lambert-Hope.

He and his colleague PC Maurice Stanford, with his German Shepherd 'Zeus', belong to the dog section at West Ham police station. PC Standford regularly patrols open spaces such as Mayesbrook Park near Barking, one of the worst places in London for attacks on trains by vandals.

Earlier this year a heavy steel bolt was hurled at a train, which smashed a window and terrified a mother with a baby on her lap. The culprits can be anything from seven to nineteen. 'We also get children playing chicken, crossing the lines – which carry a 630-volt current – which is both stupid and highly dangerous,' said PC Standford.

On Sunday 6 January 2002 the third-round FA Cup tie between Cardiff and Leeds was played at Ninian Park, Cardiff. The visiting team supporters invaded the pitch to taunt the home team supporters after Cardiff beat Leeds by two goals to one. The disorder continued at Cardiff Central railway station and British Transport Police officers were kept busy maintaining law and order. One of the officers involved in restoring order was Dog Handler PC Paul Morse and his dog 'BJ'.

On a scorching hot day, in July 2002 Mick Kinirey, a Midlands-based dog handler and his two-and-a-half-year-old German Shepherd 'Tazz' won the overall trial competition and the Obedience Trophy.

The annual competition was held at Canon Popham School, Edenthorpe, Doncaster and helped raise money for the school. Originally part of a large Railsafe day, the Railsafe Shield won by Mick and 'Tazz' was donated by Midland Mainline.

'Tazz' had been with Mick since he was a ten-week-old puppy and the pair impressed the judges, as they went through their paces in the Obedience and Criminal Work categories, competing against entrants from South Yorkshire, Nottinghamshire, and Ministry of Defence Police, as well as the Prison Service.

The obedience package included keeping the dog at heel at slow, fast and normal paces, distance control – requiring the dog to stay in various positions at a distance from the handler – speak on command and retrieving – in this case, a Wellington boot. The dog also had to run an agility course requiring him to scale a 6-foot obstacle, perform a 9-foot long jump and a 3-foot high jump. The afternoon was given over to criminal work – straight chase, stand-off and a simulated attack with a stick.

Running a Pro-active Drugs Search Dog Licensing Refresher course at Tadworth in the summer of 2002, highlighted to Assistant Dog Training Manager, Mike Jones, that these dogs were still under-used. 'Many officers still don't realise that these dogs are available to them to search buildings, vehicles and open areas where it is believed drugs may be concealed,' he told *The Blue Line*. 'These dogs have also been taught to indicate to handlers the presence of firearms and related components during searches. To date they have found many thousands of pounds worth of narcotics and, on two separate searches, one in Liverpool and one in Kent, firearms have also been recovered. The dogs have been operating with the force for little over eighteen months and have already achieved great things.

During the autumn of 2002 a dog handler in full search gear sweeping Paddington station with a sniffer dog was approached by a member of the public, who offered to lend him a hand. 'I know what it's like; I'm partially sighted myself.'

During the early part of 2003 a dedicated team of officers was set up to police the Airedale line between Leeds/Bradford and Skipton as part of the problem-orientated policing approach to reducing crime and the fear of crime. The team was made up of one sergeant and three constables, who included PC Colin Sladden and his dog 'Simba'.

Could London's transport system better meet the needs of the young? That was the question the London Transport Users' Committee set out to answer in April 2003 at a one-day youth event held at City Hall, home to London's Mayor. The Chief Constable of the British Transport Police Ian Johnson was part of the invited panel. Among others there was a workshop covering personal safety and crime on public transport. Explosives dog team Sergeant Tom Goodyear and 'Milo' and PC Jim O'Riordan and 'Jasper' made an appearance over the lunchtime period to show how they helped to keep the rail system in London running.

In 2003 John 'Corky' Hawkins won the Force Dog Trials with police dog 'Keller' and then entered the 2003 London Regional Dog Trials 21-23 February, although they were only allowed to enter as guests and could not qualify for the National Police Dog Trials.

BTP fired the first salvo in a 'clean up Brixton' campaign at the end of September 2003. As part of a year-long multi agency initiative involving BTP, Lambeth Police and Lambeth Council in partnership with the voluntary sector and resident groups, Stockwell officers took action against ticket touts who haunted the Tube station. Many of these touts were aggressive towards customers and staff, and had become a persistent nuisance at Brixton station. Intelligence suggested that most of them used the money they made to feed a drugs habit, so officers mounted an intelligence-led operation using drugs sniffer dogs.

'I think if people knew that, when they hand over Travelcards to ticket touts in Brixton, they are contributing to the drugs problem, they wouldn't do it!' said Chief Superintendent Steve Hotson, London Underground Area Commander.

The BTP operation ran over an afternoon and was supported by London Underground Revenue Control staff who mounted ticket checks. The afternoon resulted in sixty-four stops and nine arrests and was part of a wider campaign to clean up Brixton town centre, spearheaded by Lambeth Police and the London Borough of Lambeth and involving Transport for London, the Brixton Area Forum and St Mungo's.

PC Neil McEwan and drugs dog 'Marmite' took turns with PC Ray Allan and drugs dog 'Charlie' during the five-hour operation at Brixton Underground station. The 'passive' drugs dogs screened people as they went through the station.

They worked effectively for about half an hour before needing to give their noses a rest.

Towards the end of 2003 a conversation was overheard between two dog handlers at Force Headquarters. They were deep in discussion over what their job title should be in today's modern police service. After mulling over several ideas, they decided that the title of 'Cross-Species Communicator' would be better suited.

Phil Trendall retired from the BTP as a superintendent and played a key role in the development of the Dog Section, particularly in the field of counter-terrorism and the use of specialist dogs. Always a man known for speaking his mind, his recollections are as follows:

> In general terms dogs are expensive and can be difficult to manage, or rather their handlers can be, and there are always dangers of sub-cultures developing. Currently BTP dogs do not do much tracking, which is surprising and contrasts with how they are used in other forces, and how they were used in the past by BTP.
>
> In 2004 we did a lot of work on our readiness to deal with post 9/11 terrorism. I was promoted to superintendent to put together the Counter-Terrorism Support Unit, which would eventually incorporate all dogs, but at first included just the explosive-detection dogs. This was a time when the force was getting on its feet financially and a number of business cases were approved, one of which was the establishment of a full-time Special Branch, which Mike Layton (co-author) put in place. We also expanded the Specialist Response Unit, and the ESD Section. Adrian Dwyer, the Force Counter-Terrorism Risk Advisor, did a lot of work in preparing the way forward, and we both worked

closely with the Department for Transport, who provided some of the funding.

Traditionally ESDs had been used for pre-event and post-threat search, normally working under the direction of a Police Search Advisor (POLSA). What we wanted to do was to create a situation where ESDs would be used on routine patrol, allowing them to detect explosives in a public space. The attacks in Madrid in March 2004 provided a harsh reminder of the continuing dangers posed by terrorists. We were able to visit Madrid and to see the work that they were doing in the aftermath of the tragedy that killed around 200 passengers.

A series of quiz nights at Tadworth organised by PCs Phil Chamberlain, Bill Wilde, Chris Jessop and Mark Jones raised £1,161.97 for charity. The four were on a basic dog handler's course between August and November 2004 and cajoled fellow students and staff into parting with the cash.

Andy Fidgett, a retired dog handler, recalls his 'passing out' day as a dog handler in November 2004, with some amusement:

I had been training for a total of thirty-one weeks, consisting of two basic dog courses plus a driving course, and somehow our instructor PC Mark Jones, who is now at Peterborough, had got Chief Constable Ian Johnston to agree to present our licences to us.

On the big day the chief arrived and immediately apologised as we had scrubbed up, and he was in his jumper. Anyway we got out all the dogs for a picture with the chief. It would have been great – five dogs, the chief constable and the instructor; however, my dog 'Ned' started a fight, which we had to break up.

After this, one dog 'humped' the chief's leg. Being the 'gent' he was, he 'brushed it off' so to speak and then had his picture taken with each of us one at a time, just to be on the safe side. Afterwards he made us all tea.

13

'VINNIE'S' STORY –
7 JULY 2005 –
THE LONDON BOMBINGS

After the Madrid bombings on the railway in 2004, the ESD dog team was increased from six to thirty-two dogs. On 7 July 2005 suicide bombers attacked the London Underground.

The 7/7 bombings, as they are often referred to, were a series of suicide bomb attacks in central London, which targeted civilians using the public transport system during the morning rush hour. They occurred the day after London won its bid for the 2012 Olympic Games, which had highlighted the diverse nature of London's community.

On 7 July 2005 four men separately detonated three homemade bombs in quick succession aboard London Underground trains, while a fourth was later detonated on a double decker bus in Tavistock Square, just a few minutes' walk from the then-British Transport Police Headquarters. The devices contained organic peroxide.

At 8.49 a.m. three bombs were detonated on board London Underground trains within fifty seconds of each other. The first exploded on a train travelling between Liverpool Street and Aldgate, having left King's Cross St Pancras eight minutes earlier on the Circle line.

The second device exploded as a train left Edgware Road on the Circle line, en route to Paddington.

A third device went off on a train travelling on the Piccadilly line from King's Cross St Pancras and Russell Square.

At 9.47 a.m. the fourth bomb was detonated on the top deck of a No. 30 double-decker bus in Tavistock Square.

Fifty-two people were killed, and more than 700 injured in the attacks, which was the UK's worst terrorist incident since the 1988 Lockerbie bombing, as well as the country's first-ever suicide attack.

After the blast at Russell Square the scene was described as 'utter pandemonium'. The train driver took steps to apply the emergency brakes and, after doing an initial assessment in the first carriage, where the explosion had taken place, he turned his attention to making sure that the track was not live, as a sea of people with 'blackened' faces emerged from the train.

Twenty-six people died in this attack by bomber Germaine Lindsay, as the tube travelled between King's Cross and Russell Square stations. Lindsay, aged just nineteen years, detonated his bomb next to the rear set of double doors in that front carriage. A total of 340 people also sustained injuries.

One survivor told the subsequent inquest that the carriage had been crammed when an 'extremely loud pop and a very bright yellow light' was given off. The train was carrying between 1,000 to 1,500 passengers at the time of the explosion. The force of the explosion in the confined space of the Piccadilly line shattered windows and left charred and twisted metal – a very difficult environment for a dog to work in. One police officer at the scene was later quoted in the media as saying, 'I don't know what heaven looks like but I have just seen hell.'

Hot, dangerous, and claustrophobic, the scene was 70 feet below ground at the point of the explosion, with 11-foot-wide aging tunnels, which in some places were barely larger than the train. Subsequent search teams had to work in 'furnace-like' conditions where temperatures sometimes hit 60 degrees Celsius, partly because they were using cutting equipment, and also because they had to block the tunnel's ventilation to prevent clues from being blown away.

Dogs were deployed to locate possible secondary terrorist devices at the four bomb-attack sites. BTP dog 'Vinnie' was deployed at Russell Square Tube site, where he searched the tunnel to King's Cross. His handler PC Dave Coleman subsequently said, 'Despite horrific conditions, 'Vinnie' never wavered. I was so proud of him.'

PC Dave Coleman volunteered to conduct the search with 'Vinnie' prior to bodies being removed, while PC Smith with search dog 'Ross' assisted the Metropolitan Police at the scene of the bus explosion in Tavistock Square. It is difficult to comprehend what the officer and his dog would have faced during the tragic events of that day. Both were highly trained for such events but no amount of training could have prepared them for the sights, sounds, and smells that they would have encountered.

Phil Trendall continues,

Expansion of the ESD section within the new Counter-Terrorism Unit (CTSU) was rapid. Much of the early work was done by a very experienced Sergeant, who was later joined by three other members of staff. Before too long, however, we were hit by the attacks on 7/7. Like all of our officers the ESD handlers and their dogs responded magnificently, searching for secondary devices and working for long hours, with little thought for their own safety. In fact I think that they were more concerned for the welfare of their dogs than they were for their own wellbeing.

The conditions that many handlers worked in that day were among the worst seen by BTP dog handlers, probably only matched by some of the major incidents and, of course, experiences during the First and Second World Wars.

'Vinnie' was awarded a PDSA Gold Medal, which is regarded as the animals' George Cross, and, accompanied by his handler PC Dave Coleman, went to an investiture at St James's Palace. Dogs from the City of London and Metropolitan Police were also honoured and I shall never forget the sight of HRH Princess Alexandra draping medals over the necks of the dogs. An oil painting was made of 'Vinnie' and was presented to the Chief Constable.

Following these events we were very keen to increase the range of explosives that dogs could detect and we worked closely with central government and scientific advisors until our dogs became the first to be able to detect a full range of homemade explosives. This project took a couple of years and it made me very proud that BTP were once again leaders in the field.

At the same time experiments took place that allowed dogs to be trained to undertake passive detection. In other words, they could be used to scan people rather than objects, again a new departure in the use of ESDs. All these projects were undertaken by operational officers with support from the Dog Training School at Tadworth. We were also able to study and evaluate similar activities around the world. We looked closely at what colleagues in Amtrak, and other railway forces, were doing in the United States and we had the chance to visit and observe their work. Perhaps I am biased but I have no doubt that our dogs were the best in the world.

The PDSA Gold Medal is generally awarded to animals that are instrumental in saving human or animal life. The organisation's full title is the People's Dispensary for Sick Animals and it is the UK's leading veterinary charity. Marlyn Rydstrom (then Director General) said at the time of the investiture: 'Their gallantry helped save lives by ensuring medical assistance reached the casualties as quickly and safely as possible.'

Dave Coleman, 'Vinnie's' handler, retired from the force in 2012, and gives his own very personal, moving, and harrowing account of that fateful day which in itself was a very humbling experience for the authors:

'Vinnie' is still alive and living with me today. I had been a dog handler for many years but 'Vinnie' was my first ESD and I finished my course with him just before the bombings.

'Vinnie' is a Labrador and was about two years old when I had him, although we were never quite sure of his age. I finished my course with him, if memory serves me correctly, in March 2005. 'Vinnie' is now about thirteen years old. He has a black coat, which goes greyer by the day – but then so do I.

It sounds mad but I often talk with Vinnie about what happened on that day and how proud of him I am. When the call first came in as a 'power surge', I always felt that that wasn't the case – I always felt that it was a bombing.

Our first deployment was at Liverpool Street and we started carrying out an external search and setting up of cordons. Officers were struggling to set up the cordons as it was the rush hour and there were people everywhere. A man came up to me in a jacket and said he was an officer and asked if he could help. I used a pretty strong swear word to ask him to get people onto the other side of the cordons. He then took off his jacket and it became apparent that he was a Chief Superintendent. I said, 'Sorry, sir', but he replied, 'I couldn't have put it better myself – don't worry.'

While searching down to the target train I was wearing a uniform t-shirt and trousers and about 50 metres out in front of the search team, who were all wearing full bomb suits. I remember looking back and thinking something isn't quite right here.

Upon arrival at Russell Square. I was tasked to go below so searched my way down to the platform, which is where blood-stained bandages were strewn on the platform along with passengers' personal items – so now it really begins.

Power was off on the line so I searched along the darkened, smoky, sweet-smelling and messy tunnel to the train. After a couple of hundred yards I could hear a train coming up behind me – wow – panic – how come the power's not off – have they turned it back on?

I called 'Vinnie' back to me and had seconds to pick him up while making sure that we were off the power lines – the train is getting closer – it is so quiet except for this engine coming.

I was looking around for a safe place to tuck into so we didn't get hit. 'Vinnie' is not the lightest of dogs and nor am I the slimmest person. Suddenly the light comes around the bend and it is only the bloody fire brigade on their battery-operated truck that runs on the track. Well the chief with the white hat certainly got some choice words said to him and got told to go away until I had done my job.

I had to wait a second or two, although it seemed longer, for my heart to get back to normal. It was not known at this time that it was a suicide attack and it was believed that other devices were at the scene – hence the full evacuation.

I am not going to mention the first two carriages and the carnage – just to say that it was clear that the first carriage was where the explosion had happened and, as the train moved through the tunnel, the explosion hit the second carriage. I had to check for any other devices among the people there. I tried to do it in the most respectful and careful way possible and tried to treat them as if I were related to them. Basically all the people had to be moved and checked while at the same time I had to try to ensure that evidence was not lost. It had to be searched well to ensure the safety of any officers coming to the scene after me.

There was lots of broken glass and bare sharps all around the damaged carriages so I covered 'Vinnie's' paws with duct tape to protect him. Nowadays all the dogs have issued 'booties' to wear for this type of incident.

The rest of the carriages, apart from a broken window here and there and personal equipment strewn all over the place, were pretty normal. My duties did carry on for the rest of the day, although I was filthy and my clothes all the way though to my skin and underwear were soaked with blood. I just didn't stop until about 9 p.m. and that is about it.

To be honest it is difficult to talk about what happened, without it sounding disrespectful and carefree. I hope that makes sense.

By the way the very next day there was a report of a bomb attack at Moorgate station, so off we all went again. Thankfully it was just the PM at the ambulance headquarters, and they were showing him how they would deal with an emergency call – without telling us it was a test call.

'Vinnie' was on call again when, about a week later, some relatives of the bombers were 'hard-stopped' by Met police on the concourse at Liverpool Street station. The people had been taken away by the police but they had left all the cases and bags on the station concourse. The concern was that explosives might be within the bags and the station was evacuated – so again, up steps 'Vinnie' who deals with it all perfectly.

As he is asleep at the side of me now, I wake him up and tell that I am proud of him – and of course give him a biscuit ...

Retired Superintendent Phil Trendall concludes,

It is clear that several dog handlers did amazing things that day – over many hours they were the enablers that allowed everything else to follow. The tactic Dave describes of putting the dog and handler forward with the searchers in a 'V' formation behind is in place to minimise casualties – but in doing so it maximises the risk to the dog and the handler.

Even now it is hard to put into words just how immensely proud I am of the specialist resources that deployed on that day, and to the many incidents since.

Richard J. Stacpoole-Ryding has done his own research into the story of 'Vinnie' and outlines his own thoughts:

Heroes come in all shapes and sizes and not all are humans either. There are many heroes that come from our animal society. The one factor that is common to both is that neither are aware of their capacity for bravery and courage until placed in an extraordinary situation requiring extraordinary action.

Sometimes these actions are recognised by the award of medals and commendations from the state, official bodies or organisations and voluntary societies. One such organisation that recognises the bravery and courage of all animals is the People's Dispensary for Sick Animals, better known as the PDSA. Among PDSA's animal awards are the PDSA Dickin Medal and the PDSA Gold Medal.

The Dickin Medal is probably the best known of the PDSA awards and is awarded for military bravery; it is known, internationally, as the animals' Victoria Cross. It has been awarded to dogs, horses, pigeons and a cat over the past sixty years.

In 2002 the PDSA instituted the PDSA Gold Medal, which is the highest honour for outstanding animal bravery and exceptional dedication in civilian life. It is open to any animal instrumental in saving human or animal life when its own life is in jeopardy or to any animal killed or seriously injured while carrying out official duties in the face of armed and violent opposition. It is now widely known and recognised as the animals' George Cross. To date, only twenty-three of these prestigious medals have been awarded, all to dogs, and one of the recipients is police dog 'Vinnie' of the British Transport Police.

'Vinnie,' whose handler is PC Dave Coleman, was awarded the PDSA Gold Medal on 3 March 2007 for his tireless work following the horrific London bombings on 7 July 2005. There is no better way of describing what 'Vinnie' did on that day than reading the citation that accompanied the award: *'For gallantry in the service of humanity, immediately following the terrorist attacks in London on Thursday 7 July 2005.'*

Vinnie and his handler, PC Dave Coleman, were already on duty in the city when they were urgently deployed to the terrorist explosion at Russell Square tube station. 'Vinnie' immediately began a search for secondary explosive devices in order to establish a clear route for medical assistance to reach the many casualties.

Overcoming smoke and poor visibility, 'Vinnie' then searched the mile-long route from Russell Square to the bomb-damaged train at King's Cross and completed a reoccupation search of King's Cross station. Despite horrendous devastation and human trauma, 'Vinnie' did not hesitate in carrying out his duties. His skills and tireless devotion to duty were instrumental in restoring public safety and he proved invaluable throughout this tragic event.

Labradors 'Vinnie' and 'Billy' and Spaniel 'Hubble Keck' (pet name 'Jake') were chosen by BTP, City of London Police, and Metropolitan Police respectively, to represent all fourteen police explosive-search dogs working in the capital on that fateful day. The medals were presented at a ceremony at St James's Palace in July 2007 by PDSA Patron HRH Princess Alexandra.

PDSA's then-chairman, Freddie Bircher, said that it was the search dogs' turn for the spotlight. They worked fearlessly and in perfect unison, searching for possible secondary devices. 'These police explosives dogs were the unsung heroes of that tragic day.'

'Vinnie' and PC Dave Coleman were each further recognised by being awarded a Chief Constable's Commendation. Four other dogs, and their handlers, were individually awarded Chief Constable's Commendations for their part in the terrible events following the London bombings.

There have been many dogs and their handlers in the history of the force who have faced danger or have displayed exceptional devotion to duty and been recognised by Chief Constable's Commendations but none that have received such a prestigious award as 'Vinnie'.

Perhaps it is now time to consider recording the names of our brave canine 'officers' who go about their duty and show their gallantry, courage and devotion to duty alongside those of their human colleagues.

14

'RIOT' TAKES ON THE BEST AND 'CHARLIE' WINS THE LOTTERY

BTP took a leading role in the planning for 'Operation Sorbus', the coordinated policing operation for the three-day G8 summit held between 6 and 8 July 2005 at the Gleneagles Hotel, near Auchterarder in Perthshire. Explosives-trained dog teams from the force were deployed for the operation at key stations such as Haymarket and Waverley in Edinburgh, Dalmeny, Stirling, Perth, Gleneagles, Glasgow Central and Glasgow Queen Street. The world-famous Forth Rail Bridge was included as well.

Andy Fidgett recalls some of his experiences as a new dog handler:

During my basic course from September to December 2005 we would have, from time to time, the dog school manager, Mr Peter Heard, come out with us for training. On one occasion it was my turn to run for a dog. I am sure you have seen the sort of thing; you run with a padded sleeve on and the dog bites your arm and often pulls you to the ground because of his speed and weight. The art is to make sure your left arm is holding your right collar or breast pocket and don't twist your body, as you want the dog to go for the outstretched right arm.

My turn came and it paid never to show you didn't want to do it – if that came out you would be running all day long. It's one of those funny things in life that you could hate and love to do; you never heard the dog so you didn't know when it would hit.

I started running on the field at Tadworth. In those days I was pretty quick. I ran and ran and was running out of field; I knew not to turn and didn't know what to do. A man who was trimming his hedge in one of the nearby houses, which was at the bottom of the Tadworth field, and who was standing on a ladder, said to me, 'Don't worry, mate – there's nothing behind you. They do it all the time.' All the others and the instructors had gone for tea and never actually let the dog off the lead.

On the same course we had to give an input to some new recruits. One, an ex-serviceman, was rather full of himself and wanted to run for a dog. It was my turn to get 'Ned' out, but he had been ill and was not at his best.

I didn't know but our serviceman said some unpleasant things about 'Ned' behind my back as he had seen me earlier with 'Ned', who was sick and looked poorly. As I returned one of my colleagues on the course, who is still a dog handler, told me to put 'Ned' back into solitary, where he was being kept and not to let him run.

He then changed 'Ned' for our only Rottweiler, which was being trained at the time. Our serviceman almost messed himself when this monster of a dog crashed into him and wouldn't let go of his arm. All was well with 'Ned' and a couple of days later I asked him if he wanted to run again as 'Ned' was better – I can't print his reply.

During this period, as part of continuing terrorism operations in the capital, London North officers began targeting the Heathrow Express service from Paddington station. Regular patrols and the use of explosives dogs were part of the high-profile activity designed to deter and detect possible terrorist threats. Paddington officers worked in partnership with the Dog Section at FHQ with dog teams scanning the travelling environment on platforms and trains.

One such officer was PC Mel Blanford and 'Jack'. 'The Heathrow Express was undoubtedly the sort of target that terrorists might consider,' said Inspector Sue Peters from Paddington. 'The trains go into the heart of the airport and are the fastest link between London and the world's busiest international airport, so they attract a good deal of the business market. Having said that, the stations are very controlled, CCTV-rich environments and these counter-terrorist operations are designed to make the Heathrow Express an even harder target.'

In July 2005 BTP officers stopped seven times as many people under Section 44 of the Terrorism Act 2000 as they did in June. 2,900 stops were made under the Act in July compared with just over 400 in June as BTP stepped up operations following the London bombings on 7 July and the attempted bombings on 21 July. Teams of officers making extensive use of explosives dogs made their presence felt on the rail system in high-profile operations described by Deputy Chief Constable Andy Trotter as a policy of 'intrusive policing'. The highly visible policing presence seems to have had an immediate effect on crime levels, with crime down over 20 per cent.

Andy Fidgett recalls another incident:

In December 2005 we were training at a place called West Park. It was one of the many old hospitals in the Epsom area of Surrey. It appears that many years ago all the boroughs of London had to send their mental patients somewhere and one borough built an asylum near to Epsom, as the railway reached this location, and others then followed. We were allowed to train in the old buildings. One day the Instructor went off to set out some training.

An officer who got 'caught short' went the other way and let nature take its course. Sometime later the same officer took his dog for a walk before it was his turn to carry out the exercise. He let his dog off the lead to give it a run. We heard some shouting and went to see if he was okay, as there were lots of hazards in these old buildings. We saw him running towards us and the dog was behind.

It turned out that the dog had found what the officer had left, so to speak, and had eaten it. Now the dog wanted a cuddle!

New passenger-screening techniques were to be tested on the National Rail and London Underground network from January 2006, Transport Secretary Alistair Darling announced to parliament in November 2005. BTP would have a dedicated team of officers attached to the first trial of equipment taking place on the Heathrow Express platforms at London Paddington for four weeks. The tests were being carried out by TRANSEC, the security arm of the Department for Transport, using a contracted security firm. They involved a small number of randomly chosen passengers either going through a scanner or being searched either by hand, with the use of portable trace equipment, or with sniffer dogs.

Andy Fidgett recalls,

January 2006 was my first really big deployment. I was at King's Cross station when a call came in that one hundred people were fighting at Stratford. Every unit made their way and we had four dogs in there in total.

On arrival most of the fighting had stopped, but there was a rumour of shots being fired, and we found a knife covered in blood. There is a shopping precinct opposite the station and the Metropolitan Police asked us to help out by walking the dogs through from the far side to assist in bringing everyone out into the street. 'Ned' and I were put in a 'Met' police carrier and driven around the back and walked through with others. The Met then 'bubbled' the people, who turned out to be from a number of street gangs, and carried out searches on the lot; I believe some arrests were made.

The next day 'Ned' went lame and it's likely he got kicked in the incident somehow. I blamed myself but it was probably bad luck. He had three months off work and the vet's bill was £1,500.

Retired Dog Handler Kate Moore recalls one of her experiences:

There are times when it's difficult to have a working GP dog at home with you, and there are times when you're glad he is a working dog, not your own pet; like the time when in 2006 I was walking my GP dog 'Arnie' home through the park from the local police station, where I parked my van.

As it was late at night, in a familiar closed-in area with no-one else around, I let him off the lead for a quick sniff around and wee. He then, on seeing the resident fox, chased after him through the hedge, completely forgetting his well-practised 'recall' exercise, ran over the road and was sadly hit by what seemed like the only car on the road in the area.

Luckily, he was still conscious and we were able to blue-light it to the vet's. They confirmed that he had broken his front leg in two places, but with the right care and attention he would recover and even work again. So glad that he was a working dog, with the bill belonging to BTP! Seriously though, BTP spared no expense with his recovery and agreed to have his leg pinned, rather than cast, so he could recover quicker, and he even went for hydrotherapy (or swimming lessons as I liked to call them, as up until then he hated water) to assist in getting him back to being fighting fit!

While he was off sick though, we had to carry him to the local park, although he still managed to still bark at other dogs while he was in our arms – like some kind of furry machine gun. He was perhaps worried about his reputation slipping!

On 15 July 2006 a brand new and much larger new Dog Training Centre was opened at Tadworth. It was now one of the most modern in the country. London South Dog Handler Steve Madden said the new training school had made a huge difference to those attached to BTP dog units: 'This is a massive step forward for us. It creates such a level of certainty and reassurance in regards to having dogs as a future within the force. This is a purpose-built professional building and it's fantastic for the dogs and for the handlers, such a step up from the Portakabins we've been in previously.' PC Madden said dogs and handlers could spend anything from two days to fourteen weeks at the school and that it was great to now be able to work in one of the most modern training facilities in the country. He commented, 'There's heating, ventilation, washing machine areas and dog bath areas, isolation blocks – everything. There's even a custom-made machine called the 'Macerator', which helps break down and get rid of dog excrement. They've thought of everything.'

Dog-training manager Peter Heard said the dog school would be beneficial not just for BTP, but for other forces who use the training expertise offered at Tadworth. 'We train dogs for general-purpose policing, explosives, firearms and drugs searching. At the moment, BTP has seventy-three handlers based all over the country with thirty-nine explosive-search dogs, twenty-two drugs search dogs and thirty-three general-purpose police dogs, all of which come to Tadworth during the year for training.'

The school was officially opened by the British Transport Police Authority Chairman Sir Alistair Graham and Deputy

Chief Constable Andy Trotter as part of a family fun day and Police Dog Trials. On a hot and sunny Saturday in July, the trials tested heelwork, agility and criminal work and saw dog teams entered from the BTP, the Metropolitan Police, Hampshire Police, City of London and Surrey Police.

The Met took first and second spots, with PC Steve Bishop and police dog 'Ace' coming ahead of PC Graham Clarke with police dog 'Kiro-Demi'. BTP's own George Pudney and police dog 'Kaiser' took third place honours.

BTP's latest recruit was a ten-week-old English Springer Spaniel puppy, destined to become an explosive-search dog. A competition to name the new recruit resulted in some 200 suggested names, with Shirley Young of Cobham picking the winning entry 'Kookie'.

BTP's first initial explosives course to be run under the Association of Chief Police Officers' (ACPO) licensing scheme was completed at Tadworth. With the recent increase in explosives dog numbers from sixteen to thirty-nine, and the opening of the new dog school, it was decided that BTP would start to run its own courses to the ACPO standard, with an outside assessor being brought in to licence the course.

'The background was that in 1990 ACPO decided that all explosive-search dogs would be trained by regional police dog training schools and handlers licensed under ACPO guidelines,' commented Dog Training Instructor Mark Jones. 'BTP sent its dogs to regional schools in Surrey, Stafford, Durham, Lancashire and Strathclyde. As time has gone on these courses have become expensive and forces have started to train their own dogs. In May, we did that and in June the first four students were passed by an ACPO assessor from Sussex Police.'

'This was such a success that all future explosives dog initial courses will be run from the BTP Dog School here at Tadworth.'

PC Keith Smith and 'Bailey' become the first dog team to be based in Edinburgh since 1992. 'Bailey' was an explosives-detection dog and the team would be a highly visible presence at east Scotland stations, assisting with the counter-terrorism Operation 'Alert' and providing a reassuring presence to the public and staff.

During the early 1980s there were two general-purpose dogs at Edinburgh, who were deployed to great effect during the electrification of the East Coast main railway line. By 1992 work on the line had been completed and the need for police dogs at Edinburgh had diminished to such an extent that they were not replaced at the end of their working lives.

Michael Layton (co-author), who was then a detective superintendent (Director of Intelligence) with BTP, recalls,

In September 2006 I set up an operation aimed at disrupting football hooligans travelling on the UK rail networks. I borrowed the name of an undercover operation I had previously run in 1987 and thus 'Red Card' was reborn.

There was plenty of evidence to suggest that a sizeable minority of hooligans were taking Class B drugs such as cannabis, and others were taking cocaine and amphetamine. With some drugs little more than the price of a 'couple of pints', many opted for a quick fix, but this presented us with some disruption opportunities and I started to deploy 'drugs dogs' as part of our operational response to match days, when 'high-risk' fans were travelling.

From 2009, on moving to my last role as the operations superintendent in Birmingham, I used PC Colin Fowler, based at Birmingham, on a number of occasions together with his black-and-white Collie/Cross dog 'Kye', who was trained to act as both a 'passive' and 'proactive' searcher. Like many of BTP's dogs 'Kye' was a rescue dog.

In the first role he would stay on a lead and scan people. In the event of a 'positive indication' he was trained to follow a suspect or to sit in front of them, looking alternatively up at the suspect, and then to Colin. If the suspect continued walking, 'Kye' sometimes would take the rather unorthodox approach of wrapping his legs around them! As a 'proactive' dog he was trained to work off the lead, searching houses and vehicles.

'Kye' was a very effective dog and I personally saw him indicate on many occasions, leading to some great recoveries. He never got his reward until drugs were actually found but I saw that ball come out of PC Fowler's pocket many times, much to 'Kye's' delight. It was, after all, about having fun!

Normally we would put the drugs dogs out for the forward traffic and then replace them with general-purpose dogs for the return traffic where there was a higher prospect of clashes taking place between opposing fans.

PC Fowler also had a GP dog at that time called 'Vik', who was a large long-haired German Shepherd with a fierce disposition when confronted by hostility. They often worked alongside PC Stuart Rimell, also based at Birmingham and his GP dog 'Sid', and they made the perfect team with 'real teeth' with which to exercise control of unruly elements. I never personally witnessed in all my years of service football hooligans trying to stand their ground against police dogs.

When he wasn't involved with public-order situations, PC Rimell also used another working dog by the name of 'Mini', who was trained to indicate the presence of explosives.

BTP's explosive-search dogs had been very visible on the rail network since the 7 July bombings. Indeed they had proved a great hit with the public and staff, who liked to see the dogs out and about, and constantly asked the handlers how they worked, trained, and were cared for.

In 2007 PC Steve Gould of the Force ESD Section had the idea of creating collectable cards, each featuring an individual dog, to hand out. Virgin Trains's Sophie Thrussel agreed to sponsor the cards, which were so successful that they were reprinted several times.

During this period the Bank of England contributed £36,000 to help BTP train one of its newest recruits. The money was donated to help BTP's first cash dog, 'Charlie', get his nose in. London-based handler Steve Palmer said the notes had been cut in such a way that they were unable to be used in general circulation but, because the paper and the ink was effectively a bank note, they were perfect for training cash dogs.

PC Palmer, who also had a German Shepherd GP dog called 'Zehn' and a Labrador passive drugs dog, 'Gizmo', said working with a cash dog had proven challenging: 'The difference between working with other dogs and 'Charlie' is that the general purpose and drugs sniffing dogs are very public and have a lot of contact with the public, whereas 'Charlie' is very much behind the scenes. It is a different way of working when you are searching for cash.'

'Charlie' was a Springer Spaniel, donated by a member of the public in Lincolnshire, and eighteen months old. 'We've been doing a bit of a road show, going to different posts around the country to let people know that the force now has a cash dog and how we can be used to help with cash seizure,' said the officer.

Police have powers under the Proceeds of Crime Act to seize cash from anyone found in possession of £1,000 or more, who can't explain its origin. As a result, house and property searches often ensue and that is when 'Charlie' comes into his own. Already 'Charlie' had been deployed for Operation 'Drum', the national operation targeting cable theft, and during the search of a scrap yard succeeded in detecting a floor safe containing a substantial amount of cash.

'Charlie' underwent monthly training at Tadworth to hone his cash-sniffing skills and could also sniff out firearms and drugs. In one case two men were arrested in possession of a large amount of cash. 'Charlie' was sent in on the house searches and at one address indicated the bottom of a double bed. Over £2,000 was found hidden in the bed frame inside a plastic bag and wrapped in clothing.

'Charlie' was also part of a three-day operation at Waterloo International station codenamed Operation 'Cane', which targeted passengers using the Eurostar service, who were potentially involved in money laundering and proceeds of crime offences.

A joint operation with HM Revenue & Customs and BTP provided high-profile uniform visibility at both departures and arrivals at Waterloo. The operation was set up following intelligence received about more people moving large amounts of cash via Eurostar. 'Charlie' was used over the first two days, while 'Harvey', a drugs dog, covered the third.

Inspector Melisa Cunningham from FHQ Operations said,

> We had thirty-six indications by the BTP dogs used over three days. Three people were stopped with large quantities of cash in their possession – £8,000, £6,500, and £5,000 – and, after detailed questioning, were able to prove legitimate reasons for carrying the cash. Operation 'Cane' was a good learning opportunity for us in relation to future pre-planned cash operations and the difficulties of working with POCA legislation. It has opened the debate about the viability of having more cash dogs within the BTP.

Eight officers from the Search Dog Section of the Counter-Terrorism Support Unit took part in a joint operation with the Army, Air Force and Navy. Working alongside explosives officers from the armed forces, as well as search teams from twelve other English and Scottish police forces and colleagues from the North Western and North Eastern Areas, Operation 'Saton' saw the dogs working a number of search venues.

In May of 2007 the FA cup final returned to the new national stadium at Wembley. Chelsea and Manchester United fans flocked to the impressive new 90,000-capacity stadium to cheer on their teams. More than 500 BTP officers, including dog handlers and their dogs, were on duty at key stations around the Wembley area to police the crowds.

When one of BTP's dog handlers was approached on Paddington station by a well-known actor to ask whether or not his dog was really a police dog, the handler quickly retorted: 'Yes, and aren't you a really famous actor off the telly?' Rik Mayall, for it was he, was heard to answer indignantly: 'Yes, I'm Jennifer Saunders,' before rushing off.

Making arrangements for a joint operation with Merseyside Police at Southport, an officer had occasion to contact them to try and obtain the services of one of their passive drugs dogs. None were available on the day, but a helpful inspector did offer the services of a mounted patrol in order to show a presence in the area. The officer then asked: 'When did they start training passive drugs horses?'

In 2008 a drugs dog working with an Operation 'Shield' knife crime team at Birkenhead Park station, Wirral, indicated a man who was subsequently stopped and searched. Nothing was found, but the man was so agitated that the officer decided to check him out on the Police National Computer. The result came back that he was known but not wanted, to which the suspect breathed a huge sigh of relief.

Asked why he was so nervous, he replied that he thought there was still a warrant out for him and that the dog had scanned him and picked it up. Now 'Jack' was a clever dog but a 'warrant-scanning' dog – that would be a boon!

As the BTP Dog Section celebrated its one-hundred-year anniversary, BTP officially took part in ACPO regional dog trials for the first time – and produced a winner. 'This has been a very significant event for us,' commented Dog Training Manager Peter Heard. 'This year we competed in our own right whereas before we only had guest status.'

To mark the one-hundredth anniversary year, BTP was also asked to host the regional trials, which took place at the Tadworth Training Centre in February, bringing together nine competitors from Surrey, Sussex, Kent and BTP. BTP were represented by PC John Hawkins and 'Riot' from the North Eastern Area, and London South's PC Kate Moore and 'Arnie'. Both John and Katie progressed to the regional trials from BTP's own police dog trials, which were actually won by another North Eastern team, PC John Mann and 'Zeke'.

John 'Corky' Hawkins recalls in his own words how proud he was to take part in the trials:

In 2004 I began handling my last dog 'Riot', who was a natural, bought for £150. In 2008, the centenary year of the BTP Dog Section, the BTP were allowed to compete in the regional dog trials as official competitors and, if successful, then onto the nationals. In the force dog trials of 2008 I finished third with sufficient points to allow entry to the regionals.

The trials were held at Tadworth and organised by BTP between 19 and 21 February 2008, myself, PC Kate Moore and police dog 'Eric' competed and I was able to qualify for the national dog trials. So between 28 April and 1 May 2008 I competed in the 48th National Police Dog Trials, organised by the Merseyside Police as the first BTP dog and handler to do so.

This I was very proud of, especially when the Merseyside Chief Constable Bernard Hogan-Howe mentioned in his closing speech the involvement of the BTP. Oh, by the way – I finished twentieth out of twenty-four but that didn't matter.

John concludes his recollections with the following:

Apart from GP dogs I also worked two explosive-search dogs and with my first one, 'Brook', was called to a category one threat received from the IRA.

In the late 1990s, while cutting my lawn, I received a call to go to Newcastle. The IRA had sent a coded call that there was a device on the station. I arrived only to find that a dummy device had been found at the location of the incident control point. This made things totally different. When myself and the Northumbrian dog handler, who had only finished his basic course a week before, went under the police tape to start the search of the station, I looked back to where the other officers were safely stood. I thought, 'my life depends on this little black Labrador, "Brook", a year out of his basic course.' Luckily after about seven hours of searching no devices were found, but the IRA had done their job and shut the North East Coast Main Line down for hours.

In September 2008 BTP Dog Handler PC Paul Morse, along with a number of other officers, received a commendation for bravery during a serious football-related incident at Cardiff railway station.

Eleven serving dog handlers joined retired staff in Liverpool in October 2008 to celebrate one hundred years of the Dog Section in the BTP.

15

'KODA' AND 'DIBBLE' ARRIVE – COPPER THEFTS AND THE OLYMPICS

On 2 April 2009 a major operation codenamed 'Glencoe' took place in London, involving a number of police forces, which was aimed at policing large-scale demonstrations taking place in response to the G20 summit.

The BTP played a key role in the operation in support of the Metropolitan Police, and BTP dog handlers were on duty with their dogs to support the force's public order strategy. One such officer was PC Andy Fidgett, who was on duty with his dog, an Alsatian called 'Ned', and he recalls:

'Ned' and I were on the steps at Liverpool Street station exit into Bishopsgate while the demonstrations into the G20 were going on; we were faced by a large crowd, who were throwing missiles at us. There was just a barrier between us, and behind us the station had been emptied.

Another dog handler and I were waiting for back up. Outside we didn't know it at the time but an ambulance was trying to get through the crowd to help a newspaper seller, who had collapsed and died. They also threw food, and put their arms between the barriers, hoping to get bitten as they had their own photographers behind them. Behind us the station was empty.

If the demonstrators had simply walked around the corner they could have walked onto the station – due to a 'cock up' the others officers had gone elsewhere.

In July 2009 a new counter-terrorism operation was launched by the BTP, the first major change to BTP's counter-terrorism for four years, and was codenamed Operation 'Pegasus'. It fully integrated all aspects of CT policing into all areas of policing through the tasking process, which included the deployment of explosive-search dogs at key rail locations in the UK. This brought the force's approach into line with the government's 'Contest' counter-terrorism strategy.

BTP recruited ten additional explosive-search dogs for the Olympics, which were funded by the Department for Transport. In 2009 British Transport Police recruited two Malinois, or Belgian Shepherd dogs, who would be exercising the more than 220 million olfactory receptors in their noses to search out explosives on the rail network.

Police dogs 'Koda' and 'Dibble' were the first of their breed to be used by BTP, and the only ones in Britain in this role. The two passive explosives-detection dogs could monitor the environment around people and their luggage, operating in the same way as drugs sniffer dogs.

'We chose Malinois because of their high intelligence and enormous drive and stamina,' said Sergeant Bill Pearson from BTP's Counter-Terrorism Support Unit. 'Compared with Labradors and Spaniels they offer us extended-duration operations and are an important enhancement to our overall counter-terrorist capability.'

After the Olympics the BTP reduced its Dog Section to focus on the priorities of counter-terrorism, public order and cable theft.

During 2009, BTP continued with a major offensive to combat cable thefts on the rail network. One of the methods used to detect offenders was the use of lineside alarms on the track. Shortly before Christmas 2009, lineside alarms on track-earthing cables were triggered in Rainham Essex. A subsequent police search found 150 metres of cut cable and a rucksack at the base of a nearby stanchion.

'This indicated that the person or persons responsible were more than likely disturbed,' said the investigating officer Detective Constable David Stewart. 'In the rucksack was a pair of gloves and a water bottle. They were sent for forensic analysis and the water bottle returned a DNA match to a particular individual.'

Following a further alarm activation in January of 2010, a team of Land Sheriff security officers went to Creekside viaduct on the high-speed line, where they saw the suspect running away. 'The security team followed him but he evaded them by hiding in the undergrowth,' said DC Stewart.

BTP officers and a dog unit were called and they found the man, together with a pair of bolt-croppers, gloves and 300 metres of cut cable. He was later charged with attempted theft, criminal damage and endangering safety on the railway, pleading guilty to all the charges. He was jailed for three years at Blackfriars Crown Court.

In March 2010 a television programme showed BTP drugs dogs deployed at railway stations looking for controlled drugs. PC Mick Cook and police dog 'Raffa' worked at Lancaster, while PC Wood worked with police dog 'Charlie' at stations on London Underground. The programme appears on YouTube and has had over 13,000 views to date.

In 2010 the BTP dog-training moved to the Metropolitan Police Dog Training School in Keston, Kent.

In November 2011 the force conducted a review of the Dog Section, aimed at delivering a better service in the key areas of cable theft, counter-terrorism, and football policing.

Under the banner of the 'Futures' programme, BTP launched a review aimed at bringing dog operations into line with the force's Strategic Threat and Risk Assessment. As part of the initial review, dog handlers in London were brought under one line management structure and the number of secondary dogs, handlers and vehicles were reduced to compensate for the end of Olympic funding, projected for September 2012. The decision was also taken to reduce the number of drugs search dogs used by the force.

At the time three separate trials were planned, the first of which was to start using dogs cross-functionally in assisting with public order, as well as explosives-detection duties. The second trial planned to look at the issue of multi-handling, alongside that of central kennelling, moving away from the traditional approach of keeping dogs at officers' homes. The third trial was designed to assess how effective a dog trained to detect chemical markers could be in detecting stolen metal. After some deliberation the force decided to defer the decision to consider 'multi-handling' of dogs.

London South GP dog 'Ice', together with handler PC Mark Chambers, took top spot in the 2011 BTP dog trials. The trials took place in January at Keston Dog School.

National Express operator c2c helped to train police dogs through donations of old, unclaimed lost property. 'We hugely appreciate all the donations,' said Dog Handler PC Steve Madden. 'We take unclaimed lost property such as broken laptops and mobile phones, as well as old clothing, bags and suitcases. Everything is used to train our dogs in the most realistic way possible – and it's proved invaluable.'

Phil Trendall continues his recollections,

The section expanded by another ten dogs in the lead up to the London Olympics in 2012, making BTP the largest users of ESDs, with the exception of the Metropolitan Police.

The dogs were a huge success during the Games, attracting positive comments from many members of the travelling public. A couple of passengers even said nice things about the handlers as well!

One of our sergeants established an Olympics dog welfare centre near the Olympic Park so that our dogs had somewhere to rest during the almost continuous search regimes. This location was a great success and police staff volunteers from around the force helped to feed and care for the dogs.

After 2012 a new approach to the use of dogs was spearheaded by Chief Constable Paul Crowther.

Phil Trendall concludes his recollections:

Of course ESDs continued to be used in their pre-event search role and were very busy during the Diamond Jubilee, when the Queen made good use of the Royal train to tour the country. Both the ESD section and the Special Movements section were part of the CTSU and this made for a close and useful working relationship.

This relationship had been honed during the period to 2010 when senior Labour government ministers made extensive use of the rail network to travel, meaning that it was not unusual to have half of the Cabinet on one train or, worse, spread over the whole network, including the London Underground. When John Reid was home secretary he came to know all of the ESDs by name. This stood in stark contrast to his need to ask a handler the name of the Chief Constable just before he was to meet him on a train!

All the dogs had their own 'business cards' that contained a picture of the dog and details of their age and character. These proved to be very popular, with some passengers and many rail staff collecting complete sets of cards.

In 2012 a black Labrador called 'Benson' was one of the passive ESD dogs deployed to the Olympics. His handler was PC Graham Rowlstone. He was card number seven for the 'dog picture' collectors and his read:

Hi, I'm Benson, DOB June 2007, Breed Black Labrador, and Handler PC Rowlstone – Benson is a very friendly and affectionate dog who loves to get cuddles from everyone he meets. The BTP Dog Section is the oldest and largest in the country. The Explosive-Search Dog section in London consists of about sixty highly trained dogs. Most of the dogs have been rescued, sometimes from sad and abusive backgrounds. Once the dogs have been assessed they are sent on an eight-week course with their handlers where they are taught to search for explosives. Once they complete their course the dogs live at home with the handlers and their families.

Another dog engaged in similar duties was 'Pete', who worked together with his handler PC Tony Mart.

Superintendent Phil Trendall commented, 'The dogs are a tool that's effective across a range of activities, reassurance and engagement with the public, and detection – that's why they are attractive to us.'

Taking advantage of planned line closures between Gospel Oak and Stratford London Overground stations, BTP organised a week-long counter-terrorism training exercise called Operation 'Safe Return'. The exercise was based at Kentish Town West station, and involved officers with ESDs searching the lines up to Camden Road. This provided a real-life setting in which to carry out searches and hone their skills.

Dummy explosive devices were placed along the line of route, which the search teams had to find. Run as a live exercise, the scenario was of a bomb threat assessed as needing a line closure and police response. The whole exercise was carried out in real time with a simulated media presence to heighten the pressure.

In all 144 officers from around the force took part, including ESD handlers and BTP's counter-terrorism Special Response Unit. Staff that were employed by London Overground were given briefings on the management of counter-terrorism incidents and took part in simultaneous exercises at the station. Observers also attended from other agencies including the London Fire Brigade and West Yorkshire Police.

In preparation for the Olympics ten new explosive-search dogs, sponsored by the Department for Transport as part of BTP's Olympics programme completed their eight weeks' initial training and underwent independent licensing. 'These new dogs and their handling team will ensure the safety of thousands of visitors we are expecting at London 2012,' said Transport Minister Paul Clark when he visited some of the dogs at Stratford Regional station. 'Stations are expected to be very busy and we must provide security with minimal disruption to the travelling public.'

Assistant Chief Constable Steve Thomas led BTP's Olympic programme team as well as being national coordinator for Cross-Modal Transport Security, covering rail, road, maritime and air transport. 'Explosive-Search Dogs (ESD) and their handlers are a vital part of our operational planning for 2012,' he said. 'With a train arriving into the Olympic Park every thirteen and a half seconds at peak time, and

80 per cent of spectators using rail transport, any disruption will have a serious impact. We will be using these resources proactively to ensure that the network remains secure and to help keep security-related incidents to an absolute minimum.'

The new dogs, some of which were rescue dogs, and their handlers joined BTP's existing dog teams who made up the ESD section, the largest unit of its kind in any police force in Britain.

Former Olympic Security Minister Lord West also welcomed the new recruits. 'These new sniffer dogs are a welcome addition to the London 2012 security team,' he said. 'The dogs are just one part of the biggest security operation in the UK since the Second World War. They will play an important role in ensuring that London 2012 is remembered for its sporting achievements.'

More than one hundred years after the British Transport Police sought advice from the Belgian authorities about their innovative use of patrol dogs, officers from the Spoorwegpolitie (railway police) in Brussels sought the expertise of BTP's dog handlers. Tadworth Dog Trainer PC Mark Jones highlighted that the force was offering training and counter-terrorism advice to police forces internationally. 'It's amazing how things can change. All those years ago we were the force that had no established Dog Section. Now they are tapping into our knowledge and skills to improve their counter-terrorism plans,' he said.

Inspector Michel Geurts of the railway division of the Belgian Federal Police (Spoorwegpolitie) completed an eight-week training course with English Springer Spaniel 'Charlie'. The course was centred on explosives search capabilities with Michel remaining under the watchful eye of PC Jones. Four other BTP officers also took part in the course: Dougie Hird and police dog 'Banjo' from the North Eastern Area and Counter Terrorist Support Unit officers;

PC Keith Board with 'Max'; Sergeant Neil Forsyth with 'Monty', and PC Adam Turner with 'Charley Cracker'.

Michel, who was the first officer in the Spoorwegpolitie Railway Division to be trained in working with an explosive-search dog said, 'The BTP course was far more advanced than anything available in Belgium. A general dog-training course takes ten months to complete – but here we were able to do a specialist explosives course in eight weeks.' The training course centres on teaching the dogs to detect eight different substances in controlled environments and going to live venues for practice.

Michel's dog 'Charlie' was a gift dog from Hampshire and was issued with a dog passport system to enable him to travel between England and Belgium for ongoing training support over the next four months. 'We've had a lot of success in a very short period of time,' commented Michel. '"Charlie" will be the only explosive-search dog in use on the Brussels subway system and it's hoped that by next year we will have four explosive-search dogs in use in the railway division.'

'Lucky', an abandoned Welsh Border Collie, was a rescue dog who became part of London South's war against drugs. 'Lucky' was dumped as a puppy by his owners outside a Wandsworth pet shop and collected by Battersea Dogs Home. He was days away from being put down when a member of the staff alerted BTP to his potential as a police dog.

'He's such a great dog to work with and has done some amazing work over the past four years,' handler PC Chris Jessup said. 'He's had such a rollercoaster ride in his short life. He was abandoned and left for dead and then thankfully rescued but then didn't quite cut it in the cute dog stakes. But what 'Lucky' lacks in looks, he more than makes up for as a working police dog. Thankfully the staff at Battersea saw his potential as a police dog and contacted us to give him a trial. He's been brilliant to work with. He's got the nickname among the officers as being the singing dog because, whenever he's deployed, he howls. It's like he's telling people that he's here and ready to work.'

'Lucky' proved to be lucky by name and lucky by nature. Alongside Chris's other passive drugs dog, 'Amber', 'Lucky' clocked up his 1,000th arrest.

'Bruce', a two-year-old black Labrador, was an abandoned dog hoping to find a new home. He was one of BTP's newly qualified explosive-search dogs and the first working dog to be recruited from Dogs Trust Glasgow, and joined BTP in Scotland with his handler PC Raymond Martin.

'"Bruce" is already proving his worth with BTP and is a valuable addition to our team,' commented Chief Inspector Alex McGuire, describing 'Bruce' as a 'highly driven' dog. Raymond said, '"Bruce" showed an immediate aptitude for the role. He displays a natural ability and willingness to work and search.'

Canine carer Mandy McShane from Dogs Trust Glasgow was the one to spot 'Bruce's' potential. 'When interacting with "Bruce" I soon realised that he had the qualities needed to be a working dog,' she said. 'He was friendly, excitable, loved toys and was very keen to learn. Dogs Trust is very careful to only put forward suitable dogs who would enjoy the work and find it comes naturally to them. It's like one big, fun game for them but they're really doing a valuable job.'

A drugs problem in a Hertfordshire town was targeted by London North Area's Tasking Team (LNATT) as part of a joint operation with Hertfordshire Police. Local police in Cheshunt, former home to Sir Cliff Richard, and current location of Lotus Cars and a popular shopping centre on the edge of the Lea Valley Park, reported problems with drugs being brought into the town via the rail network. In addition, they registered an increase in stolen goods coming in from London.

Operation 'Fern' was set up at the station to identify gangs travelling to Cheshunt, possibly with weapons. A high-visibility deployment at the station involved BTP, Herts officers and the officers from Lea Valley Park, alongside revenue protection staff from National Express East Anglia. For this operation BTP deployed police dogs 'Ozzy' and 'Ned' with their handler PC Andy Fidgett, and Sergeant Nicholas Cladd from the Tasking Team.

Katie Moore comments further,

I also had a little Lab/Collie-cross from the RSPCA, whom I worked successfully as a drugs dog for many years, called 'Buster'. One particularly memorable job was when I was contacted by PC McEwan, who had been contacted himself at short notice by CID regarding some late intelligence about a male possibly carrying a large amount of drugs on a particular train from Scotland. They had very little information and wanted the whole train scanned and so PC McEwan had asked for our help so we could both scan the train with our passive drugs dogs and ensure that no one could slip past.

We successfully managed to scan the whole train and 'Buster' picked out the male they were after, whom you would not really have given a second glance to otherwise, and he was indeed carrying a whole case full of heroin.

Andy Fidgett recalls some of the tedium of carrying out searches:

In August 2012 I was on patrol with another officer. What had happened was that in the Stanford Le Hope area of

Southend's patch a lot of cable had been stolen. In some places the railway replaced it and it would be stolen again the next day. I had previously had a bit of luck and came across three suspects with some cable. Two of them got away but I managed to hold on to the third one, and the cable, so London North managers were happy and I then started patrolling that area a lot.

There is an oil refinery in this area in a place that I think is called Corrington and one day we received a call of 'suspects on scene'. We went to a wooded area and couldn't see anyone. The practice is to carry out a quarter and search; what you do is send the dog to the furthest point of a search area, i.e., go left, then move forward and send him to the right. All the time he is trying to scent any suspects but, as it's a wooded area, the officer can't see behind bushes or trees and you rely on the dog. It's a very tiring exercise both for dog and handler, plus you don't want anyone to get behind you and attack from the rear. On this occasion we didn't find anyone.

16

'NED' GOES QUIETLY AND 'OSCAR' LOOKS TO THE FUTURE

Andy Fidgett recalls how he experienced elation and pain in a matter of just days:

On 26 November 2012 I met up with other BTP and Met officers near to Cricklewood. There had been a robbery, I believe, at the station and some offence where the suspect was now wanted by both forces, and a firearm had been mentioned by the Met.

When we got to our RVP point the BTP were short of officers due to late-running football the previous evening. There was a general conversation about what to do regarding arrest/search and the possibility of the firearm. From memory I think we had four officers and myself, and the Met had four, all in plain clothes.

We had a vote and decided to carry on. At the address the uniformed BTP took the lead and a male was arrested. I was then tasked with searching the house; one of the Met said to me his warrant was for the house, garden, and next-door's house and garden. He told me not to worry about the houses too much as their focus was on the gardens.

I should have said this was 6.00 a.m. at the time. I searched the suspect's house as well as I could with screaming children and a wife. When I went into the garden I found that the house next-door was boarded up. The Met asked me to search that and the garden but, to make matters worse, it started to rain slightly, which can affect scent and make things harder for the dog. I did as I was asked and searched both houses and gardens.

In the suspect's garden when 'Ozzy', my 'drugs/cash/firearms' dog, got to the top left-hand side of the garden, standing with your back to the house, he started to air scent. This was a little strange as everywhere was overgrowth with weeds and bushes and looked very untidy and not used.

One of the Met lads went off to make a phone call, which I had my thoughts about, as I suspect he was talking to an informant. When he returned we went to the other neighbours and knocked on the door to ask if we could search their garden. A lady in a wheelchair answered; by now it was about 6.45 a.m. and still dark. The lady told us to go ahead and said she hadn't been in the garden for about seven months.

'Ozzy' started searching and when he got to the top right-hand side he started air-scenting again. This put him opposite where he had air scented before. I let him go further and he indicated on a small mound. When I pulled it up there was a hand gun and sixty shotgun cartridges, plus a knuckleduster, which could be used as a sort of Taser. I was 'over the moon', plus wet through. It was my best moment with 'Ozzy' in terms of working together on a long search with an excellent result. It appears the suspect had walked down his garden and leaned over the fence, putting his gun and other bits in his neighbour's garden – hence 'Ozzy' air scenting from his garden.

Two days later I went to the kennel to get the 'boys' up for an early turn, which for me was getting them up at 3.30 a.m.

'Ned' had died in the kennel. I was heartbroken.

I took his body to my vet's. She was particularly fond of police dogs, and 'Ned' in particular, and she never muzzled him. She loved him; we were both in tears. She looked at him and thought that his spleen had ruptured during the night. She said there would have been no real pain, just a gentle sleep.

The force paid for him to be cremated and I kept his ashes in my bedroom with my Long Service Medal on his casket. I often worry about if there was anything I could have done but the vet assured me there wasn't. So, in the space of two days, I went from a high to a low.

That finished me; the force was good to me and let me 'coast' to my finish date. I started on 14 March 1977 and finished on 31 March 2013.

'Ozzy' is a black, with white chest, working Cocker Spaniel. He was born on 9 March 2004 and was a gift to the BTP. He started out as a passive drugs dog and was converted to 'drugs/cash/firearms'. He retired with me.

I couldn't bear to put him back in the kennel where his mate had died, so I moved him into my utility room. I put a 'baby gate' up, which, in November 2014 around bonfire night, he found he could jump. He gives my family hell walking around the kitchen. He can jump from standing up onto the kitchen units. Recently my son said somehow 'Ozzy' had got upstairs and, when my son was lying in bed at 10.00 a.m., as it was a weekend, he saw a periscope-type thing walk into his room, remove something and walk off. It was 'Ozzy's' tail and he was just exploring as he had never been upstairs before.

When I am at home now he just sits under my chair and nods off; just as he did while I was writing about my experiences for this book, in August 2015.

Today I was playing a five-a-side match. When I got in he got his dinner and then I took him for a walk. It's a dog's life all right!

My daughter once took a picture of the two dogs together. It was taken in a field near to a place called Wrabness Woods in Essex. 'Ned' could be a bit of a handful with other animals but never harmed a hair on 'Ozzy's' head. The force supplied a kennel to handlers and my dogs slept outside. In the winter 'Ozzy' would curl up in a ball next to 'Ned's' tummy.

I completed basic training at Tadworth with 'Ozzy' in 2008. During his service with the police 'Ozzy' was involved in many drugs operations, including one at Ipswich railway station in August 2010 following intelligence that large quantities of drugs were being brought down from London by rail, to both Colchester and Ipswich. On this occasion 'Ozzy' made several successful drugs indications but no major seizures were made.

At the end of May 2013 PC Paul Morse deployed from Cardiff with his drugs dog 'Diesel' to support a joint operation with local police at Nailsea & Blackwell, and Yatton railway stations in the South West. Following indications by the dog, twelve people were searched at the two stations and one person was arrested for possession of Class A and Class B drugs.

During the course of 2013/14 the force introduced the concept of using 'cross-functional' dogs for public order and explosive-search purposes.

In 2014, as a result of enquiries by the media, it was established that many police forces had reduced the size of their Dog Sections and that the BTP had reduced the size of their section by almost half since 2009 with fifty-five dogs left.

A recent innovation has seen the training of a 'cadaver search dog', available to speed up body recovery following rail fatalities. BTP officers in C division can now call on the services of a specially trained dog to help search for body parts following fatalities on the rail network. The dog has been trained by DC Mike Dermody in Manchester CID, who volunteers in his spare time with the National Search and Rescue Dog Association. The dog is an operational 'drowned victim search dog' and is trained to find parts of and complete dead bodies.

Identifying an opportunity for innovation, DC Dermody has trained the Belgian Shepherd to search for body parts on land in addition to its primary role in water-based searches. This means that the dog can be used following a fatality on the railway where a major part of the deceased's body cannot be found, either a limb or main body part. The dog will help speed up lineside searches, enabling lines to be handed back quickly, reducing police-related disruption on the network.

DC Dermody said: 'Traditionally, the dog has been trained in water-based searches and it can locate bodies that have been in the water for anything from two hours up to twenty years. The dog is taken out in a boat and detects the scent of bodies on the surface of the water, which narrows down the area of search. Then police divers can be called in.'

He added: 'I thought the dog's skills could be very useful for the force so I have spent a further two months training the dog, in my spare time, to find body parts on land. This is a first for BTP and I am keen to ensure that the dog's skills are used to benefit BTP and rail industry partners.'

Andy Fidgett recalls a poignant moment in July 2015 during the course of which he reflected on the loss of his beloved 'Ned':

Many years ago ITV filmed a programme called *Send in the Dogs*. I think we were in the first programme, then the Met, and others. In what was a tragic episode, one of our officers was speaking to camera because her dog had died. In the camera shot behind her, I and another officer were doing obedience training with our German Shepherds in the rain.

I saw it on television again two Sundays ago. It reminded me of 'Ned' and my old friend's dog who had died. No real story there but I have to say it made my lip wobble a bit.

'Ozzy' still lives with me today. I only have 300 pictures of him; he loves the cameras and sits under my chair when I am working on the computer. In his service he found £272,000 of drugs money, four firearms and made loads of indications for possession of controlled drugs. He featured in a children's book and was on London news searching a scrap yard.

I believe, although I cannot be 100 per cent sure, that he was the first BTP Cocker Spaniel drugs dog, with the rest being Springer Spaniels.

Andy concludes: 'When the "good Lord" looked down on me and gave me these two dogs it was my lucky day.'

As the 'circle of life' for BTP's working dogs goes on, new recruits continue to join the force, which collaborates with other forces and organisations in exchanges and breeding programmes.

All training for dogs in 2015 is based around play and toys. Puppies do not begin their police-dog training and courses until they reach a level of maturity, which is normally some time between twelve and eighteen months. To support these programmes BTP run a 'puppy-fostering scheme', which has been opened up to officers and police staff.

'Oscar', a black Labrador, was one such puppy, fostered in April 2014 by one officer's family. The force looks to those fostering not to train the puppies, but to socialise them by introducing them to as many experiences as possible. This ranges from city noises, rural environments, public transport – in particular trains and railway stations – and noisy machinery such as grass-cutters or bin lorries for instance. On other occasions dogs are exposed to a police station for the day while trainers assess their reactions to such things as dog vans, sirens, and officer and vehicle radio traffic noise.

Puppy-fostering has many benefits for the dog, the force and, ultimately, the communities it will serve. For the puppy fosterers it can be hugely rewarding but the attachment to the dog in that year or so can make the 'hand-back' a little upsetting when it is time for the dog to leave the family home to start work. After all, we are only human ...

On 15 July 2015 British Transport Police officers joined with other emergency teams at a special safety awareness show in an effort to stop youngsters playing on the railway tracks and putting themselves in other dangerous situations. The pre-summer-holiday three-day event at the Emergency Services Training Centre Ltd in Birkenhead, included BTP officers talking to over 1,000 Wirral schoolchildren. The BTP session also included a demonstration featuring police dogs 'Rex' and 'Rafa' with handler Michael Cook, which proved popular with the schoolchildren.

Currently the force has a number of dogs of varying breeds for different types of work based around the country. The dogs are now trained at the Metropolitan Police's Dog Training Centre at Keston in Kent, where BTP have a sergeant and four trainers based.

The force is also involved in the Met's breeding programme. However they occasionally obtain dogs from registered breeders, outside donors and charities such as the Dogs Trust and the RSPCA.

Included in the BTP's Dog Section are a number of passive and proactive explosive-detector dogs. Some of these dogs are trained for the two disciplines. Under Home Office rules they must be licensed to carry out their work on a yearly basis and to qualify for this licence they must undertake ten training days each year for each of the two disciplines with which they are involved.

Like most other forces the British Transport Police runs a volunteer scheme. The volunteers, all of whom are vetted to police standard, come from all walks of life and get involved with a variety of work within the force. One such duty is acting as a stooge for the Dog Section, on training days for which they are a valued and integral part.

Bill Rogerson concludes his recollections with the following account:

Little did I know that in 1971, when I first acted as a stooge for the Dog Section as a young police constable in Birmingham, that I would be doing it again some forty-four years later as a force volunteer in London.

At 9.00 a.m. on Thursday 3 September 2015 I, along with four other volunteers, had the privilege to join PC Will Atkinson as a dog-trainer, and PCs Rob Smith, with his yellow Labrador 'Bruno', and Pete Beal with his black Labrador 'Bobby', in a four-hour explosives-detection training exercise on the main concourse at London St Pancras International railway station. As well as dealing with domestic services, in 2007 it became the London station for the Eurostar services to Paris and Brussels and beyond.

This was an ideal location due to the importance of the station and the diverse number of people using the station to and from the continent. The exercise concluded on the concourse of the neighbouring King's Cross railway station, which was thronging with people.

For security reasons I cannot divulge the full details of the exercise, except to say that under the supervision of the expert eye of PC Will Atkinson it was used to hone the skills of these two four-legged 'Sherlock Holmeses' and as part of their Home Office licensing.

Each time the dog made a successful indication he was rewarded with a tennis ball and there were plenty of tennis balls being handed out at the two stations.

The use of dogs and their achievements in the British Transport Force is legendary and they have quite rightly earned their place in its history.

Michael Layton and Bill Rogerson

BIBLIOGRAPHY

Every attempt has been made to seek permission for copyright material used in this book. However if we have inadvertently used copyright material without permission/ acknowledgement we apologise and we will make the necessary correction at the first opportunity.

Articles

Austin, L., 'The Police Dog – From Pre-Palaeolithic to Present Times' in *BTP Journal* (1962)

Christopher, John, 'There's just no escaping Major' in *Daily Express* (1983)

Harrison, John, 'Police Dogs – Use or Ornament'

Morris, Mick, 'A History of the Dog Section'

Mulville, Paul, 'One man and his dog' in *BTP Journal* (1986)

Murray, Dick, 'Playful pet is really an undercover police dog' in *London Evening Standard* (2001)

Senior, Ben, 'A quiet weekend' in *BTP Journal* 80 (1968)

Toal, Eddie, 'Grim role for BT Police at Lockerbie' in *Railnews* (1989)

Unknown, 'The North Eastern Railway's Police Dogs' in *The Railway and Travel Monthly* (1910)

BONZO, 'Our Four-Legged Policemen' in *BTP Journal* (1978)

Books

Appleby, Pauline, *A Force on the Move: The Story of the British Transport Police 1825-1995* (1995)
Campion, Dorothy, *The Perfect Team* (1959)
Head, Viv, *Between the Sea and the North Star* (unpublished)
Philbin, Harold, *Rail Revelations* (2002)
Whitbread, J. R., *The Railway Policeman* (1961)

Other Resources

Blue Line, a BTP magazine – various editions
BTP Journal – various DVD copies and hardcopy editions
British Newspaper Archives
Crewe Chronicle
The Line, a BTP magazine – various editions
LNER Magazine
Modern Transport XC1, No. 2332 (1964)
North Eastern Railway Magazine
Proctor, Alastair, portrait entitled *Vinnie*
Railnews magazine – various editions
Railway Observer 36, No. 446 (1966)

ACKNOWLEDGEMENTS

John Harrison – Retired Inspector (BTP – Leeds)

Tony Parkinson – Retired Dog Handler (BTP – Manchester)

Malcolm Clegg – Retired Detective Sergeant (BTP – Cardiff)

Pete Hempton – Retired Detective Sergeant and former Dog Handler (BTP – Crewe)

Colin Sinclair – Retired Sergeant and member of BTPHG (BTP – Leeds)

Ed Thompson – Retired Sergeant and member of BTPHG (BTP – London)

Ian Murray – Retired District Inspector (BTP – Aberdeen)

Colin Thomas – Retired Superintendent (BTP)

Richard Jones – Former Special Chief Inspector (BTP – Cardiff)

Mike Morris – Retired Inspector (BTP – London)

Viv Head – Retired Detective Inspector (BTP – Birmingham)

Phil Trendall – Retired Superintendent (BTP – Force HQ London)

Andrew Fidgett – Retired Dog Handler (BTP – London North)

Paul Majster – Retired Detective Constable (BTP – Birmingham)

Bob Cook – Retired Dog Handler (BTP – Hull Docks)

Kevin Gordon – Retired BTP A/Sergeant and member of BTPHG (BTP – Tadworth)

Megan Gilks – Internal Communications Officer (Media & Marketing) 'C' Div., BTP

Fred Keeler – Retired Senior Civilian Manager (BTP)

British Transport Police Retired Officers Association – *Retired Lines* publication

Paul Robb QPM – Retired Assistant Chief Constable (Crime) BTP

Tony Thompson – Retired Superintendent (BTP – Force HQ)

Jack Wintle – *Railnews*

Mike Dermody – serving Detective Constable (BTP – Manchester Piccadilly)

Katie Moore – Retired Dog Handler (BTP – London South)

Acknowledgements

Roger Wilkes – Retired Dog Handler (BTP – St Pancras)

Frank Street – Retired Dog Handler (BTP – Birmingham)

Mollie Street – wife of Frank Street

Ivor Kerslake – Retired Dog Handler (BTP – Birmingham)

Alan Morecock – Retired Dog Handler (BTP – Birmingham)

Neil McEwan – Retired Dog Handler (BTP – Tadworth)

Thomas Park Sergeant Nottingham – author of the PARK cartoons – *BTP Journals*

John McBride – Chief Superintendent (BTP – Glasgow)

Dave Coleman – Retired Dog Handler (BTP – Force HQ)

Mel Harris – Retired Dog Handler (BTP – Birmingham)

Gil Tyler – Retired Detective Sergeant (BTP – Cardiff)

'Maggy' Lyall MBE – Former Dog Handler (BTP – Glasgow)

Henry Wreathall – Ex-Dog Handler and retired Sergeant (BTP – Hull Docks)

John Warner – Retired Dog Handler (BTP – London Euston)

John 'Corky' Hawkins – Retired Dog Handler (BTP – Leeds)

Richard J Stacpoole-Ryding – Retired Sergeant (BTP London – Victoria)

Steve Gardner – Retired Dog Handler (BTP – Leeds)

Allan Beddoe – Retired Dog Handler (BTP – Cardiff)

PC Catherine Trunley – BTP Dog Trainer at Keston & BTPHG

The British Transport Police History Group

The British Transport Police website

PDSA Website

'WARD' – author of cartoons in *Railnews*

Sim Harris – editor, *Railnews*

Grace Hampson – critical reader

PERSONAL BIOGRAPHY
OF CO-AUTHORS
AND DEDICATIONS

Michael Layton QPM joined the British Transport Police as a Cadet on 1 September 1968 and, after three years, was appointed as a police constable in 1971, serving at Birmingham New Street station. In 1972 he transferred to Birmingham City Police, which amalgamated in 1974 to become the West Midlands Police, where he eventually reached the rank of chief superintendent in 1997. On retirement from that force in 2003 he went on to see service with the Sovereign Bases Police in Cyprus, and then returned to the British Transport Police in 2004, initially as a detective superintendent (Director of Intelligence), and then in his last two years as the operations superintendent at Birmingham, where he continued with his passion for combating football violence, until finally retiring again in 2011. In the January 2003 New Year's Honours List he was awarded the Queen's Police Medal for distinguished police service. He is the co-author of a book entitled *Hunting the Hooligans – the True Story of Operation Red Card*, which was published in July 2015 by Milo Books, and the author of *Violence in the Sun – a History of Football Violence in Cyprus*, which was published as an eBook, also by Milo, in May 2015. More recently he has co-authored a book called *Tracking the Hooligans – the History of Football Violence on the UK Rail Network* with Amberley Publishing and *Birmingham's Front Line: True Police Stories*, also by Amberley. Michael is a self-employed consultant, engaged predominantly with crime and community safety issues.

Bill Rogerson MBE is a native of Morecambe, Lancashire and began his career with the British Transport Police on 5 April 1971 at Birmingham New Street, serving at Coventry, Leicester and Heysham harbour in the rank of constable. On 3 September 1979 he was promoted to uniform sergeant at Crewe. In October 1985 he transferred to Holyhead. While serving at Holyhead he also performed duties at Dun Laoghaire Harbour, which was a British Railways Board harbour in Southern Ireland, in connection with sporting fixtures and thefts. On 1 February 1989 he became the officer in charge at Bangor, North Wales. He was appointed an MBE in 1995 for charity and work within the community in North Wales, something he described as 'a huge surprise and quite an honour'. He retired from the force in September 2001. However, four years later, he returned to the force after being offered the position of Community Partnership Co-ordinator, which he filled until the role become redundant in July 2011. This did not deter him, as in September 2011 he returned to the force for his third career as a volunteer, visiting schools and delivering safety messages. Bill is also a founding member and current secretary of the BTP History Group. He edits the group's monthly newsletter, *History Lines*. In his spare time Bill devotes a majority of his time to charity work, assisting a number of organisations in North Wales.

Dedications

Michael Layton – to my grandchildren Christina and Henry, and to my wife Andry for her continuing support and encouragement to write about some of my experiences.

Bill Rogerson – to the whole of my family, especially my grandchildren William, Aaliyah, and Brodie, who are my pride and joy, and to my wife, Shirley.